Let's Ask Betka

Let's Ask Betka

A Story of Survival

Regina Betty Eber

As told to Jacob Eber

Full Court Press
Englewood Cliffs, New Jersey

First Edition

Copyright © 2018 by Jacob Eber

All rights reserved. No part of this book may be reproduced or transmitted in any form or by any means electronic or mechanical, including by photocopying, by recording, or by any information storage and retrieval system, without the express permission of the author, except where permitted by law.

Published in the United States of America
by Full Court Press, 601 Palisade Avenue
Englewood Cliffs, NJ 07632
fullcourtpressnj.com

ISBN 978-1-946989-19-2
Library of Congress Catalog No. 2018956799

Editing and book design by Barry Sheinkopf

Cover art and interior photographs courtesy of the author

To the Eber and Sadin families

Special thanks to my lifelong friends:

Eva and Hyman Abrams, Bianka and Zisek Adler,
Regina and Baruch Czarnoha, Cela and Mark Feinstein,
Inga and Peter Gershonowicz (Gersh), Sonia and Avram Hurman,
Gutcha and Yakov Jacobson, Hana and Anchel Kantor,
Lyka and Lutek Karp, Anja and Sam Krausman,
Susan and Marco Levi, Yadja and Sam Pfeffer,
Grace and Jerry Posluszni (Pahl), Frieda and Morris Rabinowitz,
Layele and Moishe Schwartz, Esta and Yulek Schwebel,
Lily and Nathan Shapelski (Shapell), Eni and Aaron Topiol,
Sophie and Motek Topiol, Manya and Henyek Usherowicz (Usher),
Helen and Max Wakshlag, Fela and David Waldman,
Sala and Max Weisbrot (Webb), Rachel and Victor Weistuch,
Naomi and Karl Weistuch, and
Gutcha and Henyek Zimberknopf (Zimber).

In Memory

of my families who perished in the Holocaust

Wygodski
Rosenstein
Feinstein
Eber

PROLOGUE

THE DICTIONARY DEFINES "MOTHER" as a female parent, but she is often much more than that. She goes by different names—Mom, Mommy, Mama, Ma, etc.—and is the focal point of the family. It is her job to nurture and guide her children, and to create a home for her family to thrive in. It is one of the hardest jobs around, and not everyone is up to the task.

I was born very lucky. My mom, known to the world as Betty, is an amazing woman. She's the only member of her family to survive the Nazi regime, immigrated to several countries where she didn't speak the language or understand the culture, and built a life for herself and her family.

My mother is not only very capable but extremely independent and has an insatiable thirst for knowledge. Physically, she is a beautiful woman with a small chiseled nose that accents her prominent cheekbones that never need rouge.

Wrinkles appear with the warmth of her smile. Her most outstanding feature are her large hazel eyes, which always sparkle like moonlight reflecting off a lake on a clear night. However, behind those eyes one can see strength, determination, and sensitivity...along with much sadness.

She never smoked and instinctively ate healthy. She has no computer, no microwave, no cable. She never learned to drive—the New

York subway was her limousine—yet she is smart, savvy, and hip. At ninety-five, she remains as sharp as ever, and is an adored mother, grandmother and great-grandmother. As I approach my own retirement years, I am blessed to still have her influence in my life.

Growing up, I didn't realize how special my mother was and believed that everyone had parents and a home like I did. Many years later, I came to understand how unique my mom and dad were, and how blessed I am to be their son.

My parents' love affair began in the ruins of Poland following the Second World War and continued every day until my father died. Even now, some thirty-six years later, my mother is still very much in love, and very much married to my father.

Together they raised me, educated me, and protected me. They taught me what it means to love unconditionally and gave me the skills to survive in the world. I would not be the man I am today if it weren't for their guidance and love.

I only wish I'd had more time with my father. He died suddenly of a heart attack at the age of sixty-two, not long after I got married. It was especially heartbreaking when, only a few months later, he would have become a grandfather when my wife and I welcomed our first child.

As I have grown older, my relationship with my mother has changed in ways I could never have imagined. I have come to appreciate her more and better understand all she has been through and everything she has done for me. We speak every day, even when there's nothing new to say. She's more than just my mother these days; she's my friend, my confidente, and my greatest source of inspiration.

She survived the worst of times, triumphed during the best, and did it all with tremendous courage and an unbreakable spirit. Most people who meet her recognize immediately that she has a unique quality about her, something that's almost impossible to describe. She wears a glow on her face and an energy that radiates from within. Both men and women tend to gravitate towards her and not only want to be near her but seek out her opinion and advice. Over the years, I've been pulled aside by countless people—family, friends, business colleagues, and the like—to talk about my mom. It's always the same thing. They appreciate her outlook on life, her attitude, and her wisdom. Almost every one of them ends the conversation with the same words, "Your mom has a certain something," but are never able to define it.

For a long time, I couldn't understand what they meant. It was nice to hear, but to me she was just my mother, the woman who raised me, the woman she had always been.

That all changed in the spring of 1993 when, together, we traveled to Washington, DC, for the opening of the Holocaust Museum. The night before the ceremony, I met several of her co-inmates from the Ludwigsdorf camp in Poland. That night, listening to their stories and hearing their descriptions of my mother, I finally saw her for who she really was.

Her life didn't begin when I was born, and she became my mother; a lot—more than I ever realized—happened before I came along, and shaped who she was. She has always been special, always had those unique qualities, and that was never more apparent than during her years living under Nazi German rule. The people she lived among then, those who had been tortured and brutalized too, remembered my mom as the calming influence and a big reason why they survived. A lot of them used the same wording—"A certain something"—when trying to figure out what abilities she possessed.

"Your mother was our leader," one of them told me. "She made us laugh and took care of us when we needed it most. We followed her because somehow she knew what was right."

My mother made light of these compliments and took them in stride, claiming she only "did what had to be done." But that night awakened something inside me, something I'd been hiding from since the day I was born.

As a child, I avoided learning about the Holocaust and all that was done to the Jewish people. In school, we studied it, and I knew the facts, the what and the why, but refused to believe it was real, that it had happened to the people I love. I saw my father's tattoo, the one branding him a Jew, and knew he and my mother were survivors, but didn't let it go further than that. Thinking anything else, imagining my parents being treated with so much cruelty and bigotry, was unfathomable. I couldn't go there.

But after attending the opening of the Holocaust Museum, listening to other survivors tell their stories and relive their memories, I had to know. I was ready to listen, and my mom needed to tell her story. She wanted her family—me, my children, my children's children—to know all about what happened so they too would never forget. . .and never let it happen again.

Not long after we returned from Washington, the two of us sat down at her kitchen table with a tape recorder, a cup of tea for her, and a cup of coffee for me, and talked for hours. It became a weekly ritual, and I began learning things about my mother that I never knew. Though decades had passed, she remembered every detail, all the pain, all the laughter, and all the cruel and inhumane experiences.

I listened to every word she spoke, and finally understood what those horrible people had done to my parents and anyone else born Jewish or any other human being opposed to their ideals. I began to realize the extent of their cruelty as it directly influenced me, questioning when I was young, *Where are my grandparents? Where is my family?* Those questions were being answered as the story unraveled.

After years of being unable to listen, let alone comprehend how anyone could harm the people I love most, I became addicted to the story she was telling. After every conversation I went home, sat on the couch, and stared at nothing while reliving parts of her story. I let the facts penetrate my soul and sometimes felt sad and empty and sometimes cried.

And though it was depressing, I returned each week for more.

Because I needed to hear it.

Because she needed to tell me.

Because the world needs to know.

I began this journey so that my children and my children's children will know and understand the strength and courage that flow through their veins.

The pages that follow are what I learned. They are a transcription of events with roller-coaster emotions and feelings. They comprise the story of a woman—a daughter, a sister, a friend, a wife, and a mother—who has been through so much more in her life than most people can imagine and come out stronger on the other side.

She has lived through unspeakable tragedies and done so with unwavering strength, courage, and dignity. She is an amazing woman, a source of pride and inspiration, and a witness so that the next generation won't forget. She had to remember.

I want to thank Tom Mechin for his invaluable help in making this book a reality

—J.E.

LET'S ASK BETKA

CHAPTER 1

I REMEMBER—I REMEMBER everything and everyone. The images in my head are as clear today as they were then, and I will never forget. It's still hard to believe that it's real, that it all happened, and that I am the only survivor of a large and prominent family.

I was known as Rega and affectionately Regusha by family and close friends. When thinking back to the days before the war, I remember how happy we were. My first thoughts always seem to drift back to an evening in December 1929. I was eight years old, sitting around the table with my family, enjoying a traditional Sabbath dinner. My mother, Sonia Rosenstein Wygodska, loved beautiful things. I can still smell my mama's cooking, still see the reflection of the crystal chandelier in the perfectly arranged plates and crystal goblets—Mama liked everything to be perfect. Her china closet, filled with mementos, reflected good taste and a high quality of life.

The curtains were drawn, and there was an aura of warmth from the lit candles. Seated at the head of the table, the place of respect, was my father. He may have had faults, but I never saw any. Rubin Wygodski was a wonderful and honorable man who took care of his family and always made time for his daughters. He was busy and hardworking, but there was room still for us to curl onto his lap to talk or cuddle whenever we needed. My father enjoyed challenging us and encouraged discussions and banter on a wide range of topics. He made a conscious effort to make my sisters and me feel special and important.

That night was like any other Friday night dinner—I, my two older sisters, Vanda and Irenka, my parents and grandmother, Elka Rosenstein, all seated around the table...with one exception. At twenty-two, Vanda, my eldest sibling, had brought home a guest. Her boyfriend, Stasiek Mushkat, had come to meet the family and, hopefully, gain our approval.

My first impression of Stasiek was positive, and I immediately noticed how handsome he was. He was very impressive with his height, strong physique, and dark movie-star features. It was obvious that he never had trouble attracting the ladies. Even with Vanda's dazzling beauty, flawless complexion, emerald eyes, and goddess-like figure, she was smitten with him. However, it would take more than looks and charm to win over my father.

Hoping to impress us, Stasiek dominated the table conversation, talking about his interests and love of military life. He had recently returned from Belgium, where he had completed his studies in international business and language. Stasiek spoke seven languages fluently and at the time was an officer in the military reserves.

Unfortunately for him, he fell short of his goal that night. Living in a home where education, business, and the arts were important, endless stories about military life fell on deaf ears. By the time Vanda and Stasiek left—early, before dessert had been served, because they had tickets to the theater—my father's boredom was apparent. When the door closed behind them, he finally spoke up, ending the family's silence that night. "What kind of man talks about himself for two straight hours?" he asked. His voice was rich and cultured, but a frown framed his lips.

Mama didn't answer him but offered insight of her own. "I think she loves him, Rubin."

"Maybe so, but don't you think there is something else to talk about other than military life? He had to notice that no one else was participating in the conversation, yet he went on and on."

"Vanda loves him," Mama repeated. But it didn't matter; Daddy had left the table shaking his head.

The truth was that, although Stasiek came across as self-centered and narcissistic, he loved Vanda, and she adored him. If one day they decided to get married, our father would welcome Stasiek into the family with open arms.

CHAPTER 2

GROWING UP IN WARSAW, POLAND, a large metropolis, could have been overpowering, but my world was small and ideal. I had a great family, a strong group of friends, and I was a happy child. In school, I was popular, and at home my sisters and I were close. Even though Irenka was seven years my senior, and Vanda fourteen years older, we shared our dreams and goals and would spend hours talking and playing together.

Our home was also the central hub for almost every holiday and festivity. Family from all over—cousins, aunts, uncles, and grandparents—would get together to celebrate. We'd listen to music, laugh and sing, dance and party.

We had a good life, in part thanks to my father and his strong work ethic and business skills. He had many business ventures in his life. He managed two sugar refineries, and since he excelled as a talented calligrapher, he was hired to script all important government papers. In his spare time, and during his years in Russia, he became the controller for the Tzar, his final one being the owner of a wholesale coal distribution center—*Carbomontana*—which he ran with his brother-in-law, Misha Rosenstein. With separate locations adjacent to the Gdansk and West railroad stations in Grochor Praga, the business thrived; trains came and picked up the coal, then delivered it to businesses and factories along the route.

As an employer, my father was every bit the man he was at home. He was honest, strong, and hardworking, and he didn't let his employees think he was better than them. He exuded confidence and warmth and earned the trust and respect of almost everyone he was in contact with.

With the summer of 1930 came an epidemic of influenza sweeping across nearly all of Europe. Few families were left unscathed, not even ours. My father had been a heavy smoker most of his life. It came as no surprise when he developed a severe cough which left his immune system vulnerable to an attack.

As the temperatures increased that summer, so did my father's cough. His congested lungs produced an intense sound, so loud that it announced his arrival home from work each night. He soon began losing his strength and vitality, and by the end of August he had a full-fledged case of influenza.

Bedridden and barely able to stay awake, my father's condition worsened quickly. Two months later, on the thirtieth of October, Rubin Wygodski succumbed to the illness. He was fifty-two and left behind a family—a wife who loved him, three daughters who adored him, and a mother-in-law whose love and respect he cherished.

The months that followed were agonizing. Nothing was the same without him, with holidays and celebrations being the worst. I was nine at the time and couldn't understand why my father had been taken away from me. I loved him more than anything, and even though I knew he cared for us all, I was the special one, his baby girl.

All these years later, I still remember sitting on his lap, talking and laughing. It's been nearly a century since I was a child making memories. I remember his distinct smell and the way his arms wrapped around me made me feel, happy and safe. It's been nearly a century since, and I haven't felt that warmth or safety again.

Luckily my father had been an excellent businessman and left his family financially secure.

CHAPTER 3

A LOT OF THINGS CHANGED after my father's death, and in some ways, it's good that he wasn't around to see what became of his homeland and family.

The next several years passed slowly, and many people around the world were suffering. The worldwide economic hardship that worsened every day didn't affect our family much.

After the traditional year of mourning following our father's death, Vanda and Stasiek were married in December 1931. Although Stasiek never lost his affection for other women and sometimes indulged himself, he and Vanda loved each other. Four years into their marriage, her pregnancy brought excitement to the entire family.

But not all news was good that summer. At the age of sixty-seven, my grandmother, the woman who openly dreamed of a great-grandchild, passed away before that became a reality. She died in her sleep and, as matriarch of the family, Elka Berkowitz Rosenstein left a big hole in it.

I was especially devastated by the loss. Grandma Elka and I shared a special bond that had only strengthened after my father died. She protected me when I was in trouble, often slipped me extra money for the movies or candy, and made room for me to accompany her on trips to stores, to visit friends, even on weekend getaways. She was revered for being a smart and successful businesswoman, and I adored her vibrant and vivacious personality. I loved my grandmother and hated that she was gone.

Several months later tragedy struck the Wygodski household again. The excitement of a new little one running around ended when Vanda gave birth to a stillborn child. She and Stasiek were devastated, and their marriage suffered. Stasiek's taste for extramarital affairs continued, and Vanda learned to turn a blind eye to reality, accepting her husband's indiscretions.

I went through many phases too, from pigtails to perfume, from puberty to maturity. Soon the innocence of life was evaporating and the reality of the world began settling in.

Despite the turmoil, my teenage years were filled with exciting plans and hope for the future. I graduated from high school and wondered where life would take me. My parents and teachers often said I was smart and had a bright future, but what did that mean? *Would I be lucky like Vanda and find a handsome man to sweep me off my feet? Would I settle down to raise a family or join the workforce?* I imagined becoming a teacher or a lawyer and making a difference in the world. I had big plans and big dreams.

Unfortunately, as my expectations grew so too did anti-Semitism in Eastern Europe. When Adolf Hitler became Chancellor of Germany, he began to openly express his hatred of the Jewish population. Not long after taking office, he called for the boycotting of all Jewish-owned businesses and approved the random beatings of Jewish men in the street.

In 1935, Germany passed the Nuremberg Laws, which essentially classified the Jewish people as less than human. It became a punishable offense for Aryan citizens, those of European dissent but not Jewish, to marry or have extramarital relations with any Jews. As a result, many Jews living in Germany began fleeing across the border into Poland.

Soon Poland wasn't safe anymore. Tensions were escalating daily, and the hatred spread into my homeland. An anti-Semitic group calling themselves the '*Endeks*' began publishing a newspaper—the *Shtafeta*. It was filled with lies and hate, blaming the Jewish people for all the world's troubles. We were the reason for the economic troubles, the reason Germany had lost the Great War. We were the guilty, the scapegoats, and eventually we became the sacrificial lambs.

Soon the universities became segregated, and there were reports of Jewish students being beaten for no reason other than their religious heritage. It was a frightening time, and things only got worse. Before long, the massacres of Jewish people began happening in earnest and out in the open, in the streets, but no one did anything about it. The perpetrators were careful and made sure that their attacks were spread out enough to look like random incidents.

The streets of Poland were not safe for Jews anymore, and hardly any of us—male or female—walked them alone. The slow deterioration of our neighborhood was devastating. The windows of Jewish-owned stores were smashed, their doors broken into. Garbage was dumped on the pavement in front, and slogans of hatred were painted on the walls and street.

Don't Buy From Jews!
Dirty Jews!
No Jews Allowed!

Hitler spread venom throughout every city in Poland, and soon it became terrifying to be a Jew living in Poland. We survived under a cloud of hate, and the fear that Germany's Nuremberg Laws would soon impact us, too. Our dignity, our pride, were disappearing before our eyes, and nothing was being done to protect us. The belief that the violence toward the Jewish people was only a passing trend soon ceased to exist. The authorities turned a blind eye. (Some of us believed—*knew*—that the people in power, those responsible to everyone, were condoning the attacks and violence. The poison was in the system.)

CHAPTER 4

DESPITE MY FATHER'S EFFORTS to keep the family financially secure even after his passing, Mama knew our savings wouldn't last forever. Sometime in the mid-1930s, during my teen years, Mama and twenty-one-year-old Irenka, seven years my senior, opened a retail store. They had received approval for a Telefunken franchise, a popular radio brand at the time, and registered the store to Irena Wygodska—believing her Aryan features and Polish-sounding name would quiet any whispers that they might be Jewish. The store sold radios, cameras, and bicycles, with a repair shop in the back.

Mama was smart and ran a successful business, but Irenka constantly worried about the family. Money wasn't the concern, but rather the growing tensions and violence in Warsaw. She continuously pressured Mama to consider leaving Poland, but Mama wouldn't hear of it. "Nonsense, Irenka. You needn't be worried about these things." She tried reassuring us. "These actions are committed by a small group of vandals."

"Mama, these are not random incidents." Irenka pleaded. "This is happening more and more around the city." She went on to explain the details of the university beatings, the attacks on city streets, and the vandalism to every Jewish-owned business. "These people hate us and will not stop until we've been robbed of all our dignity. They're careful, and they know what they're doing. We're not safe, Mama."

Mama was unyielding on the subject. "This will not continue. The government will not let us down. We are, after all, *Polish citizens*."

At the time, I was young and still full of hope. I wanted to believe that Mama was right, that the government would step in and protect us, and stop the craziness. Maybe I *had* to believe that because I wasn't ready for what was coming.

It was at times like that that my father's absence was really felt. He had been the center, the core, of our family, the stabilizing and comforting figure, and he would have known what to do. Mama would have listened to him, and he would have made the rest of us feel safer too.

Although it hadn't been said, my family knew that I would take the reins and lead us. In many ways, I had been born with equal parts my father and grandmother. I had my father's innate sense of logic, his ability to see the bigger picture and make decisions accordingly, and I was blessed with my grandmother's spirited personality and mental strength. If things continued in the course they were heading, and the situation became bad enough, it would be up to me to decide the path our family would eventually take.

Irenka and I weren't the only ones in Poland worrying about the growing threat of Germany. Under absolute secrecy, all Polish officers were summoned to a meeting to discuss the possibility of a German invasion and prepare for war.

Stasiek was notified at his home before dawn and, like every other officer, given only a few hours to be with his family before reporting for duty.

Later that night, he and Vanda came to the house. Before they could even say a word, their expression told us they had not come with good news. Vanda was rigid and obviously stressed; Stasiek's face and eyebrows were crinkled, and he had difficulty making eye contact.

Mama led us all to the dining room, where we sat around the table praying silently and staring at each other. The silence in the room wasn't like any silence before; it was eerie and scary, and I swear I could hear everyone's hearts beating. The room took on a strange and mysterious aura that sent a chill up my spine.

It was Stasiek who finally broke the silence, and then the family spent the next two hours discussing the details of the impending war, the fate of the Jewish people, and what preparations we should be taking.

"Things are going to accelerate rapidly," Stasiek warned, as he himself had been warned earlier.

The following day, my mother went shopping. She returned with more food and supplies than we had room to store, but insisted it was necessary. As I was helping unpack the groceries, I found several packages of rope. Because the apartment was filled with little more than dread, I hoped to lighten the mood with a joke, but instead my sarcasm came out.

"Mama, the groceries I understand, but the rope? Is that for us to hang ourselves in case the Germans get too close?"

She apparently didn't appreciate the sarcasm, gave me a scolding glare, and didn't respond. I knew I had struck a nerve, getting a little too closer to reality than I should have, and didn't pursue the conversation any further.

CHAPTER 5

GERMANY INVADED POLAND on September 1, 1939. For the next month the German army, one of the most powerful military machines the world had ever known, unleashed a deadly attack designed to overpower the entire country. The newspapers were inundated with details of the invasion. The radio was constantly giving step-by-step details of our impending future. The Wehrmacht hit the areas just inside the border first, reclaiming former German provinces that Hitler had signed away in the Non-Aggression Pact of 1934. Then they moved farther inland.

The sounds of gunfire and artillery echoed in the distance, and news that the Nazis were closing in on Warsaw spread. As Poland's largest and strongest city—and the one best equipped to thwart a Nazi invasion—Warsaw would likely give the Third Reich its toughest battle. Even so, none of us inside the city limits were confident that our citadela (fortress) would be able to stand up to the German Army forever.

Some chose to flee instead, illegally crossing the border into Russia. Since the Soviet Union was not at war with Germany, many felt it was safer there than staying home. My mother and her brother, Misha Rosenstein, discussed running but didn't have the stomach for it. They worried about what was coming but feared getting caught trying to escape even more.

When the Germans finally reached Warsaw, the results were catastrophic. For weeks, the city remained under siege, being attacked from the ground and air. The Germans didn't limit their targets either; in addition to municipal buildings and industrial areas, they attacked schools and hospitals, too.

The Polish Army did everything they could to save Warsaw, but their efforts were futile. The German military was simply too powerful. No one in Poland was safe. Because our apartment was on the ground floor, we were not forced to evacuate, and our home became a place of refuge for those who were. We taped the windows to prevent the glass from shattering and were thankful Mama had purchased the extra food and supplies. That, and the radio providing updates on the invasions, were the only things keeping me, Irenka, and our mother sane—that is, until the Germans knocked out the city's power, leaving us terrified and in the dark, never knowing what was going to happen from one minute to the next.

For days on end, we sat huddled together, listening to the constant bombings and explosions, hearing them get closer and closer, and fearing we were going to be killed. Aware of the danger, we feared for our lives. Mama had each of us pack a bag—filled with necessities in case we needed to make a run for it—and placed them by the door. We were more fortunate than others. We had candles for light and a water tank powered by gas, making it possible to cook.

On the final night before Warsaw surrendered, our building was hit with a bomb. The explosion was so terrifying, so loud, that even to this day, when I think back, I can still feel it. The walls and floors shook, the windows shattered, and things went flying. All our paintings and pictures, Mama's knickknacks, and everything that makes a house a home erupted from the walls and tables, crashing onto the floor. In the kitchen, the cabinets flew open, dishes and crystal plummeting to the floor.

The three of us cowered there, covering our heads to protect them from flying debris. It felt like an earthquake, but worse. Our home was in shambles, the building seemed on the verge of collapsing—and all of it took a matter of seconds, and I was left with questions, but never got any answers. *How is this even possible? How could someone do this to other human beings?*

The moment we could, Irenka and I grabbed our bags and made a dash for the door. However, Mama panicked, and instead of her bag, she took a bar of soap and a towel from the bathroom and ran out of the apartment in fear for her life.

We took shelter with others in a nearby basement while the Nazis destroyed our city. The bombings continued relentlessly, fires erupted on every street, and explosions could be heard throughout the night. There were a few periods of calm and quiet, but somehow those were even more terrifying. Not knowing what was going to happen, or when it was going to happen, was not good for anyone's anxiety. Even the rats and cockroaches seemed scared, hiding in the shadows instead of creeping out in search for food.

During the silence, some managed to sleep, but I couldn't. I was exhausted, stressed, and sleeping would have helped, but I couldn't close my eyes. Every time I did, I relived it all, every terrifying moment.

When daylight came, so did three hundred German bombers. They were relentless, and the roar of the planes jolted everyone in the basement, even those lucky enough to be sleeping. I opened my eyes to look around the room, seeing several people crammed together holding their loved ones.

One woman was screaming in terror, "We're all going to die! They're going to bury us alive!"

Her husband slapped her in the face, and she wilted into his arms. The hysteria was gone, but the fear was still alive in that face, in all our faces.

Soon the city had had enough. The bombing left everyone and everything shaking uncontrollably, and despite the efforts of our troops, Warsaw fell to the enemy. Our city surrendered to the German soldiers on September 29, 1939.

CHAPTER 6

Before the German invasion, the city of Warsaw was a bustling metropolis, the center of Polish culture housed in fine old buildings with classic architecture. The city had all the modern conveniences and a hold on its past. The opera house was majestic, and the concert hall had a quality of grandeur. In a lot of ways, Warsaw was the perfect place to live.

Then, in only a matter of weeks, it was all gone—burned, bombed, and destroyed. A city of culture and beauty was transformed to a state of complete disorder and destruction. If I hadn't seen it myself, I never would have believed it possible.

When the bombings finally ended, those left alive were forced to deal with the consequences. While insisting my mother and sister stay in the safety of the shelter, I ventured aboveground to see what remained. Throughout everything that had already happened and most of what was going to, I remained as strong as I could. I knew that, if I let it get to me, let those feelings overwhelm me, I wouldn't survive. But that morning, walking those streets and seeing what those bastards had done to my home brought tears to my eyes.

The air was thick and gross, with a black funnel twisting upward towards a filthy sky filled with gray clouds of smoke and dust. Several buildings were still on fire, and many more had been demolished. I was stunned as I looked up at that sky, as dark as the ebony swastika on the

Nazi flag. It made me sick and turned my stomach.

I stood there for several minutes in a complete daze, my feet frozen to the concrete. I was jolted out of it by people screaming and running in every direction, frantically searching for loved ones; others were lying on the ground, bleeding. Parentless children wandered the streets, looking for someone to comfort them now that their mothers and fathers had been taken away.

Everywhere I looked, I saw dread. One mother raced by, calling her child's name with tears streaming down her cheeks, while another lay holding her dead husband's head in her lap. There was nothing but horror.

Within minutes of arriving, the planes were gone, but the chaos continued. More explosions came, destroying more buildings and sending broken glass and debris ricocheting onto the street; flames spread like fiery coils into the sky. It didn't seem real, none of it did. It couldn't be real.

For the first time in my life, I felt fragile, that I couldn't handle this. A cold air chilled my body, and the closeness of death brought with it a strange feeling. In that moment, I wanted nothing more than my mother's arms around me, holding me and telling me that everything was going to be all right. Though I knew she couldn't make that promise, and that I wouldn't believe her if she had, I wanted to hear it and pretend to believe it.

Since our building hadn't been destroyed, we were able to return home. It didn't feel as it once had and probably never would again. The Germans had won. They added Warsaw—Poland's strongest city—to their list of victories.

The Nazis came, conquered, and stayed!

CHAPTER 7

CARRYING OUR SUITCASES, we returned to our apartment. No matter what happened to me, no matter what the circumstances, I had always felt safe in our home, but at that moment and for the first time, comfort and security were gone. We found a few rooms in shambles, which we used exclusively for shelter, but what we had known as home was gone. Irenka and I insisted that Mom rest while we straightened the furniture and cleaned up the debris.

Within days of being conquered, Warsaw had been transformed from a beautiful modern city into a vast wilderness filled with dread, apprehension, and devastation. The streets became clogged with men in foreign uniforms, speaking an unfamiliar language.

My blood ran cold the first time I saw the parade of Nazi soldiers marching through the city, our city. They were rigid and uptight, marching with precision and proud of what they had done. The image of the wooden soldiers from the 1934 film Babes in Toyland flashed before me. Hate and danger marched into my city while fear was entering my world. It was an image that I knew I would never forget, and I never have. It's been burned in my memory and outlasted many others.

There were others standing around watching that day, seeing all that I had seen. They too were frightened, angry, and bewildered. To many, it was the moment of realization that nothing was ever going to be the same.

Everything after that changed quickly. Soon signs in German appeared everywhere, and the swastika logo was a constant reminder of the new regime. I'm sure it meant something different to them, but to all of us it meant nothing more than destruction, suffering, and death. Their flags flew on every major building, and the swastika logo was on the armbands of all the soldiers' uniforms, including the most inhuman group of all, the Gestapo—better known as the SS.

The Gestapo was the secret state police of the Germans that had carte blanche to operate as they saw fit. It was made up of ruthless SS officers who took pleasure in the deliberate destruction of other human beings simply because we believed in the Old Testament. They hated Jews and got satisfaction from watching us suffer and die. They had no hearts, just souls surrounded by sadism and vindictiveness.

Within the first two weeks, the Germans ordered the establishment of a Judenrat (Jewish council). It was headed up by a Jewish engineer named Adam Czerniakow. As chairman of the council, he would soon administer the establishment of the ghetto and implement all new orders. The process was slow and calculated.

The first order of business was to limit communication and news. They confiscated all radios, including ours. Then, the Nazi soldiers raided individual homes, demanding all valuables while helping themselves to anything they deemed worthwhile.

I don't remember exactly when, but one early evening when we were all home, I froze with the first knock on the door. It was not a normal knock—it was a continuous loud banging. We immediately knew who was at the door. Irenka let them in while Vanda and I huddled with Mama. One soldier, rifle in hand, asked our names and demanded jewelry and money while the other one rummaged through our closets, specifically looking for furs. Furs were collected just before the winter months, months that were brutally cold in Warsaw.

The entire transaction took less than five minutes. As fast as they had come, they left, and we began breathing again. The frightening incident was over. I felt defiled. The thought that a stranger, especially a Nazi, going through my clothes, touching my things—even now that thought makes me quiver.

The surprise home visits by the Nazis were always frightening, but Mama was particularly unnerved. We were never sure what was on their minds. Although sent by their supervisors, their behavior depended on their mood. Would they just rob us? Did they plan to hurt us? Was there more on their minds than collecting valuables? Mama hid money and jewelry throughout the apartment—in the ice box, the stove, on the closet floor, inside pockets of suits.

I remember her saying once, after a surprise raid, "This time they didn't make too bad a mess." With that statement, Irenka and I started to straighten up the living room. To steady her nerves, Mama busied herself making dinner. She lit the stove, and within five minutes, we heard yelling. She had totally forgotten that, at the last minute, when the Gestapo knocked on the door, she had hidden 300 zlotes in the stove.

One of the Germans' final decrees was to order all Jewish-owned businesses to be closed and the premises sealed. As a result, the Wygodski family's Telefunken store, although successful, was shut down.

Soon Poland was divided in half, with the Germans occupying one side and the Russians on the other. It was an impossible situation, made worse in the Wygodski household because Vanda had not heard from her husband in weeks. She didn't know whether he was alive or dead, and since many of the soldiers who had left were returning to Warsaw, she feared the worst.

Finally, news came. A soldier who had been under Stasiek's command reported that their unit had been separated while they were in the Russian zone just days before the Soviet Union occupied Poland. The soldier had been able to tell Vanda exactly where he last saw Stasiek.

Vanda was determined to find him, and despite the inherent risks, she left the safety of our home and smuggled herself into the Russian zone just days before the Soviet Union occupied Poland. I don't remember the exact details of how it happened, or if I ever knew them. What I do know is that Vanda was able to locate Stasiek. No doubt her fluency in Russian helped, but I think it was her will and determination that led her to him.

He was weak and dehydrated when she found him. After being separated from his unit, Stasiek had roamed the woods for several days without food or water. He'd had to move quickly and often to avoid discovery, and even though he was outside the grasp of the Germans, he knew the Russians could not be trusted either.

Cut off from civilization, he almost died of thirst and starvation, but through little more than willpower and a little luck, he found his way to the other end of the forest. It was there that he came upon an old church, collapsing at its entrance. The priest who found him attempted to nurse him back to health. He gave Stasiek fresh clothes to replace his Polish military uniform, then food and water to rebuild his body.

When Vanda found him—and I have no idea how she did, given all the circumstances—Stasiek was still extremely weak. She stayed by his side, helping him slowly regain his health and strength.

When he was healthy enough to travel, the two of them decided it would be safer to stay in Russia. They planned to go to our father's family for help. When questioned, Vanda explained to the authorities that she and her husband were traveling to her grandparents in Slutzk, but because of her fluency in the language, they believed she was a spy. It was a time in history when everyone was mistrusted, and the fear of espionage was high, and many people were refused entry into Russia. Vanda and Stasiek were no different, and although it disappointed them, they were ordered to return to Poland.

CHAPTER 8

My mother's cousin, Yakob Tannenbaum, may have had a way out of Poland for our entire family. He was in possession of several blank certificates that would enable us to enter Palestine. As the head of the bookkeeping department at the Polonia Ship Lines—one of their regular course of travel was Poland to Palestine—he had the connections to get us there. Yakob had already registered his wife and children, and his sister—claiming she was another daughter. He himself planned to leave within the next few days, and if the passage was safe, his family would follow.

Pinsk, 1930. Left to right, my sister Irenka, and Vanda, Ola, and Yakob Tennenbaum

Our family gathered around the table in November 1939 to discuss it. A teenager at the time, I sat without speaking. I was permitted to listen but not expected to take part in adult discussions. My mother and her brother Misha were skeptical. Together they formed a united front, unwilling to leave Poland.

Yakob soon became frustrated with their negativity and naiveté but understood their fears. He continued his plea, begging the two of them to register their families. He explained everything we would need to do to go to Palestine. Since England was not at war, and Palestine was under English rule, the first step was to present the certificates to the British Consul. Yakob assured them that all the necessary stamps and seals were already affixed to the certificates, and that all we had to do was add our names. Then he spoke of his experiences with the appointed officials and the accommodating way in which everything had been handled.

The next stop would be at Gestapo headquarters, and, since we'd have to travel through Italy to get to Palestine, the Italian consul.

It was this part of the discussion that brought silence around the table.

"I implore you to make an immediate decision," Yakob said. Exasperated, he took a long pause before making one final plea. "Once I leave Warsaw, my hands will be tied, and I will no longer be able to help you."

But it didn't matter what he said—I glanced at my mother and realized she wasn't even listening anymore. Once the Gestapo was mentioned, she had frozen in fear; no pleading or promises would change her mind. She declined the offer and declared that returning to Russia was unthinkable too.

"The Germans are a gentle race," she said in a slow monotone. "We are women. Nothing will happen to us here."

After the family left, my mother remained at the table, sitting with her chin resting in the palm of her hands. She continued to stare at nothing and seemed lost in thought. I remember the next moments vividly as she put both hands on the table and her head fell forward as if her neck no longer had the strength to hold it up.

"Are you all right, Mama?" I asked, my hand on her arm.

A few seconds passed before she answered, then looked up from her deep concentration and studied my face. "Yes! Yes, I'm fine," she said, patting my cheek.

Once again, we lost Mama to her memories. She turned away from me and began thinking back to her life in Russia—her sister Leah, the city of Pinsk, the pogroms—and it all crystallized in her mind.

It was a clear, sunny day in the city of Pinsk, situated on the Pena River in Poland. Leah, seven months pregnant with her second child, went shopping. On her way home, she got caught in the middle of a pogrom—an organized massacre of Jewish people. She was kicked by a soldier, dropped her packages, and fell to the ground in agony. She closed her eyes and remained very still, hoping that the Russian hoodlums would assume her dead.

When she stopped hearing the thunderous noises of the horses, she opened her eyes and stood up. Many people in the street had been beaten and bloodied, and several storefronts and windows had been smashed. It was a horrible sight.

Aching and exhausted, she staggered home. She told her family of the incident, leaving out only the part of her being kicked (she didn't want them to worry too much). However, Leah would not feel safe again until she was in the arms of her husband, Rubin Wygodski.

Not long afterwards, she began spiking a fever, and then shocking news came that she had developed gangrene and was carrying a stillborn child. Devastated, Rubin buried his wife and child, then, with his only living child, eighteen-month-old Vanda, moved in with his mother-in-law, Elka. She had two other children, Sonya and Misha.

Elka owned several businesses, and Rubin helped her run them. There were two sugar refineries, one in Pinsk and one in Kiev. As time passed, Vanda began calling Sonya *mamouchka* (mother). Sonya and her deceased sister, Leah, shared a strong resemblance, and after months of living together, she and Rubin fell in love and married.

Before the outbreak of the Great War, Sonya became pregnant while her brother Misha left home to study engineering in St. Petersburg. With less help, the businesses became a burden, and Elka decided to liquidate them. Afterwards, Sonya and Rubin joined Misha in St. Petersburg, believing there were better opportunities there for employment. Because Vanda was of school age, they decided it best to leave her in Pinsk with her grandmother.

Sonya and Rubin enjoyed life in St. Petersburg. The city was rich with history and culture—theaters, museums, the opera house—and they took full advantage.

Having her brother close by was an added benefit that helped convince Sonya and Rubin to make St. Petersburg their permanent home. Rubin became employed by the government, obtaining the position of Controller for the Tzar. He was charged with overseeing government warehouses, and carried the title *Byelo-Guardist* (the Tzar's Man.) Life was good for them, especially when Irenka, a beautiful and healthy baby arrived.

In the winter of 1917 rumors began to circulate that a revolution in Russia was imminent. Living in Pinsk, a place she had no ties to, Elka began worrying about her and Vanda's safety, and moved to Warsaw. She enrolled Vanda in school, and soon thereafter her intuition proved timely. While she was settling into her new home, the Russian Revolution had begun. All who worked for the Tzar were arrested, including Rubin. He did not have papers proving he was a Polish citizen, as Sonya and Misha had, and the Communist Party scheduled him for execution. But while he awaited the firing squad, Misha bribed high officials and obtained paperwork declaring Rubin a Polish citizen, and they all headed back to Warsaw.

Crossing the Russian border into Poland had become extremely dangerous. It was decided that it would be safer for Sonya to take Irenka and make the trip without the men. If questioned, she was to say she was a Polish citizen returning home to her husband after visiting family in Russia. If she needed money along the way, she could sell or trade the jewelry that had been sewn into Irenka's clothing.

Eventually, they made it to Warsaw, but the journey was not without hardship. They had very little food or water, and ended up traveling most of the way on foot. Only during the final stages of the journey did things become easier. At the Baranovitz railroad station in Poland, Sonya bought milk and rolls, and then procured a private compartment on a train to Warsaw. Then and only then did she begin to relax, but her concern for her husband and brother had just begun.

Rubin and Misha's trip across the border was much more difficult. They were constantly running and hiding, trying to avoid the Communist army. It was an endless ordeal of searching for food, shelter, and protection, and of trying to stay alive. But they made it. Eventually, they all met in Warsaw, safe from the Russians.

While on the road to Poland, Misha met Erna Feinstein and her family, who were also hoping to make Warsaw their home. Despite Misha's tendency to be a womanizer with no intention of settling down, Erna became infatuated. Once they were safely in Poland, she continued to pursue him, intent on making him her husband. Eventually, they fell in love and married. Grandma Elka loved telling the story of their courtship and the determination of a young woman in love, but mostly she enjoyed ending the tale with a laugh. "She attached herself to him like a wet rag to his ass."

It did not take long for the Wygodski family to make Warsaw their home. Vanda was fourteen and in high school; Irenka was seven and enrolled in Indrichkovka, a private elementary school, and soon another member of the family arrived. On June 4, 1921, Regina was born.

LET'S ASK BETKA

CHAPTER 9

One last chance to leave Poland and the Germans behind came to the Wygodski household. It was an unusually warm December evening when twenty-four-year-old Irenka returned home from a date with her boyfriend, Rafael. Their love affair blossomed quickly, beginning as friends and soon becoming more.

Irenka was stunningly beautiful, A combination of elegance and the girl next door. On the piano, she had a master's technique and personal style. Her slender arms and beautifully tapered fingers moved freely on the ivories with the speed of a jaguar and the accuracy of a gymnast. When Irenka played, she was one with the piano. Her talent mesmerized anyone that listened.

Their love was not meant to be. Two hours after her date, she was standing at the window of her bedroom, staring out at the courtyard, her eyes fixed on the filigreed wrought iron gate that led into the courtyard of our apartment building. She had been crying, and with every word she spoke, more tears flowed. "I told Rafael about Mama's cousin Yakob," she said, "and how he left for Palestine. I explained that he's safe now and has sent word for his family to follow. Rafael was happy for them, but something seemed to be bothering him."

She went on to explain that their walk home in silence had been awkward, neither sure of what to say or what they wanted. It was Rafael who had finally spoken up. There was no way to tell Irenka easily, and he knew he would be hurting her when he did.

"My brother and I are escaping to Russia," he had blurted out.

Irenka had been stunned instantaneously. Their relationship had developed quickly, but they meant a great deal to each other. How could Rafael leave her? How could she let him? They wanted a life together. The situation, every situation, had become unbearable.

"Come with me, Irenka," he had pleaded. "Come with me to Russia, as my bride."

Her heart had skipped a beat, and she could feel goosebumps all over her body. Everything she had wanted was standing in front of her. She wanted to accept Rafael's marriage proposal, fall into his arms, and live happily ever after.

However, her life wasn't just hers anymore, and she had other people to consider.

"I can't. I can't leave my mother and sister," she had explained.

"They can come with us," Rafael had insisted. "They can all come. It will be much safer for us in Russia, and you and I can have a future together."

The conversation had taken them to the courtyard of our home, Irenka fighting back tears. She'd looked deep into his eyes and said that she could never go to Russia with him. She had told him about Mama's fear of the Russians, and how she was convinced they'd be safer under German rule.

"Things are only going to get worse here, Irenka. It won't get better."

"Regusha and I made a pact that we will never leave our mother. We can't." She had hugged him tightly, whispered her goodbyes, and watched him disappear into the night. It was the last time she ever saw him. Before the new year arrived, he and his brother had escaped to Russia, leaving her lonely and depressed.

CHAPTER 10

THE ARRIVAL OF THE NEW DECADE only brought more fear, violence, persecution, and the establishment of what would become known as the Warsaw Ghetto. I remember it all too clearly for my own good. Watching the Germans construct a stone-and-brick fortress around the entire city was terrifying. They trapped us behind a ten-foot wall topped with barbwire, and surrounded every gate with armed guards.

And that might not have been the worst part. Upon its completion, the Germans ordered all Jews from surrounding cities and villages to immediately relocate to Warsaw, fully separating us from the Aryans—the obviously superior race. If there had been any question about what the Germans' intentions were or what they thought of us Jews, there was no disputing it then.

With the sudden influx of thousands of Jews from outside the city, there were far too many people and not enough space. We were crammed together so tightly it became almost unbearable.

Some on the outskirts of Warsaw were lucky. They managed to escape into the woods or forest before the Germans came—but they were forced to survive in the wilderness without access to food, water, or shelter. It was a chance that many of us were willing—or should have been willing—to take.

But for those in Warsaw, there was nowhere to hide. Once the Germans invaded Poland, and specifically after they began constructing the Ghetto, our chances of escaping evaorated. There were those who temporarily succeeded avoiding the inevitable. Most were caught escaping and were either beaten, tortured, or killed.

Warsaw had been turned into a prison. The city was hemorrhaging with people, and it was nearly impossible to find shelter for everyone. Two, and often three, families were forced to share an apartment. Vanda and Stasiek were lucky; they lived in a one-bedroom unit with Stasiek's mother.

The rest of our family was not so blessed. Irenka, our mother, and I had been living in a large apartment on Holdna 40 with plenty of space for us and our maid. With everything that was going on, and knowing that the Nazis were inching closer and closer to fully taking over our lives, our home gave us a protective shield. Even if it was only a mirage, we felt better being there. When the Ghetto was constructed, we too were forced out of our home and made to move into a much smaller unit at Nalefski 13—a room with four walls and three cots. We shared a kitchen and bathroom with another family. We were permitted to take a few personal items with us as mementos, but we still felt naked and exposed.

It was shocking how many people were still in denial about what was happening, my mother included. She, along with countless others, believed that this was a passing situation, that eventually the Germans would be overpowered and we would go back to our normal lives. But I knew differently. The construction of the Ghetto, and the way they began treating us, clearly revealed German intentions. We were second-class citizens, practically less then human. The Nazis would never be satisfied with just watching us suffer and be humiliated. This was genocide plain and simple. Hitler and his Nazi party were laying the groundwork for the extinction of the entire Jewish population.

Once the Ghetto was installed, the brutality of the Germans increased dramatically. Our every move was restricted; we were told where we could go and when. Pushcarts were the only means of transportation. Each of us was forced to wear the Star of David, the Jewish Star known in Hebrew as the Shield of David, on our clothing. The symbol that had for centuries stood for unity, security, and faith among Jewish people had become nothing more than an animal tag, a way for the Germans to tell us apart from their own, better people.

Any Jew found not wearing the symbol was subject to severe punishment and beatings, but wearing it wasn't much safer. It exposed us to criticism and attacks by any hoodlum, thug, or anti-Semitic maniac who used violence as a form of power.

Life inside the Ghetto was beyond horrible. It was overcrowded, we had no means of transportation, and there wasn't enough food or water to feed everyone. Starvation became rampant, and disease spread quickly. Many people died, and that was before one accounts for all those the Germans killed.

The first victims of the Nazi brutality were ones the Germans feared the most, the upper echelon of the Jewish community—the doctors, lawyers, and wealthy businessmen. The Germans worried about these people and their influence and leadership qualities, believing they could threaten a coup, and knew they had to be dealt with immediately. Up next on the Nazis' list were all the young, smart, and single men—men without the responsibilities of marriage or children, and who had nothing to lose.

They all quickly learned the Nazis' one and only method for dealing with any potential threat to their power base—cold-blooded murder.

Before long, any and every Jewish person became target for humiliation, and not just by members of the Nazi party. Anyone who wanted to feel powerful could attack us without consequence. Random beatings, shootings, and looting became regular occurrences, and the authorities turned a blind eye. (Thankfully, the Nuremberg Laws forbade personal dealings or association between Jews and Aryans, or I'm certain more advantages would have been taken of us Jewish girls.)

A seemingly favorite target for attack were older men with long beards. The Germans would force them to sing or dance in the street, do tricks or other tasks, and then be rewarded by having their facial hair cut off. The only crime these men, or any of us, committed was being born into a Jewish family and believing in the Ten Commandments.

It took every ounce of my strength not to interfere each time I witnessed the inhumanity of the Nazis. I took offense at the evil and hatred of the entire population and couldn't understand how they could be so morally corrupt. Watching innocent people being hurt and killed for no other reason than religious faith—our religious faith— caused my blood to boil. I knew the day would come when I wouldn't be able to contain it and just explode.

There was so much death and destruction all around. The first time I saw a dead body lying in the street, I took a quick glance at it and clenched my teeth and fists. It was morbid curiosity. The image of a smashed, bloody skull made me sick to my stomach. The back half of his head was gone. Through my teary eyes, I saw a pool of blood flowing on the cobblestones, the same street where children had played ball, where women's high heels clicked and the sound of children's laughter echoed, the same street where there had once been so much life, and where I had played as a child.

Sometimes I wanted to explode, to lash out, to scream or hit something. I wanted to let them know that this was not okay, that they could not do these things to other human beings. Inside I was seething, but outwardly I remained calm and rational. Anything else would only have brought about my own beating or death.

Eventually, there were many more bodies in the streets. Seeing it was sickening. I was repulsed, angry, and sad at the same time, and it changed something inside me. I learned to hold my anger, bury my emotions, and restrain tears in public, all because I didn't want to become their next victim.

CHAPTER 11

WE BELIEVED THEN THAT THINGS couldn't possibly get worse, so of course they did, and significantly so. Soon after the Ghetto was completed, the Germans introduced a new horror into our lives—*selection*.

None of us knew what selection was at first, only that it gave the Nazis some new kind of power to wield over us and their officers control over the fate of the Jews. Like alcohol to an alcoholic, selection fed into an inner need of these men to regulate and dominate another person. It gave them the authority to hold the reins tight and exercise power over life and death. They became judge and jury.

Every day, two hundred men, women, and children were chosen and taken to the railroad station at Stavki Square—a large oval area the Germans named Umschlag Platz (market place), with the capacity to contain thousands of people. An aerial view gives the impression of an octopus, as several roads led into a central hub surrounded by buildings. At one time, the area had been used by merchants to traffic goods in and out. But the Nazis closed off all the exits and used it for an entirely different purpose.

Many of those selected in the beginning went willingly, believing they were being sent to farms where food and shelter would be available. At first, the process seemed random—anyone could be picked out.

But the selection process was much more cynical than that. People were not chosen at random but rather on the basis of their perceived ability to work. Those deemed fit were left behind in the Ghetto, and those not were taken away—to somewhere none of us remaining in the Ghetto knew.

Luckily or unluckily, I was deemed fit to work and therefore kept prisoner in the Warsaw Ghetto. At the time, I may have been disappointed, but months later, when everyone learned what was really happening, I was relieved. Those trains weren't heading to farms or anywhere with food and shelter; they were heading northeast about fifty miles, to a town named Treblinka.

The first Poles who arrived at Treblinka must have been confused. It was nothing like they were expecting, and when I later learned the truth, I was horrified. There were no farms or even prisons in Treblinka; it was an extermination camp, used for the sole purpose of murdering as many Jews as possible.

Suddenly, the true meaning of selection, or choosing who would live—at least for now—and who would die, became clear. This was the first phase in the Nazi's Final Solution, the extinction of the entire Jewish population. (During the Holocaust, hundreds of thousands of Jewish people were killed in the gas chambers at Treblinka. The victims would think they were simply at a railroad station to switch trains, but then were quickly led to the gas chambers and murdered.)

Everyone in the Warsaw Ghetto feared selection. When the Germans issued a ruling that would spare an entire family from selection if at least two members were working, my mother set about to get Irenka and me jobs. She contacted an old high school friend, Mr. Moravchik, who was an administrator for the Countess Vilanovska Estate. The estate had several acres of land used for agricultural production, and Mama secured work positions for both of us. We received passes from the Germans to leave the ghetto and go to work each day. Those positions saved us and our mother from selection. (Of course, deep down I knew the rules could change at any time and we could be selected, but I allowed myself the comfort of believing we were safe.)

In the mornings, Irenka and I left our apartment and walked to the Nalefki Gate, only a block away. Most farm workers used this gate daily. Two trucks waited in the mornings to bring laborers to the estate.

It wasn't a long walk, but every day it was a horrible one. The images in the ghetto were grotesque and always the same. Dead bodies lay all over the place in pools of blood, covered with flies and insects. The sight of a rat gnawing on the arm of a corpse became a permanent image added to my dreams. I saw death and despair every day, everywhere I went, and it never got easier. My stomach twisted and turned at the horror, and it was all I could do not to throw up.

Thousands of men, women, and children died in the ghetto each month. Some were murdered by the Germans, but many more succumbed to starvation, disease, or exposure to the cold. Those who weren't already dead were dying a slow death anyway. Sometimes, I thought the dead were the lucky ones, knowing that they wouldn't have to face this horror anymore.

Many people walked around like zombies, too lethargic to move, and without purpose or destination. On every corner there were drooping bodies, people leaning awkwardly against walls or collapsed on steps, people with sunken eye sockets, hollow cheekbones, and open sores. Nearly everyone had the same haunted look in their eyes, the look of anger, frustration, and even surrender. Then, there were those who had just given up; they sat by the side of the road waiting for death to come.

I should have gotten used to it all but couldn't. Every night as I lay on my cot, hoping for sleep, I relived all those horrible images. It was the children who tormented me the most, the ones so hurt and hungry they literally wobbled back and forth simply walking in the street. They didn't look like children anymore but rather someone's used-up rag dolls that they had discarded like trash.

Before long, there were so many dead bodies piled up in the streets it became difficult to walk anywhere without stepping on one. It was so bad that even the German soldiers recognized the problem and gathered up some men in the ghetto to remove them. It was a disgusting job but only temporary, and the men chosen hoped it would shield them and their families from selection. They dug trenches large enough to hold hundreds of bodies, carried the bodies out of the city limits, and dumped them.

Countless Jews, unknown and unimportant to their killers, were buried in these mass, unmarked graves. *How can people be so cruel? What happened to humanity and compassion? How can these people hate us so much without even knowing any of us?*

Within months, the situation became insufferable. Those who hadn't reached their breaking point were dangerously close. To fill the quota, I remember the Nazis offering extra food—two pounds of bread and one pound of marmalade—to anyone willing to go to work in Treblinka. By then we all knew what Treblinka was and what our fate would be, and still many people volunteered; the Nazi soldiers found it amusing. *How could this be happening? What do they know that I don't?* With their bruised bodies, their swollen feet, protruding bellies, sunken eyes, and hollow cheeks, people walked, ran, or crawled. They boarded trains willingly going to their death. Either they had given up completely and figured a quick death in a gas chamber—after filling their bellies with food—was better than slowly dying in the ghetto, or they convinced themselves they would somehow escape or be saved.

Thankfully, I had not reached that point yet and did not volunteer. Neither did Irenka, Vanda, or Mama. We still had some fight left in us.

CHAPTER 12

Working at the Countess Vilanovska Estate was difficult, and the days were long, but it gave us an opportunity to earn money and receive additional food. Mr. Moravchik had always been extremely fond of my mother and extended courtesies to Irenka and me as well. Whenever possible, he gave us extra food. (He was generous with many of his workers, not just us.) He gave us milk, butter, potatoes, fruit, and vegetables that we smuggled into the ghetto. It was dangerous, and if we were caught, the food would be confiscated and we would be beaten. Luckily, Irenka and I were never caught.

Although we had passes to leave the ghetto to work, doing so was still dangerous. The Nazi soldiers with rifles on their shoulders and clubs on their belts were always within reach of us. They could attack anyone for any reason.

There was one Nazi soldier who scared us all. He took immense pleasure in murdering Jews and often did it just because he could. He was known in the ghetto as *Morderca* (The Killer). One day, I witnessed him ring the doorbell of the apartment to our building's superintendent and then shoot the man who answered it at point-blank range. He had no reason, no motive, other than his desire to kill. I didn't see the actual heinous act, only heard the pop of the gun and thud of the body. It was enough to make me shudder and cry, turn my blood cold with the sheer madness of it all.

Morderca was a big man, slightly overweight but powerfully built. With shaggy eyebrows set above sharp, glaring eyes, and a thick crown of matted hair, he looked like an out-of-shape wrestler. He was a man to be feared, a man without a conscience who had been given the right to torture and kill.

Each night before returning to the ghetto, the head of the work group would contact the Jewish Police to verify which gate was safest for returning to the ghetto. (The Jewish Police was a unit of men inside the ghetto that were given the responsibility by the Germans for orderly deportations of those selected to go to concentration camps. They had no real authority but took on many additional responsibilities in the hopes of keeping themselves and their families alive and all of us a little bit safer.)

The police only warned us once that Morderca was posted at the Nalefki Gate. That night the workers, including Irenka and me, re-entered the ghetto through a different gate, one much farther from our apartment.

However, with curfew time close, Irenka and I hired a young man with a rickshaw—a type of wagon used to transport people—to take us home. He moved quickly, but as we neared the entrance to our apartment building, we saw a soldier approaching. We both feared for our lives, Irenka grabbing my hand tightly.

"*Halt!*" was the only word I heard.

The young boy escorting us trembled as he pulled the wagon to a stop. We knew immediately it wasn't just any soldier, but Morderca. He came toward us slowly with his rifle pointed at us, ready to shoot. Up close he was even more intimidating, his voice powerful and scary.

I felt the blood drain from my body and turned to Irenka. Noticing she was white as a ghost, I whispered, "Don't say a word."

Worried that Irenka and I were late, Mama had been watching for us through the window. As curfew time approached, she'd become anxious, then relieved when she saw us coming in the rickshaw. However, seconds later, as Morderca approached the wagon, she had panicked again, and fainted.

Morderca's boots sounded loud on the cobblestone streets. "*Was haben sie dort?*" he barked, demanding to know what I had in the bag I was carrying.

Inside, my heart was pounding against my ribs, my throat so dry I could barely utter a sound. Although I didn't speak German, I understood every word he said. In Polish, I explained that our boss was satisfied with the work we had done and had given us some extra food. As the words came out, I remembered one of the things Mr. Moravchik had sent was *zanne*, a cream used in coffee. It was a gift for my mother, but knowing the Germans considered it a delicacy, I removed it from my bag and offered it to him.

His eyes lit up upon recognizing the item. "*Du hast shvine!*" he snarled as he grabbed the bottle.

I picked up the word *shvine*, knowing that it meant "pig" and not understanding the German expression was slang for "you have luck," and immediately responded in Polish, "*Ya nei yestem swinia!*" ("I am not a pig")

He was momentarily confused, then began laughing. It was a loud and sinister laugh, followed by an explanation that we were lucky because it was his *geburtstag*, his birthday, and that he would not dirty his hands with Jewish blood on such a day. Then turned to the young man with the wagon and told him to *verschwinder*, to get lost, before turning and heading to the main gate himself.

I congratulated myself for remembering the cream, but outwardly I wasted little time—I grabbed Irenka's hand and ran toward home. Once we were safely inside the building, I dropped my packages and bent over, waiting for my heart to stop pounding.

She rested her back against the wall and tried to catch her breath. With one hand on her chest and still breathing heavily, she asked, "Regusha, you never cease to amaze me. How in the world did you stay so calm?"

"What makes you think I was calm? I was so calm I peed my pants!" Sarcasm had always been my strong suit.

With nothing but nervous energy to keep us going, we both began laughing hysterically. We laughed all the way to our apartment door, where we found several neighbors trying to revive mama.

CHAPTER 13

As the fall of 1942 approached, a new ruling came down from the Germans: Jews were no longer permitted to work outside the ghetto, and anyone without a job could be subjected to transport to Treblinka. People were being taken from their homes at random and sent to the extermination camp. It was the beginning of mass annihilation.

With no other way to stay alive, Irenka and I had to find work inside the ghetto. There was no analyzing the situation, no family discussion. The task was all but impossible because there were tens of thousands—too many people for too few jobs. Some Jews were working for the Gestapo and able to buy jobs for their family and friends. But we didn't know anyone who could, the cost was exorbitant, and we certainly did not have the money.

Uncle Misha, Aunt Erna, and our cousin Yerzik lived about a mile away, on Electoralno Street. Because Uncle Misha had a friend who owned a factory, Irenka believed he could help us get jobs. She went by herself, not afraid to walk the streets of Warsaw alone. As dangerous as it was, her physical appearance helped keep her safe: She was a brunette beauty with Aryan features. In some ways, she was fearless; she appeared quiet and delicate most of the time but had a silent strength that came whenever she needed it.

I was nine when Papa died, and I remember how Irenka held the family together. We were devastated. She immediately exercised control. She temporarily set aside her grief and took care of all the necessary details. She notified everyone, arranged the burial customs, and met with Uncle Misha, Papa's partner, and the foreman to make sure the workers felt secure and the business could thrive. Lastly, she comforted me and Mama and gave us the emotional strength we needed.

Several hours passed after Irenka left for Uncle Misha's home, and Mama became worried. I tried calming her, to no avail. She was pacing the apartment, wringing her hands, and probably thinking the same horrible thoughts I was. When neither one of us could sit around and wait any longer, we decided to go to Uncle Misha's home ourselves to check on Irenka. (Well, Mama decided to go check on her, and there was no way I was letting her go alone.)

Three blocks away from our house, on Leshno Street, I noticed a bunch of Ukrainian men setting up barriers throughout the area. When I heard yelling—Nazi soldiers barking orders in German—I grabbed my mother and froze. In addition to the voices of the Nazi soldiers, I could hear men and women screaming, and their children crying. We hid behind a corner building and watched one family after another pushed out the front door of their apartment building, the Germans dragging people from their homes and tossing them into the middle of the street. As a woman fell to her knees, trying to protect her child, I felt Mama squeeze my arm. I immediately felt her fear or anger. The woman kept being pushed, but she continued to hold her child close. Mother and child held each other tight, hoping that, if they squeezed hard enough, they would become invisible. Those who didn't move fast enough—adult or child—were clubbed. The Nazis were in the middle of another round of selection.

Although we were hidden from their view, it was only temporary.

Being out in the open, even far enough away that the Germans couldn't see us, was still too dangerous; we needed to find somewhere permanent where we would be safe. I thought returning home might be best and had reached under Mama's elbow to pull her along when I noticed a door with a double zero (00)—the designation for public bathrooms—on it. In less than five seconds and all in one motion, I grabbed her hand, opened the bathroom door, and hurried both of us inside. We held each other tight and prayed in silence.

It was too dark to see anything, but whatever was going on outside was a nightmare. I heard nothing but terror—the sounds of wooden clubs connecting with human flesh and bone; a child wailing as she was dragged away; a father pleading to sacrifice himself to keep his family safe; a mother begging for the mercy of her child. All falling on deaf ears. None of it was heard, not by the German soldiers anyway. They were murdering bastards filled with nothing but evil and hate—men without a conscience.

Mama and I bit our lips and trembled whenever another set of boots passed the doorway, sure we were the next to be dragged away to the gas chambers. Every cell in my body wanted to scream, but silence was the only weapon that could save us. My adrenaline was high, my blood flowed cold, and sweat was dripping off my skin. Mama wasn't doing much better. With both her hands clamped on my arm, I could feel her shaking. As ripples of sweat rolled down my back, I could almost feel her fear.

Watching innocent people being dragged into the street to be taken away and murdered was crazy, but even more terrifying was hiding behind that bathroom door, waiting. I kept my eyes closed, too afraid of what I might see if I opened them, but my ears heard everything.

Slowly things calmed. The screaming and pleading faded away, the children's cries were gone, and orders were no longer being barked. We waited in silence until we were certain that the quota of Jews had been filled and the trucks had left. Safely behind that bathroom door, my mind was playing tricks on me, making me believe I had heard things. Was that a gust of wind? Was that a soldier's boot pounding on the cobblestone street?

There wasn't a sound in the area, an all-consuming silence that was anything but comforting. My mind was racing. Were there any German soldiers lingering behind, hoping to catch one last hidden Jew as his prize? Should Mama and I stay hidden longer just in case, or was I being too cautious? I didn't know whether we had been trapped inside that bathroom for five minutes or five hours. Either way, it was too long.

We were drenched in perspiration, shaking, and scared out of our minds, but I had to look outside, I just had to. I reached for the knob, slowly turned it, and pushed the door open barely enough to poke my head out. Both sides of the street were calm and quiet, totally deserted. The leaves on the trees weren't even rustling, and the only sounds were our rapid heartbeats.

Stepping outside, I could only wish that it had been that calm all along, that what I had witnessed hadn't really happened. But it had, and I knew it, and I would never be able to get those images, or those sounds, out of my head.

"It's all clear, Mama," I said. "They're gone. You can come out now."

Everything seemed to move in slow motion. Mama stepped out of the bathroom just as I had, slowly and timid at first, taking in the quiet a moment at a time. She looked around cautiously, as if to reassure herself that the Germans were gone.

"That was just too close for comfort," she said. "Now I'm more anxious than ever to see Irenka. Let's go find her."

There were still several blocks to go, and while my legs had begun moving, I had no control over them or any part of my body. My heart was thumping against my chest, and my blood was racing too fast through my veins for me to think. Mama squeezed my hand, and we covered the entire distance in silence.

At every corner, we stopped to look around, making sure there weren't any soldiers left. There were none, but that didn't ease our panic much. I was tempted to run, to get to Uncle Misha's home as quickly as possible, but thought better of it. We didn't see anybody, but that didn't mean no one was seeing us, and we wanted to remain as inconspicuous as possible.

We were out of breath by the time we reached Uncle Misha's place, but—thankfully—Irenka had arrived there safely, too. The factory owned by our uncle's friend had, though, been closed by the authorities, taking away another option to keep us out of the grasp of the Germans and their selection process.

Gathering around the dining room table, we considered the options we still had, and what we could all do to ensure our survival. At one point, there was mention of a fur factory that was hiring workers. The plant was assigned to make hats, gloves, and ear muffs for the soldiers on the Russian front.

Before the statement was finished and all the details were known, I jumped up from my chair. "I'll meet you back at the apartment!" I exclaimed.

"Where are you going?" Mama called in my direction, but I was already halfway out the door, and too far gone to respond.

I heard Irenka saying, "Just let her go," but I knew Mama would worry anyway. That's what mothers do. Mama always worried about me and my sisters, and she always would, but that wasn't all she did. She had always been there for us growing up, too, caring about us and willing to listen when we needed to talk. Like my father, she welcomed open discussion about anything and everything, and I felt comfortable seeking her advice or complaining to her.

One topic I often complained about as a child was doing my chores. I hated them, and since we had a maid, I argued that she should be doing them for me. Mama listened as she always had—attentively and without interrupting—and then told me she loved me before kissing my forehead. "The maid is for me, not you," she explained. "Now go and clean your room."

I was angry at the time, but Mama's insistence on me working hard, and pulling my own weight despite whatever advantages we had, might end up saving our lives.

Mama would also listen and offer encouragement when I rambled on and on about school and my ever-changing dreams for the future. Two years before the Germans invaded our world, she had insisted I take a course at the Jewish Trade School. Being good with my hands, I took up sewing and hat-making, finishing the course of study earlier than anticipated. Little did I know then those six weeks would literally be the difference between life and death one day soon.

Leaving Uncle Misha's apartment, I ran all the way back home, not caring who or if anyone was watching, to get my diploma, the proof of my skills.

With my life and my family's literally in my hands, I went in search of the factory. But when I reached it on Orgadova Street, I became overwhelmed and disheartened by the sight of hundreds of people in line ahead of me, all whom had the same thoughts I did.

There was a lot of yelling and shoving, and the cacophony of sounds was deafening. It was almost impossible to hear anything. Desperate and in the middle of total chaos, I began pushing my way through the crowd. Running frantically from side to side, scrutinizing every face, I finally made it to the front.

There, standing in front of me was a very tall, husky man with broad shoulders, large hands, and a deep voice, yelling at the crowd to stop pushing. I retreated from the mob and looked up to find myself facing him. At the same time, he looked down at me, towering over my four-foot-eleven frame, with a dubious look. His face crinkled into a smile, and he almost laughed.

"Little girl, what are you doing running around here? You could get hurt." When I didn't move, he bellowed at me, "Go home."

Annoyed by the slight, I said in the most uppity tone I could, "Sir, I am not a child. I am twenty years old, and I am a professional who wants a job, so that I can continue to eat and stay alive. Do you have a problem with that?"

I flashed my diploma and informed him about my ability to make hats. His name was Bzeznitski, and he was not only a furrier but the supervisor of the Tobbens Factory, where I wanted a job.

Later I learned that he saw something in me that very first moment we met. Days later, he told me that, looking in my eyes that day, he knew I wasn't a mischievous child but a young woman filled with determination and spirit. I had an energy raging through my whole body that told him I had what it took to survive even in the worst of times.

"Come with me!" he demanded, an amused grin on his face, slipping his considerable arm under my elbow and pulling me away from the crowd. My feet were barely touching the ground—I was essentially being dragged—but there was a gentleness in his touch and an honesty in his voice.

Before I realized what was happening, I was inside the building, standing in front of a desk, and facing an SS Officer, Director Marmor. I handed him my diploma and, after he took a quick look, he returned the paper to me with a work pass attached. With the transaction completed, he dismissed me and yelled, *"Nachster!"* for the next supplicant in line.

Instead of moving along as instructed, I remained there, staring at the man in charge, the man who could have me killed for even the slightest infraction or simply on a whim.

"I also need a pass for my sister," I said with great determination. In that moment, I realized that Bzeznitski and two women that were working in the office had frozen and were staring at me in disbelief. "She is an excellent stenographer and typist," I continued with a quaver in my voice.

Director Marmor leaned back in his chair and folded his arms across his chest, staring at me with curiosity. It was obvious he was stunned, but he must have admired my courage and fortitude, too. We kept staring at each other. The next few seconds passed in absolute silence while he considered my request—the longest few seconds I could remember up to that point in my life. My fear wasn't going to allow Director Marmor's stare to intimidate me. Inwardly, I was trembling, not sure whether I was being brazen or just plain stupid.

"Does your sister have a typewriter?" he asked, finally breaking the silence.

I nodded. My throat was too dry, my tongue like sandpaper, and I knew if I tried to speak, my fear would have been unmistakable.

Director Marmor leaned forward, placed his elbows on his desk, and calmly told me to go home and get my sister. As I turned to leave, he added, "And don't forget the typewriter."

CHAPTER 14

All Tobbens Factory workers were required to live near the factory, and the three closest streets—Tzeglana, Valitzouv, and Ciepla—were evacuated to make room for all of us. Eventually, the area became known as the "Little Ghetto."

Irenka and I worked in the factory—she in the office, I on the assembly line—but spent most of our time thinking and worrying about our mother. We needed to find a way to keep her safe from the Germans. She had *zonder* (special papers) omitting her from selection and allowing her to come and go freely, but we couldn't trust that they would be honored indefinitely. The danger was increasing by the day, and no one knew what rules or regulations the Nazis would suddenly come up with to fill the quota for Treblinka.

Working in the office gave Irenka opportunities to use the telephone, and even though she feared punishment if caught, she sometimes did. One afternoon, in the middle of typing a document, she noticed there were no other employees the office, and took advantage. With a trembling hand, she reached for the phone and dialed a number from memory.

The receiver on the other end was picked up immediately. "Good morning. Countess Vilanovska Estate."

"Hello, Mr. Moravchik?" Irenka asked nervously.

"Yes."

Afraid to be overheard, she spoke just above a whisper, but calmly. She identified herself and quickly got to the point: our concerns about our mother's safety, and as Mama's long-time friend, he sympathized. He promised Irenka that, if we could smuggle our mother out of the ghetto, he would keep her safe, working on the Vilanovska Estate as a cook and maid.

Irenka was relieved when she hung up the phone, but had a difficult time concentrating on her work while formulating a plan. She was too busy figuring out how to get Mama out of the ghetto.

A handful of people were still being permitted to work outside the ghetto. Irenka and I bribed the leader of that group to smuggle Mama out. We paid with some of the money and jewelry we had kept hidden, and one quiet morning she passed through the ghetto gate between two workers.

Once she was safely on the Aryan side, Moravchik procured the necessary papers, with the proper stamps and signatures, allowing her to enter and exit the ghetto.

But Mama didn't come back to visit us often, and Irenka and I preferred it that way. We loved having her around and missed her terribly when she was gone, but it was too dangerous. Even with the legal paperwork, you never knew what the Germans were going to do, what regulations they'd change without notice, and it wasn't worth the risk. Above all else, Irenka and I wanted her safe. (Whenever possible, Irenka did use the office telephone to call the Vilanovska Estate to check on her.)

Having Mama safely on the other side of those walls was helpful. It gave us one less thing to worry about, and we could concentrate our efforts on working and surviving.

Two days after she left, we moved into a new apartment—not that we had much choice in the matter—to be closer to the factory. We packed up the meager belongings we had left and hired a man with a pushcart to help us move.

Of all the terrible days and things I lived through in the ghetto, walking to our new apartment that morning may have been the worst. The horror in the streets was unavoidable, but this one was especially gruesome. It was the blood dripping from the bricks that first caught my attention, and then someone told me that was what had remained of a baby's head after a Nazi soldier smashed it against the wall. I gasped and couldn't speak, and when I closed my eyes I could see it happening.

The thought of something so barbaric made me nauseous, and it wasn't exceptional, even rare. Stories of Nazi soldiers grabbing little children and babies by their ankles and hurling them against brick and cement walls were common. I never had to witness it, but that didn't stop me from seeing it in my dreams.

There were more dead bodies than usual on the street that day, all of them bleeding, dripping, and oozing, but the ones who were still alive haunted me more. It was the worst reality imaginable, and I was unable to tear my eyes away. The looks of confusion and anger, hunger and fear, were all around. Irenka and I were luckier than most; we had jobs that gave us a temporary safety net, and not many had that. No one deserved the kind of evil the Germans were dishing out.

Once we made it to our new apartment, we entered and slammed the door, shutting out the rest of the world. Saying it felt safe would be a stretch, but I was oddly secure. Irenka and I had shelter, we had jobs that would keep us alive for the time being, and our mother was out of harm's way.

Our new home was a single room in a building on Tzeglana Street. It was small, and we had to share it with two other women and a child.

It wasn't anything like we had been used to before, and other than a couple of mementos, there wasn't much connecting us to our old lives.

The work at the factory was tedious. I spent hours sitting in the same position sewing, cutting, stitching, pinning, and trimming. The work was nonstop, and there were no breaks and little relief. Everyone there was in agony, feeling the pain in different parts of their body. Sometimes the pain was in the upper or lower back; for others in the neck. Sometimes the pain was dull and constant, and at other times it was sharp and piercing, but it was always there. So often I wanted to stand up and stretch, take a short break, or have a second or two to regroup, but never did. I knew better; the consequences could be disastrous.

Although short, I packed a lot of strength in my tiny body, which helped get me through those days. When I returned to our apartment at night, I was exhausted and on the verge of collapsing. The pain was everywhere—my back, my legs, my arms, even the nerves that ran up and down my spine, pricking and tingling me until I couldn't take it any longer.

I can't say I was alone in my suffering either. All the workers employed at the Tobbens Factory went home with similar ailments. At least the lucky ones did; the unlucky ones never went home at all.

At the end of the day, when work was done and I was safely tucked into my bed, it should have been easy to sleep but rarely was. My body was tired enough, but closing my eyes only stirred up those horrible sounds and images. The voices of children screaming in terror, visions of dead bodies lying in the street, or Nazi soldiers chasing me haunted my thoughts. No matter what I did, I could not rid myself of those thoughts—then or now. They're forever burned into my memory.

CHAPTER 15

For weeks, nothing changed; the routine was the same every single day. The days were spent in the factory endlessly working—sewing, cutting, stitching, pinning, trimming—while I battled my demons at night.

Then a fatal note from Stasiek reached the office for Irenka: Vanda was taken to Treblinka.

The words buzzed in my head over and over. I heard them clearly and understood them but could not process what they meant. It felt as if I'd been slapped across the face. Vanda, my eldest and beautiful sister, was gone, and I would never get to see her again.

That night, though nothing would console us, Irenka and I sat up crying, talking, and reminiscing about our sister. We talked about the good times, the memories before the war, and I felt the tears would never stop, that we would never be whole again.

However, as dawn approached, so did our mourning end. We had to turn everything else off and return to our jobs in the factory, for our own survival.

After Vanda's death, the weeks passed as quickly as they had before. Our lives were horrible, but at least we still had them. Irenka and I were also worrying more and more about our mother. We hadn't seen her in a long time, but at least she was safe outside of the ghetto.

It's been said that it's darkest before the dawn, but that's not always the case. I remember a day in September 1942 that challenges that notion.

It was a warm, clear day, and many of the Tobbens Factory workers remained outside in the streets rather than returning to their homes after work. The sun was still shining late into the afternoon, and the warmth as it hit our faces was exhilarating. Many people were huddled together talking about the latest rumors circulating throughout the ghetto. There was belief that workers were no longer safe from selection, and then the worst rumor of all: "There may be a roundup?" Someone asked in surprise. Several other people had heard the same thing but were too afraid to believe it or say it out loud.

If the previous two years had taught me anything about rumors, it was that they often became a reality.

I was considering my thoughts on the subject when I looked up and saw a tiny figure coming through the ghetto gates. With the bright sun shining in my eyes, it was difficult to see. I stopped talking and squinted to see the slender figure approaching. Between the moment of doubt and confirmation, I grew chilled despite the warm sun on me.

It couldn't be. It better not be. Oh, god, I hope not.

As I raised my arm above my forehead to shield my eyes from the sun, my fears were confirmed. It was Mama. She was weighed down by packages and walking slower than usual, but I would recognize her swagger anywhere.

I motioned to Irenka, and both of us ran to greet her. My pulse still hadn't returned to normal even after we'd gone inside and unpacked the groceries she brought. "Mama, this is too dangerous, and you are not to come here again!" I reprimanded her.

"When it comes to my children, I can easily confront any danger." It was a simple reply, a simple fact.

"There are rumors about a roundup. Is there a reason you came today?" I questioned.

Even seeing her, feeling her arms around me, comforting me and providing me with a warmth I hadn't felt in so long, was wonderful. But I didn't want her there. I wanted her safe.

"With God's help, if you will survive this and have your own children one day, you will understand a mother's feelings and emotions," she said tenderly.

I appreciated her response, but it wasn't an answer. It was a statement of love more than anything else.

And she was right. It wasn't until years later, when I was fortunate enough, not only to survive the worst of the worst, but to become a mother myself, that I truly understood her. A mother's love, a mother's desire to see her children, even in times when it is inherently dangerous, is more important than anything.

Mama had heard all the same rumors we had, and spent most of the rest of the afternoon sitting on a cot, filling us in on her fears. Irenka and I tried assuring her that our jobs were secure and we were temporarily safe, but she still worried.

As curfew approached, she decided to stay the night. She loved us too much, she missed us too much, to leave so soon after getting there, especially since it would likely be a long time before we saw each other again. It was safer for her on the Aryan side, but her life there was empty and unfulfilling. Mama had lost her husband, her mother, her home and her safety, and finally her daughter. She couldn't take any more loss, and Irenka and I were the only family she had left. The sparkle that once lived in her eyes was gone, and in its place I could see an agonizing pain and sadness. Even when she laughed and smiled, it was with dead eyes. It was heartbreaking to watch, and I realized in that moment that she had abandoned all hope of purpose for a future.

The next morning, when Irenka and I left for the factory, Mama stayed behind in our apartment. The other woman who lived with us—including her five-year-old son—usually left the boy with a neighbor, but Mama volunteered to watch him. She planned to stay until after lunch, so we could see her once more, and despite the risk it was a welcomed idea.

On our way to the factory that morning, there was more chatter on the streets than usual. People were nervous. We passed a group of men and women in the middle of a deep conversation, and I overheard parts of their discussion.

"I'm afraid there's going to be a roundup," one of the men said. "Believe me, there will definitely be another selection any day now."

Another man spoke adamantly. "Oh, come on. They need us at the factory."

"I think we'll all be safe," someone else opined.

We continued walking toward the factory. At the entrance, I turned to Irenka. "I hate listening to all these rumors, because they always come true."

We weren't even an hour into our workday when faint sounds in the distance caught our attention. One by one, everyone slowed their work and began looking around the room with dread. The noises were still far away, but the thunderous trot of hooves on the ground was unmistakable: Soldiers galloping on their horses, singing songs, were approaching the ghetto. They were the same songs they sang every time they came into the ghetto, which only meant two things—more beatings and another round of selection. Everyone stopped working momentarily, scared and frozen into silence, a tomb-like silence. With the belief that factory workers were no longer off-limits, the entire warehouse became filled with terror and anxiety.

CHAPTER 16

As the soldiers came crashing through the barrier that caged us in like animals, the stampeding of the horses slowed, and the rhythmic hums of their songs ceased. Their boots hit the ground with force, and they began marching through the ghetto, shrieking commands into the air. There was a new quota, and these soldiers had been sent to fill it.

They weren't strong enough to fight on the front lines, not when their enemies were equally as armed, and they didn't have the smarts to handle the interrogations of the Gestapo. Instead they were filled with a psychotic and unquenchable thirst for blood and torture, and Hitler offered them us—the Jews—as a means of fulfilling their desires. They looted what little we had left, then beat, tortured, and murdered.

Upon entering the ghetto, they ordered everyone out of the buildings surrounding the factory, and then realized there weren't enough bodies to fill the quota. Just as we had feared, they turned their attention toward the Tobbens factory workers, and one of them shouted, *"Jeder aus der fabrik!"*

We obeyed them and left the factory.

"Alle. . .euchaufstellen!"

We did as we were told and lined up in absolute silence as the commando leader strutted back and forth in front of us. He was a short, stout man with a ruddy complexion and rigid jawline. He was tense, his nostrils were flaring, his jaw clenched, and he appeared to be on the verge of having an epileptic attack. As he passed us, he began pointing at people and shouting commands. There was no method to his madness, just random insanity.

"*Sie...links!*" he barked, ordering some people to the left, and others to the right with a sharp, "*Sie...recht!* The selection went on and on. Many of the first to be chosen were the elderly, but overall there was no rhyme nor reason to the process.

The man behind the scenes, the one running the ghetto, SS Officer Marmor, had approached the crowd to watch the younger commander pick and choose who would live and who would die.

He had been staring at Irenka from the moment he stepped outside in the sunlight. Was she going to be selected? But before I could do anything, not that I could do anything, he grabbed her elbow and pulled her aside. I don't know how, but I was certain he was saving her. He exuded position and power, and his authority was not to be questioned. He stood with my sister a few feet away from the crowd and as far away from the man selecting people to go to Treblinka.

"What about my sister, Regusha?" she asked.

"She will be fine," he whispered, barely moving his lips. "I will only intervene if it becomes necessary. Now be quiet."

I wasn't quite sure what to make of him. He was SS, the enemy, but he also seemed protective of Irenka and me, although I had no idea why. That day, I was pleased he was around to intervene and watch over her. I had always inwardly been the stronger one, and physically strong outwardly, and didn't need to be protected the way she did.

His intuition that day was correct; I was not chosen for the group that was sent to the slaughter camp. He watched me carefully throughout the process, not once taking his eyes off me, and making sure I followed every order. I tried not looking at him and causing any suspicion, but I'm sure he had to notice.

Once the quota for selection was met, one final command was given: All remaining Jews were ordered to sit down with their legs crossed, heads lowered, and eyes on the ground. Just before I sat down, I glanced at the officer issuing the orders and choosing those marked for death. His neck was strained, his veins bulging out, and he was leering at us with a sinister non-smile. He was enjoying this, and he had every intention of hurting someone.

"Keep your heads down!" he bellowed into the crowd. "Eyes on the ground!"

A long silence followed, probably an attempt to wait us out, see if someone would break, and he'd have a reason to do something evil. "Follow my orders!" he snapped. "Or-you-will-be-shot!" Each word was enunciated with a cold and calculating indifference.

I was frozen, unable to move. Mrs. Rosenberg, my direct supervisor at the Tobbens Factory, was sitting next to me. With her head remaining lowered, she moved closer, and without moving a muscle, she whispered to me, "My husband was chosen."

She was devastated to the point of shaking uncontrollably. Had there not been several people surrounding her, she likely would have toppled over. As the SS officers marched the selected Jews out of the ghetto, she turned her head to catch one final glimpse of her husband, the man she loved.

It happened in an instant. I didn't see the commander raise his weapon, and at first I didn't even hear the shot. I saw the blood, felt warm droplets land on my arms and the back of my neck, and then Mrs. Rosenberg's body deflated like the air from a blow-up doll. She fell forward with her shoulders slumped and head between her knees and collapsed to the ground, dead.

It took a couple of seconds to process what had happened, and everything moved in slow motion. The commander began barking more orders, making more threats, but I didn't hear anything. The gun's explosion was echoing in my ears, reverberating against the buildings, and getting louder and louder until I couldn't take it any longer. My mind was refusing the image that my eyes had just seen. I closed my eyes tightly. I clenched my fists, scraping my knuckles on the ground to the point of bleeding. Our knees made contact, our arms were touching, and my body felt numb. My heart was pounding, my breathing was uneven, and my throat felt raw. Bile rose from my gut, and I forced it back down with a sharp gulp. I wanted to scream, to lash out, but knew my life depended on my silence.

I had seen so many horrible things the Nazis did, but this was the first time I had witnessed a cold-blooded murder up close. The body of that sweet lady lay next to me, her knees still touching mine. I felt physically ill. Even though it wasn't chilly, I was shivering and shaking, feeling nauseous while doing everything I could to avoid vomiting. The world was standing still. I felt as if I was falling into a bottomless abyss, sinking lower and lower until I could no longer breathe. The image of Mrs. Rosenberg's murdered corpse remains with me to this hour.

The hatred that led to such cold-blooded murder was staggering. As the commander stood over the body of the woman he killed, the gun still in his hand, I stared at his boots. Petrified of being next, I dared not look up. He wasn't a man but a creature without a conscience who had fulfilled his desire to kill and torture. Despite the horrors he inflicted on so many, not just the woman he had just murdered, he would sleep easy that night.

The silence was finally broken once again: "Return to your living quarters!" he ordered, his voice loud and offensive.

As I rose to return to our apartment, I tried to appear calm and not frightened, but I was anything but. I was scared out of my mind, barely able to walk without toppling over, and the desire to throw up was overwhelming. I kept feeling dizzy, the walls of the buildings seeming to close in around me, and Irenka had to help me home.

Well, no—not home. Home was gone, a place cataloged in my memories, and something that I was sure I would never have again.

CHAPTER 17

WE WEREN'T FORCED TO RETURN to the factory that day. I couldn't have even if they had ordered us to. I was mentally drained and too physically exhausted to even think. I needed to take breathe, to somehow clear my mind of the horror I had just witnessed if I was going to find the will to survive.

By the time we made it back to the apartment, all I wanted to do was escort my mother back to the Aryan side and then lie down on my cot and forget everything that had happened.

"Mama?" I called entering the apartment but heard nothing. A few moments later I called again, and again got no answer. The silence in the room, the kind you hear when no one else is around, was unbearable.

"Mama!" I called, this time as loud as I could without screaming.

But there was no Mama, and no little boy she had been watching. The neighbors were gone, too. Frantically, I searched the other apartments, hoping to find her hiding somewhere. After the ordeal in the factory courtyard, I needed her to wrap her arms around me and tell me everything would be okay, even if neither of us believed it. But she wasn't anywhere to be found, in any apartment on any floor.

No mama. No little boy. No neighbors.

While I looked for her, Irenka ran back to the office to use the phone to get word to Stasiek. He worked at the railroad station with a man we all knew from school, Leiken. Growing up, Leiken had been our neighbor, a childhood friend of Vanda's, and with the German invasion had found himself elevated to commander of the Jewish Police Force. If anyone could help, it was Leiken.

Stasiek arrived at the deportation railroad station just as everyone was boarding the cattle train, the preferred transportation method of the Third Reich. He ran up and down the platform, cutting through lines of people, peering into each car, and finally he managed to locate his mother-in-law. She had already been loaded into one of the cars.

He immediately ran to find Leiken, explained the situation, and begged him to intervene. Leiken refused. He practically ignored Stasiek, acting as if his long-time friend was speaking a foreign language he couldn't understand. When I found out, that angered me more than anything else. It was a time when there weren't many Jews who had the power to do anything, but Leiken had that power. He could have stepped up, saved my mother from the death camp, but chose not to.

It's likely he became hypnotized by the power given to him and captivated with his position of authority. Stasiek tried one final time to plead with his friend, and finally got an answer.

"No!" Leiken yelled, then turned his back and walked away.

Stasiek was so enraged that he almost attacked him, but thought better of it. He spat on the ground toward his former friend's back, mumbled something under his breath, and returned to deliver the horrible news. (During the liquidation of the Warsaw Ghetto, Leiken was shot and killed by the Jewish resistance fighters. Several million Jewish people were murdered during Hitler's reign, but Leiken's death isn't one I will ever be sorry about.)

What had begun as a warm and sunny day ended in horror. A dark cloud hovered over the ghetto, while, inside our small and dingy apartment, four women sat on their cots, staring at the floor in disbelief. How could any of this be *happening?* None of us spoke for the longest time, and I didn't have any tears left to cry. All I felt was an emptiness inside my heart, a place that would never again be filled. My thoughts made my head spin and within a moment, I was drained.

All my thoughts merged into one. It seemed as if flash cards were jumping before my eyes, each a vision from the past. I saw my parents, alive and at happier times, and Vanda and Stasiek young and vibrant, obviously very much in love. We were all sitting in the warmth of our home, safe, happy, and listening to Irenka playing the piano. I saw the children of Warsaw playing in the streets of a happy city before the Germans arrived.

Then, all at once, those thoughts turned black. Dad and Grandma were gone, and now Mama and Vanda had joined them. They were gone, dead, murdered by an evil, hate-filled regime that planned to kill all of us sooner or later. Our streets were littered with dead bodies—men, women, and children, even one woman who died simply for glancing at her husband. I was too young to have seen so much horror, and it had created an enemy of my own thoughts.

I was shaken out of this reverie by the sound of uncontrollable sobbing from the woman who lost her son, the little boy who had been taken along with my mother. "My husband is fighting in the south with the Polish Army. If we survive this horror, how will I explain to him that I allowed them to take our son?" She continued crying and mumbling under her breath, not that much of it was comprehensible.

Following several minutes of silence, Irenka spoke up. "If Mama had left last night...." She didn't finish the sentence.

"I know, I was thinking the same thing. She would be safe at the estate right now."

The hours passed slowly; tears came and went, but our thoughts haunted us. We knew sleep was not something we'd have the luxury of that night.

If Mama had stayed at the estate...

If she would had listened to Yakob and gone to Palestine, we'd all be safe!

If, if, if!

If one or a thousand things were different, we would all be safe, millions of Jews would not have been murdered, and the world wouldn't have lived through this terror. Our lives and thoughts became filled with ifs, but none of them mattered. What mattered was that we were all marked for death—like it or not, accept it or not. It was just a matter of time, and of how bad it would be.

LET'S ASK BETKA

CHAPTER 18

SO NO ONE WAS SAFE from selection any more, not even the workers at the Tobbens Factory. The raids became more frequent and came without warning. Anyone and everyone was ripe for the taking, on nothing more than the whim of a soldier.

Prior to the war, Adam Cherniakow was a distinguished member of the Polish Senate. A few days after Warsaw surrendered to the Nazis, Cherniakow was appointed head of the Jewish Council, made up of twenty-four members charged with implementing Nazi orders in the newly established ghetto.

I remember the day he was given a direct order he could not follow. They told him to fill and deliver a daily quota of six thousand Jews to the Treblinka extermination camp. Rumors had it that he had managed to get exemptions for several groups but failed in his attempt at saving the orphaned children of Warsaw. When he realized he would not be able to save them, he chose a route many others did—suicide. He swallowed a cyanide capsule, freeing himself of the Nazi regime.

Killing ourselves wasn't something that Irenka and I seriously considered, but the thought sometimes crept up on us. Would death at our own hands be better than this?

As 1942 was drawing to an end, I received word that my Uncle Misha and his family had purchased illegal papers and were living as Aryans on the other side of the wall. Around the same time, another note came from Stasiek. He was tired of living life as a Nazi pawn, and without Vanda he had nothing left. Instead of continuing that way, waiting for the Germans to turn on him and kill him, he had decided to join the underground. Food, shelter, and the basic necessities were almost impossible to come by, and for some it was better than the alternative.

The constant tension in our lives, not knowing what horror any day would bring, only created more stress. The work at the factory became harder and more intense, if that was even possible, and living every day in fear was a nightmare. Hitler was a madman with the demonic goal of eliminating an entire race from the globe, or at least from Europe, where only the Aryan people should survive in his twisted mind.

Waiting for the next raid or selection was maddening. Maybe that was the end game; maybe driving us all to kill each other instead of wasting their energy doing it for us was what the Germans really wanted.

Irenka and I, like Stasiek, could no longer live that way. The nightmares needed to stop. We had to find a way to escape.

Only days later, we began formulating a plan. One of Irenka's office co-workers, Mrs. Paula Ojzel, approached her. She had been one of our mother's many friends, which is why she'd felt safe coming to us. "I know you and your sister are trying to escape to the other side, to live as Aryans, and we would like your help to escape, too."

Irenka became alarmed and could not respond. If Mrs. Ojzel knew of our plans, how many others did? Was it safe to even attempt it? Instead of denying it, Irenka took a leap of faith, believing in the woman's history with our mother, and nodded in agreement.

After a pause, Mrs. Ojzel explained how Irenka and I could help her family. "We could never pass as Poles. One look at our faces, and anyone can see our Jewish heritage. What I am asking you to do is to find an apartment to keep us hidden. If you can arrange that, my husband will pay all the expenses."

Irenka could only nod again, but Mrs. Ojzel's pleading eyes told her she had to help this woman if she could. Everyone deserved at least that much.

Prior to the war, the Ozjels had been a prominent, wealthy couple. He owned the only franchise in Poland that distributed Swiss-made Patek Philippe watches, the most exclusive brand in the world. When the Germans invaded, they had confiscated the franchise, assigned a worker to supervise it, and then relocated the Ojzels to the ghetto. They were an older couple with a teenage son who also had distinguishing features and could never be hidden in plain sight.

After work that very day, I returned to our living quarters and found Irenka sitting on her cot, deep in thought. My arrival startled her, and she told me to be quiet as soon as I entered. After a few minutes of silence, she told me what she'd been thinking about. "I'm going to do it," she said. "The next time Marmor gives me a pass to run an errand for him outside the ghetto, I'm going to do it."

"...Do what?"

"Do you remember Mr. Woitczak?" she asked, the details of her plan still working themselves out. "Yes! Yes, now I know exactly what to do."

After that confident statement, she left quickly. I was totally confused. I remembered Woitczak very well. He had worked for my father as a railroad conductor. He'd become an underground social worker for Jews, but I wasn't sure exactly what Irenka planned to do.

Several days passed before the opportunity to leave the ghetto arose, and Irenka made her move. Director Marmor asked her to run an errand outside the ghetto, and once she was free of those walls, she began her mission. It took some time, but eventually she found Woitczak, introduced herself, and told him what she needed.

He was shocked that a Jewish girl was getting in and out of the ghetto as easily as she was and invited her to his home. Sitting together at his dining room table, Irenka explained that she would need new identities for both herself and me, and related the details about hiding the Ozjel family. "What we will need is a narrow railroad apartment, with each room leading to the next."

This was a thing Woitczak was familiar with.

"The last room will need to be sealed off with a bullet-proof wall. It will also need a movable panel that can be closed and crawled through when necessary."

He listened intently, made notes, asked some questions, and when she finished, confirmed his involvement with three words: "Consider it done!"

Everything came together in the latter part of March. All the necessary documents were ready. Irenka and I were given the birth certificates of two dead women. Their identities were strikingly similar to our own. I took on the name Albina Sofia Voitchuk, a woman who shared my exact birthday—June 4, 1921—while Irenka became Irena Novitzka. The coincidence with our new identities was uncanny. The irony was either an omen or a curse.

Living in the ghetto, seeing the harm and cruelty the Nazis were inflicting on people every day, I often wondered whether it was just happening in Poland, or had the hate and savagery spread to other countries as well.

If it hadn't, did the rest of the world even know what was happening here? Were they coming to rescue us? Not a hint of gossip was spread, not a word was discussed, not a whisper was heard. Had Hitler and his venomous anti-Semitic idealism infiltrated other countries?

LET'S ASK BETKA

In the middle of all the brutality and inhuman cruelty, the one person who gave us hope, the one man who made us realize that not everyone was insane or utterly evil, was Director Marmor. Irenka and I often discussed him at length, but had trouble understanding his behavior—a near-devotion toward us and others. He was an SS officer, the enemy, and yet he took great risks to protect us when he could.

I reasoned that, at one time, he had fallen in love and under the spell of a Jewish woman, and honored that love by doing what he could to keep as many of us as he could safe from harm. I could never completely trust him because of the uniform he wore, but he was as close to a miracle as we had in the ghetto.

What had brought Marmor into our lives? Was it just a matter of fate, or luck?

Yet he was the reason Irenka and I were still alive. He had given us our jobs in the factory—Irenka's on my word alone, the word of a Jew!—and on more than one occasion saved us from selection. He turned a blind eye when Irenka used the office telephone to check on our mother, and subtly he watched over us. In many ways, he was a godsend.

When Marmor learned of our impending escape attempt, he offered to assist. There was nothing in it for him—not money, not jewelry, not even his own freedom—and had he been found helping a Jew, his own people would have turned on him and treated him no better than they treated us. But he helped anyway, because he wanted to.

He was a subject of much discussion that often left Irenka and me more than a little confused afterwards. He was a question we could not answer. He was a puzzle that we could not solve. However, we accepted him and everything he did with a leap of faith. His private chauffeur drove us in Mr. Tobbens' car to a prearranged place where Irenka and I met several members of the Polish underground.

The money we received from the Ojzel family afforded us the luxury of contacting men in the underworld who set us up on the Aryan side. We managed to secure an apartment, furnish it, and acquire the necessities to live. Then, Director Marmor helped us leave the ghetto, escape into the night, and hopefully find freedom.

Everything had been thought out precisely, but even then I couldn't relax. Danger lurked around every corner, and one mistake could be lethal. My senses were in overdrive the night we escaped and moved into our new apartment. It was dark, but somehow I managed to see, hear, and feel everything around me.

Before bringing in and unpacking our new belongings, Irenka and I went inside to familiarize ourselves with the place. Our unit was on the third and top floor, laid out as we planned.

We entered a large vestibule. The door to our right revealed a closet. To the left, my eyes took in a large kitchen with a table and four chairs situated in the middle of the room, surrounded by cabinets and appliances. Irenka stayed in the entrance hallway while I crossed the archway into the next room, a sparsely decorated space with an old sofa, a few chairs, and a table with a lamp in the corner. Behind that was a small bedroom with no windows and only three items—a bed, a nightstand, and a lamp, sufficient enough for our needs.

I stopped and stared at the bulletproof wall protecting the bathroom—the room that would hide the Ojzels. Unless you knew of its existence, it was almost impossible to see the trap door at the bottom. The opening was barely two feet by two, like a dog-door, and no member of the Ojzel family was overweight. Luckily, malnutrition plagued many more people in the ghetto than obesity ever could.

A nightstand stood in front of the bathroom entrance, protecting the Ojzels family's haven. Three adults living in a bathroom would be cramped, and it would be difficult to avoid bouts of claustrophobia, but they would be safe. Anything was better than living under Nazi rule.

We began our new lives that night, Irenka and I taking on unfamiliar identities. We became new people to ensure our survival and safety. It was difficult, every day was filled with fear and panic, and I knew danger existed everywhere, but at least we had a place of refuge. Regardless of who we had been before or where we had come from, we were now Aryans, although we felt like aliens, walking on a distant planet.

CHAPTER 19

THE MORNING AFTER MOVING IN, we went to the housing administration office. Anyone changing their address or getting a new job was required to register. While we were standing in line. listening to the answers others were giving when the officials asked questions, a concerned Irenka whispered into my ear, "What do we tell them when they ask what skills we have?"

"Just tell them we're whores, loose women on the make." Blessed with a wry self-deprecating sense of humor, I had always managed to cover my fears with wit and sarcasm. Fortunately, the line moved quickly, not leaving much time to build up more worries.

"Albina Sofia Voitchuk," I responded when asked my name.

"Why did you come to Warsaw?"

"We are seeking employment," I said, turning my head to include my sister.

The man gave us a once-over, stamped our papers, and spoke quickly in a flat voice. He was obviously bored with the repetitious practice. "If you get a job or move again, you'll need to re-register. If you have any overnight visitors, they must also be registered. Do you understand?"

Relieved that the official didn't care enough to thoroughly vet all the information or ask more questions, we nodded and returned to the apartment to wait for the arrival of the Ojzel family.

Later that night, again with Marmor's help, the Ojzels arrived in the

Tobbens' limousine. They familiarized themselves with the apartment, walking through each room, touching each wall and surface, and then crawled into the bathroom that would hide them. Then the three of them—on hands and knees—took turns crawling on the floor and slithering in and out of the trapdoor, making sure it worked.

Once they were content that the space met their needs, Mr. and Mrs. Ojzel thanked us. Their sixteen-year-old son, Romek, wasn't as pleased. He looked gloomy, as if he was standing at his own grave site, waiting to jump in. Could I really blame him? He was still a child, and his childhood was being taken away. Living in our bathroom represented safety from the Germans, but it was no way for a family or a teenager to live. In his mind, I'm sure he was thinking his parents were simply exchanging one prison for another. He stood leaning against the wall, probably mourning all the freedom he'd lost, while his parents sat at the kitchen table, embracing each other and thankful for what they had gained.

CHAPTER 20

NOT A MOMENT AFTER WE STARTED TO RELAX and become comfortable, the doorbell rang, and we froze in terror. Who the hell could that be? I wondered in a panic. Someone would have to be insane to be out after curfew, unless they had an extremely good reason. As cold beads of perspiration trickled down my neck, I felt a chill. There was no time for the Ojzels to slip into the bathroom to hide. If it was the Germans, they wouldn't wait long—they would shoot first and ask questions later. I had to answer the door quickly or risk being killed.

Irenka pointed toward the closet and the Ojzels ducked inside—three adult-sized people crammed inside a too-tight room with barely enough air and scorching-hot temperatures was not pleasant, but you do what you must to survive.

As I forced myself to the door and opened it, I felt a burning weight in the pit of my stomach.

A stranger stood on the other side, not with a gun, not even in uniform, and for a moment I breathed a sigh of relief. "I'm sorry to bother you, ma'am. Mr. Woitczak sent me. He wants me to check the gas valve."

I invited the young man in, not sure whether he was being truthful or had been sent by someone more sinister. Just as I closed the door behind him, but not before sneaking a peek outside, the muffled sound of a cough came from the closet. Mrs. Ojzel had some respiratory issues, and being confined to the airless closet didn't help. Somehow, the young stranger didn't hear or notice, and went about finding the gas valve. Either he was deaf, a very good actor, or an even better spy, and would be able to report back to his superiors without letting us know we had been found out.

On the inside, Irenka and I were both panicking, imagining every horrible scenario in our minds and communicating with each other through our eyes. In the silence, the sounds of Mrs. Ojzel's cough—apparently, she was doing everything possible to suppress the noise—only seemed magnified.

I wondered about the stranger. He would have to be a fool to not know something was going on, which only left two options. He was either a sympathizer and didn't want harm to come to young Jewish girls, or he was a Nazi collaborator, unwilling to reveal himself until he reported back.

On the off-chance he didn't hear the noise, I attempted to divert his attention by pretending to cough. I winked at Irenka to let her know, and she rolled her eyes in disbelief. At the same time, as his wife's coughing spasm continued, Mr. Ojzel placed the palm of his hand across her mouth.

It only took two minutes for the stranger to adjust the gas valve. Once finished, he smiled and left. The moment the apartment door closed, the closet burst open, and all three members of the Ojzel family spilled out, and not a moment too soon. Mrs. Ojzel was gasping for air, and her eyes were tearing. Romek ran to get her a glass of water; after several gasps of fresh air the coughing fit stopped, and the color returned to her cheeks. As relief set in, the five of us began laughing uncontrollably. It was probably stress, but amusing in a way, too.

Who could imagine such a ridiculous scenario—two young Jewish girls living as Aryans, pretending to be something we weren't, and all the while hiding another Jewish family in a tiny apartment? No one would believe it, I thought, if we ever live long enough to tell.

Once we were officially registered with the housing administration and the Ojzels had settled in, I began letting myself relax a little. However, tension and worry were constant, and there never seemed to be a moment without being afraid. Irenka and I had to watch every move we made, process every scenario, study every possibility. On the surface things appeared normal, but we were bursting internally with anxiety. The entire charade could explode in our faces at any moment.

Early in our first week, Irenka and I hoped to reunite with Uncle Misha and his family. Before he and his family escaped from the ghetto, they had given us their new address, suggesting we seek them out if we got out, too.

The building wasn't difficult to find, but the anticipation of seeing him and his family again was replaced with dread when we arrived. The front door was boarded up, and there was a sign—a huge, can't-miss-it-if-you-tried sign—with only two letters: SS. It was a message for everyone, but especially for Jews or anyone hiding Jews: The people who lived here were enemies of the Third Reich, and were now property of the Gestapo—their hiding place found, their future gone. They would likely be tortured, if they were still alive, or murdered.

We returned to our apartment, adding depression to the growing list of emotions we had to conceal from the world. But as painful as it was, it didn't matter what was going on, we had to remember that our priority was being careful not to arouse suspicion of any kind.

LET'S ASK BETKA

CHAPTER 21

THE ORDER TO ANNIHILATE THE WARSAW GHETTO as part of Hitler's Final Solution came on April 19, 1943. It was also around that time that Stasiek, through his underground connections, sent us his final message. He, along with several hundred young Jewish fighters, were preparing for a counter-attack, a showdown with Nazi soldiers.

The idea wasn't new. Many Jews imprisoned in ghettos throughout Eastern Europe had tried similar tactics against the Third Reich forces. They had smuggled in guns and weapons, created homemade grenades, and prepared for all-out war. Most had failed miserably, but most weren't as organized or as strong as the one by those living in the Warsaw Ghetto.

The young men and women of Warsaw were strong and capable, determined to stand against a regime of lunatics and murderers, prepared to do whatever they had to do to survive, or die trying. The German soldiers significantly outnumbered them, but they weren't going down without a fight. The Germans learned quickly that the most dangerous enemy of all is the one who has nothing left to lose.

When German troops entered the ghetto with the purpose of rounding up and deporting all remaining inhabitants to Treblinka, they were surprised to be met with resistance. Seven hundred and fifty men and women, armed with pistols, rifles, a few automatic weapons, and mostly their own homemade creations attacked those troops with such force they managed to hold out for an entire month.

Because of his military training and experience, Stasiek became a leader of the Warsaw Ghetto fighters. Together, they fought with every ounce of strength and determination they had, and even managed to overpower the Nazis a time or two, but they couldn't outlast them forever. The Germans had more soldiers and more firepower.

Eventually, the Nazis decided to systematically destroy the ghetto, one building at a time, until there were none left and nowhere for Jews to seek safety.

In the end, several thousand more lives were lost, including those of a number of German soldiers. Stasiek was among the Jewish casualties, but I'm sure he died proud, knowing he was standing up to the enemy.

During the final days of what became known as the Warsaw Ghetto Uprising, German soldiers set fire to a historic Jewish temple just outside the ghetto. It was a purely symbolic gesture, letting everyone know they had won.

Looking through the window of our apartment, Irenka saw black clouds in a sky ignited with a mixture of red, yellow, and orange. "The ghetto is burning," she said, and called to me to join her to watch.

That was the beginning of the end of the Warsaw Ghetto. Many of the residents were killed inside those walls, and those who weren't were taken to the Treblinka shortly thereafter. It was devastating. The Jewish people of Warsaw tried, but in the end, Hitler won. Again.

LET'S ASK BETKA

CHAPTER 22

LIVING ON THE ARYAN SIDE was not as easy as I had hoped. Irenka and I managed to blend in, but things were more difficult, especially emotionally, than I imagined they would be. The Polish people, the legitimate ones not hiding behind forged paperwork, were a suspicious group—and, considering the circumstances, who could blame them?—and would not hesitate to report anyone to the Germans. Irenka and I had to appear as normal and happy as possible. We had to laugh, smile, and behave like all other young, single, and free Aryan girls. We played music in our apartment all day, and to further the act, we arranged for visitors too.

Director Marmor came to visit often. We learned more about him and his reasons for helping the Jews once we were safely outside of the ghetto. The suspicions I had proved correct about him and his motives. He had a soft spot for Jewish people because he was in love with one. Halinka Briskin was her name, and she and Irenka had been friends for years. Director Marmor often stopped by our apartment before or after visiting with Halinka. How she came to be involved with a German SS officer was beyond me, but their relationship cleared up a number—if not all—of the questions we had about him. As an SS officer, his allegiance was to the Nazis, but he showed compassion toward people, toward Jews. He was not only a sympathizer, but a man who protected us when he could.

I liked him a lot and appreciated everything he had done for us, but as an officer of the Third Reich, I remained suspicious. His relationship with Irenka's friend was confusing. Halinka falling for a German officer made no sense, but a German officer falling for a Jewish girl was even stranger. He claimed to be very much in love, but the idea that love conquers all is something I was not ready to accept. Had Director Marmor been found to be having relations with a Jewish girl, there would have been nothing he could do to save himself. He would have been treated as if he were a Jew, and promptly executed.

He had arranged for her safety with a new identity, and hidden her as an Aryan girl in the suburbs of Warsaw. Had they been caught, they would have been shot—no excuses, no questions, no trial.

Many other families succeeded in escaping to the Aryan side and living as Poles. Irenka knew of another friend, Halinka Greenspan, who was also living on the Aryan side. She and her husband had smuggled themselves out before we escaped. They weren't difficult to locate, and arrangements were made for them to come and visit.

Bernard Greenspan, known to everyone by his last name—as many men of that era were—was an invalid. At the age of nine, he had lost both legs in a trolley accident. He hadn't let it stop him. He exercised daily, developed tremendous upper-body strength, and fueled with a burning desire to succeed, managed to walk on his own with the use of artificial limbs.

The day Halinka brought him home to meet her parents was identical to Vanda's experience when she brought Stasiek home. Halinka was in love and determined to marry the man of her dreams no matter what her parents thought.

Now, we were all in the same boat: pretending to be Aryans. Greenspan's condition was in some ways a blessing for him and Halinka.

In addition to having all the necessary legal papers proving they were Polish citizens, his injuries made people assume he had been a war veteran, hurt while defending his country. He lacked many of the stereotypical Jewish features, and no one asked questions or looked further into his past; as a respected ex-soldier, he was free to come and go as he pleased. Personally, I found him very handsome, with a powerful personality. He exuded authority and yet was a sincere, gentle, and thoughtful man.

When they escaped from the ghetto, Halinka's parents had already died, but his parents and sister were still trapped behind the ghetto walls. I remember clearly the day Greenspan came to visit in an extremely apprehensive state. We sat around the kitchen table, and he took a large gulp from the tea cup in his hand and sighed as the warm liquid trickled down his throat. He'd been trying to work up the courage to say something all night, and finally did. "If I can get my family out of the ghetto, could you hide them, too?"

Knowing what we had gone through in the ghetto, what his family was still going through, there was only one answer. Irenka and I nodded and answered simultaneously, "No problem."

So, over the next two and a half months two Jewish girls, posing as Gentiles, protected and gave shelter to two other families—the Ojzels and Greenspans. The only means of income was the money Mr. Ojzel received from the supervisor at his old factory, a devoted friend and decent human being. Had the authorities caught him helping a Jew, he would have been arrested, tortured, and shot.

Arrangements had been made for Irenka to pick up the money every two weeks. Because of her appearance, she didn't have to sneak out in the dead of night. Instead of lurking from building to building or skulking from alcove to alcove, Irenka walked freely in the middle of the day, exuding an air of confidence. There was no doubt that she feared being recognized as an impostor and possibly picked up by the Gestapo, but she focused on her mission instead. During the hour she was gone, I paced the apartment, praying and worrying.

Though it was difficult enough for her and me to spend most of our time pretending to be carefree and happy, it was nothing compared to what the Ozjels and Greenspans were going through. The six of them—four adults and two teenagers—spent the daylight hours in the last room of the railroad flat, trapped inside a claustrophobic bathroom, taking turns sitting and standing up to stretch their limbs, and only coming out at night. It was better than being beaten and tortured, but I don't know how they kept from going insane.

CHAPTER 23

IN MAY 1943, THE RUSSIANS began to bomb Warsaw. Whenever another bomb hit, everyone ran to find shelter. People yelled for us to leave our apartment and join them in the basement where it was safe, but we were afraid to. If a fire broke out and water was needed, anyone who came to our apartment looking for water would find that there was no bathroom. If they looked further, they might find the bulletproof wall concealing six Jewish people, all whom would be marked for death—along with Irenka and me.

To avoid the potentially lethal situation, we stayed in our apartment during the bombings, explaining to the neighbors that Irenka was claustrophobic and would not go into the basement even in the worst of circumstances.

Having to pre-plan and pre-think out every moment of our life was stressful. We couldn't risk saying or doing the wrong thing in front of the wrong person. Even small things, minute everyday tasks and normal routines, became burdensome. We had to keep up appearances and not allow anyone to think we weren't what we were trying to be. It was tough.

To keep up with the illusions, I sent myself a birthday card and bouquet of flowers in early June, signing it an "admirer." Marmor and Greenspan visited often, stopping in to say hello or to make sure we were okay, and the neighbors assumed they were dating us. We allowed the rumors to persist, and thanked god the charade was working.

We had to find a way to keep our tenants occupied, too. Six people living together in a tiny room with no means of entertainment or distraction was bound to cause problems. The only solution was reading, but that meant supplying them with about twenty books a week, a number that would seem odd for any one person. To avoid suspicion, Irenka and I each joined four different libraries to borrow the books.

Halfway through the month of May, Warsaw was still burning. My sister and I had grown somewhat accustomed to the constant pressures and secrets, but it was still a hassle. During one of his many visits, Greenspan shared his latest news: "A number of South American families are sending authorized visas and properly stamped papers to their relatives here in Europe, so they can migrate to Argentina, Brazil, Venezuela as well as other countries in South America. This could be our way out."

From the beginning it sounded suspicious—I was both skeptical and confused. As doubt crept into my thoughts, I interrupted him. "Wait a minute. You mean the Germans are allowing Jews to leave the country?"

Because Germany was not at war with South America, the idea sounded plausible, but the Nazi regime didn't want the Jewish people somewhere else—they wanted us dead.

Mr. Ojzel voiced his own skepticism. "What does this have to do with us?"

"Well, it seems that most of these families have already perished, and the German officials are offering those papers to anyone—for the price of ten thousand *zlotes* each."

It seemed improbable that the Germans would so easily allow Jews to walk away freely, even at such an exorbitant price. They had certainly shown a general inconsistency in their overall behavior, changing their rules and regulations on a whim, but I often wondered whether that was their intention. Were they truly a regime led by unpredictable maniacs, or were they simply trying to confuse us and make us believe that? It was a perfect way to keep us off balance and always guessing.

However, the one thing the Nazis were consistent in was their overwhelming desire and effort to eliminate the entire Jewish population. As a result, it was hard to believe they would let any of us leave for South America.

After some discussion, the Greenspan family decided to go to South America. They were tired of the never-ending fear and believed it would be better to either be killed trying to escape or get away once and for all. The Ojzel family weren't as easily swayed, and they feared the Germans more than the rest of us.

"How can we trust these people?" Mrs. Ojzel asked her husband. "These are the same people who are trying to kill us and will do anything to flush us out."

She dropped her head into her hands, let out a loud and exasperating sigh, and continued questioning the situation. "No matter how much money they want or what we can give them, how can we trust them? They don't just want our money, they want to exterminate us."

There was a momentary silence while Mr. Ojzel comforted his wife and stared directly into the eyes of everyone in the room. Then he spoke. "We've decided not to go, not to chance it."

While his decision was calm and decisive—rational, even—it was devastating to Romek. Upon hearing his father announce they would not even try, he stood up, walked slowly over to his parents, and stooped down to where they were sitting, working hard to keep his tears in check. "I am sixteen years old and a prisoner in a bathroom!" he screamed, his voice breaking. "I am going to lose my mind." The tears started to flow as he walked away.

But the Ojzels had made their decision, and as far as they were concerned, the discussion was over. They were not swayed by the Greenspans' decision...but Romek was a different story. Their son—a gift for an older couple, the child they never thought they would have, the center of their universe—was agitated, angry, and riddled with anguish. During the evening hours when they were freed from their bathroom cell, Romek paced and muttered under his breath, which added additional stress to his parents.

Several days later, after listening to their son's relentless pleas, they said they would all go. They offered to pay for Irenka and me as well, registering us as their daughters.

Talk of going to South America, a new continent, and starting a new life consumed an entire week. We questioned everything, discussed every possible answer, and then did it all over again. Who? Where? When? How? Should we? Can we? Shouldn't we? Trust? Mistrust? Entrust? It was a never-ending internal debate. We'll stay here! We can't stay here! When the two families reached their final decisions, they were leaving for South America. Irenka and I remained as confused and unsure as ever.

With time running out, we had to decide. But we couldn't do it alone and decided to seek out Marmor's opinion. During one of his visits, we pulled him aside to pick his brain. Irenka did most of the talking, asking all the important questions from several different angles.

But even he couldn't tell us the right thing to do. "No one can, and I certainly won't presume to do so. The decision has to be yours." As he spoke, I leaned forward to listen carefully, and he also leaned toward me, placing both elbows on his knees. "But if you decide to stay, I will advise you to register as Poles wanting to work on farms or in factories for the Germans."

"In Germany?" I blurted, louder than I had intended.

"Yes. The Germans are hiring Poles to work for them. With Warsaw burning and the Russians bombing, it will be safer than staying here."

The idea of turning to the Germans, the people responsible for all the horror, for anything was shocking and scary at the same time. When he left that night, we secured our tenants in their hiding place and went to bed. Neither of us could sleep; instead, we talked late into the night about every possibility.

Sometimes I hated being the person I had been born to be. In times like that, when one decision would mean everything, I wanted to be a follower so much more than a leader, to look to someone else to carry that burden. I wanted my father back to tell me what to do.

People had always said I was the strong one among my sisters, the one who could be counted on when things got tough. I think I only appeared that way because I was opinionated and not afraid to speak my mind. Because I was independent and self-sufficient, and took care of myself, Irenka looked to me for guidance, even wisdom. She considered me logical because I had the ability to see the bigger picture before reaching a conclusion, and despite being seven years older, she left all the major decisions to me.

Just before we gave up talking for the night, she turned to me in the comfort of our bed and whispered in my ear, "Your instincts have always been better than mine, so whatever you decide is fine with me."

Sleep never came for me that night. I was unable to stop the thoughts from invading my mind long enough to relax. My father had taught me to assess and evaluate situations—hopefully, to make the right choice, which had seemed all my life to come easier to me than to many. I spent the entire night living out every scenario in my head. None seemed to be appealing, and the one idea that kept creeping its way into my thoughts was joining the underground. I was young, strong enough both mentally and physically, and would be an asset. Fighting back against the Nazis and causing them at least some of the pain they had caused was tempting. I hesitated because I wasn't sure Irenka was up for the challenge and I couldn't leave my sister.

Taking the Ojzels up on their offer, and joining them and the Greenspans on their trip to South America, might have been the safest choice. If we made it out of Europe, we would likely be free and clear to start new lives. But I wasn't sure I wanted that; I had lost my family, my heritage, and was already pretending to be someone I wasn't. Would living another lie be any better than this one? I asked myself. That's assuming we make it out of Europe alive, and that the Germans aren't simply using the offer of legal papers as a ploy to round up and murder any Jews they didn't already have in their custody.

The other two options involved keeping our assumed names and either remaining in Poland and hoping for the best or taking Marmor's suggestion and going to Germany to seek work on farms. Staying in Poland was not a good idea. The Russians were unlikely to give up their assault, and even if they did, it was difficult to imagine a future that didn't include getting caught by the Nazis. . .eventually.

The only option that didn't include an automatic death sentence—at least not right away—if it didn't work out was going into Germany as Poles and working for them on their farms. But we would be putting all our trust in a regime that wanted nothing more than our extinction. How could we do that?

I needed a sign. What would my mother say? What would my

grandmother suggest? Most of all, what would my father do? I needed help—more than ever.

Irenka woke at dawn to find me sitting up at the foot of the bed. "Are you all right?" she asked.

I couldn't speak. I'd been sitting there staring at the walls for hours, lost in a trance and hoping to find the right answer.

"You didn't sleep at all, did you?"

It was a statement and a question—that didn't need a response—at the same time. She reached for my hand and squeezed it.

"Regusha, your insight into human nature is usually on target. What does your intuition tell you?"

"Just like Mama didn't trust the Russians, I don't trust the Germans. Yet here we are about to leave on a journey halfway around the world or work as Poles, for the Germans, at the suggestion of a Nazi SS officer."

"So far he's done right by us." Irenka said. "I don't know why, but he has."

"I know, but he's still one of them. The only thing I know for sure is that we've survived this far being someone else. I hate it, hate pretending to be someone I'm not, but it's worked this far. I don't even want to think about starting another lie, and living someone else's life all over again, but I'm not taking back my Jewish name either."

There was silence for the next several minutes. I was torn, too frightened to make the wrong decision, too frightened to make the right one. As stupid as it sounded to go to work for the Germans, I'd be doing it as Albina Sofia Voitchuk.

"I'm not going back," I stammered. "I'm not going back to my old life and telling them who I really am. I'm not going back. I can't. I'm not going back."

"Okay, then. That settles it. We're going with your intuition."

That Irenka placed so much faith in me and my choices was both heart-warming and unsettling. She was a lot surer of me than I was. But what if I was wrong?

LET'S ASK BETKA

CHAPTER 24

WITH THE NEW DAY CAME A NEW REALIZATION, a new dilemma. Buying visas for the South American trip could become problematic, potentially lethal. The only stipulation was that anyone purchasing these special papers had to come to the Royal Hotel in person and report where they had been hiding. If that occurred, and the two families were honest, Irenka and I would have been condemned as Poles harboring Jews. There would be no coming back from that, and we would be shot.

It was Marmor's suggestion that she and I make plans to leave at least an hour before they did, to ensure we were safe before they purchased their way out of Europe.

When we first appeared before the magistrate to register as Poles seeking work permits, it was nerve-wracking. We had to lie and do it convincingly. The wrong answer, the wrong reaction, the wrong move would make someone suspicious, and we'd be exposed as frauds. I was also frightened that some German sympathizer might recognize either one of us and report us.

As the result of the Russians bombing Warsaw, the people wanting out of Poland multiplied. The lines for those registering to work in Germany were enormous, and it took forever to get to the front of the line.

The man behind the desk stamped the papers and gave us our instructions. "You will travel to Vienna and will be assigned work once you arrive. When can the two of you leave?"

I told him we would be packed and ready to go in three days, then thanked him for his help. We chose to leave the same day the Ojzels and Greenspans were planning to leave, hoping we'd all make it out of Poland unscathed.

"That's fine," he said, handing us back our authorization papers.

Once our plans were set in motion, the remaining three days were brutal. All of us were eagerly awaiting the next phase of our journey, this one resulting in our long-term survival—we hoped.

The morning of our departures came, and we all wished each other well. As planned, Irenka and I left before the others, arriving at the railroad station and checking our luggage. With our train not scheduled to leave for another few hours, we walked over to the Royal Hotel to check on our former tenants, to make sure they were safe.

Standing in a doorway across the street from the hotel, the image was spine-chilling. There were hundreds of Jews lined up, even some that Irenka and I recognized. They were families and people we had known before the horror of this war. Most looked nervous but relieved. They hoped their terror was about to come to an end.

As I watched from a distance, doubts slowly crept into my head. My senses were telling me we were witnessing something significant, and that something big—good or bad—was about to happen.

As we left for the train station, I began questioning whether I had made the right decision. Would it have been better to be among those standing in line waiting to leave? They are all about to start new chapters in their lives, while Irenka and I had signed up for more of the same. Had I picked the right journey for us? We were pretending to be other people and would undoubtedly spend the next phase of our lives, however long, looking over our shoulders and hoping not to be recognized as imposters.

Being safe in South America sounded so good, I could almost taste it. But something was holding me back. Maybe it was the stipulation of having to bare my soul, to tell the Germans who I was, and entrust them with my safety. No matter how much I dreamed of a better life and living on a different continent away from the Nazis, I just couldn't do it.

With a valise in one hand and our signed papers in our pockets, Irenka and I boarded the train for Vienna. We found a compartment with an empty bench and, with our luggage stowed above us, we began to relax—as best we could in an uncomfortable situation. I thought about my decision the entire way.

Later, I learned that the twelve thousand Jewish people who were lured from their hiding places had been duped. They were given a farewell dinner, and then taken to the Paviak Prison under the guise of immunization. At the prison those poor, unsuspecting people had been lined up and murdered. Thousands of innocent Jews had gotten their hopes up and perished while Nazi soldiers stood around emotionless. It was the cruelest of hoaxes.

Despite having made a different choice, one that meant I was still alive, I didn't feel any better. The train ride was long, hot, and uncomfortable. Irenka and I didn't talk out of fear of bringing attention to ourselves. Having others take notice of us was the last thing we wanted.

Thoughts of dread kept entering my head, and I tried pushing them away but couldn't. I grew suspicious of anyone who looked at me, became anxious whenever someone offered me a greeting. It was doing me no good, and I knew I was making myself crazy.

I opened the window for some fresh air, hoping that the scenery would distract me. It was quiet in the European countryside the train passed through, the only sounds the monotone clanking of the wheels on the track—*Kchink-kchunk! Kchink-kchunk! Kchink-kchunk!* I got lost in the steady vibrations and the motion of the train, and closed my eyes. *Kchink-kchunk! Kchink-kchunk! Kchink-kchunk!* Moments before falling asleep, many visions of the past flashed before me. Mrs. Rosenberg! Mama! Papa! Selection! Bombs! Director Marmor! Dead children! Treblinka! Selection! Dead children!—all of it, over and over in my head. My thoughts, my enemies. *Kchink-kchunk! Kchink-kchunk! kchinck-kchunk!* The train roared on.

The first stop, Zavierch, was the border between occupied Poland and Germany. It was also the first Gestapo checkpoint. The contents of our luggage would be examined, our papers would be re-checked, officially stamped by the German authorities, and we would board a different train to Austria. Once in Austria, we would receive our working papers, and board yet another train—this one heading for Germany—our final destination.

As Irenka and I emerged from the train, carrying our bags, an officer stepped in our path and, with an outstretched arm, pointed to the left.

"*Warten dort mit den anderen Frauen!*" he shouted, and pointed to where a group of other women were already huddled together.

As I turned to the left, I saw the group the officer was pointing to—damn it! I froze in place as an icy chill ran up my spine. It's not in my nature to panic, but had I been a person easily overpowered by fear, this would have been the moment of dread. I recognized a couple of people. One was a woman I had known, an acquaintance from Warsaw, named Halinka. Standing next to her were two men who had also been caught. The one who caught my eye was Bzeznitski—the man who had brought me to Director Marmor, who helped me get the job in the ghetto, the supervisor of the Tobbens Factory.

My heart tightened inside my chest, I felt nauseous, and the palms of my hands began to sweat. This was it. Our future, whatever was left of it, was about to dramatically change—and not for the better. My heart, along with my hopes, sank lower and lower with every step. Up to this point, we've been lucky, I thought. Had it run out? Pretending was over, dreaming of safety was over, and our freedom and lives were over.

On the way to join the others, I whispered to Irenka, "We are in serious trouble."

CHAPTER 25

STANDING AMONG ALL THE OTHER JEWS, all I could think about was how we landed in that situation: *What did I miss? Did someone recognize us at the train station? On the train? Were our new identities traced back to the dead women? Should we have gone to the Royal Hotel with the Ojzel and Greenspan families?* (At that point, I didn't know what had happened to them.) It had been my decision, my choice to go work for the Germans, that put us where we were.

I made eye contact with Bzeznitski, and a vision of Director Marmor flashed before me. Surely, he could have used his influence to save Bzeznitski—or had I been wrong about Marmor? *Was he truly our friend and looking out for us, or was this his plan all along? How could I have missed it? How could my intuition have failed me so badly?*

I thought about the Ojzels and Greenspans, and wondered if they were safe, on their ship, and already halfway across the Atlantic Ocean on their way to freedom in South America. *Should Irenka and I have gone with them?*

None of my questions had answers, but that wasn't important. Every option was a shot in the dark, and even if I had known which choice was the safest, it would not have helped us.

As nightfall came, the men and women were separated into two groups. Our luggage had been confiscated, but we'd each managed to keep a few mementos. Irenka took pictures of our parents, while I held onto a small bag Stasiek had given me as a graduation present. It was made of leather, ornamented with ostrich feathers, and shaped like a billfold. I used it to carry my comb, toothbrush, and cosmetics.

I don't know what happened to the men, but we were taken to a barn near the railroad station. The place stank; the moment we entered, Irenka gagged, and I hoped it was only temporary, and that they would move us somewhere less awful.

"What did they keep in here, pigs?" she asked, covering her nose.

"I actually believe it may have been a place for storing fertilizer."

Behind us, somewhere in the dark, several rodents were scurrying around. Was that the next stop on this train to hell? Were we to be feast for rats?

"Who knows how long we'll be here? Come on, let's see if we can find someplace to sit," I suggested. We roamed around the barn until we found a spot that wasn't muddy or covered with animal excrement. We managed to find a dry area, and the others followed. But the seating area did nothing to quell the odor, a combination of stale urine, burned copper, and a decaying corpse of something that had been alive a very long time ago.

Sounds of swarming rodents were audible—like nails tapping on a wooden table. But the rats seemed to stay away, and, fortunately, I never encountered them. They scrambled to find food and a passage to escape. There was no food or escape for us. We were unable to sleep, and the night passed slowly. Irenka and I began chatting with the other women, discussing our lives and hardships. We each had stories about how we had escaped the ghetto and where we had hidden afterwards. Most were similar, and we wondered what kind of twisted fate had brought us all together at the same place and time.

As we were about to close our eyes and try to sleep, I turned to Irenka and whispered in her ear, "Remember, no matter what happens tomorrow, we are Poles."

Early the following morning, we were taken to Gestapo Headquarters. I wasn't sure which was worse—the anxiety, the fear we had felt when escaping the ghetto, hiding from the Germans, or getting caught and waiting to see what they would do to us.

It didn't take long to realize we were being taken to be interrogated. Irenka and I were terrified of being questioned, of giving them our real names. We had family in Zavierch, and since we didn't know if our cousins were alive or dead, we didn't want to take any chances that might jeopardize their safety.

CHAPTER 26

I ENTERED THE INTERROGATION ROOM with trepidation. It was awfully hot, and the air was stagnant. The room was badly lit though a few bulbs were scattered around and it did not take long for my eyes to adjust.

Two SS officers stood at the doorway, and several others were dispersed around the room. They stood at ease but were heavily armed and no doubt would quickly kill any of us should the need—or their interpretation of need—arise. Each was wearing the formal uniform of the SS, symbolizing fear, threat, and intimidation.

Other than the blood-red armband with the Nazi insignia, the uniforms were black and somber. The tailored tunic jacket was belted and had epaulets, and their collar patches denoted position and rank. Their high leather boots were shined to perfection, and the military style peaked hat finished off the ensemble. The uniform was designed to project authority and foster fear and respect. As far as I was concerned, all I saw in it was hate.

At the far end of the room, the head SS officer waited for us. Tall, thin, and muscular, with a blond crew-cut, he made interrogation an art form, and began immediately—intimidating us from the moment we walked in. His look was at once one of hatred and amused curiosity rolled together. He stood with one foot on a chair, his elbow resting on his knee and an oxtail whip in his hand. I could not help but stare at the whip, its long leather strap with knots all along it was frightening. I knew the intention was to give the officer holding it an even more intimidating presence, and he succeeded. After all, we were unarmed, scared, and helpless.

Once we were lined up, the officer took his foot off the chair and approached us with confidence. His lips curled into a sinister smile and stared at each one of us. Back and forth he walked, from one to the next and then back again. When he got close enough for me to smell him, I almost threw up. The combination of cigarette smoke, liquor, and body odor emanated from his pores. Bathing was not a daily ritual for him.

As he passed me and moved on to the woman next to me, I stifled an urge to laugh. He looked like a cartoon character; the veins at his temples were bulging, and his neck muscles were tightening while his face turned red and twitched. He looked like he was about to explode. As he stopped to question each of us, it was obvious his blood pressure was rising, and the tension in the room followed it.

Irenka reached for my hand and squeezed it. Both our palms were hot and sweaty.

The officer stopped and looked down at my sister. In a quiet and overly friendly voice he asked, "*Ahh—und wem haben wir hier?*" (Ahh—and whom do we have here?)

Unlike me, who could only guess and make assumptions based on tone, gesture, and facial expression, Irenka understood a little bit of German. She wasn't fluent but capable of understanding what the officer asked. "Irenka Novitzka," she answered as their eyes met.

"Irenka Novitzka," he repeated as he spat out her name with disgust. For a long moment, he stared at her, contemplating his next move. "*Sie willst fur das Vaterland arbeiten?*" he asked with a distinct note of sarcasm in his voice, as if wanting to work for the Fatherland was an impossible aim for the likes of her.

"Yes. My cousin and I are assigned to work in Germany."

"Germany?" He paused, as if appreciative of the gesture. "How nice." A smile crossed his lips, although it was more of a grin, a repugnant smirk. Then he took out the picture of our father, which had been confiscated from our luggage. It showed a handsome man standing tall with Aryan features, a pale complexion, light eyes, and a thick mustache that curled at the ends.

"*Wer ist der Mann auf dem bild?*" he barked.

Without hesitation, she replied, "That is my father."

The acknowledgment only enraged the SS officer further. He managed to keep his physical outburst in check to ask another question. "*Wo ist dein Vater?*" he spat, with a loud and thunderous vibration like venom from a snake.

Where indeed was Father. Irenka said with even confidence, "He was a Polish officer who was killed while on duty."

Her answer only fueled the officer's anger more, and as his eyes widened, I felt the hair on the back of my neck stand up, and my heart was pounding like a jackhammer. He was a grenade ready to explode. I knew what was about to happen to Irenka, and I couldn't let that occur.

"*Wie kannst du es wagen zu die beleidigen—*" he screeched, demanding to know how she could so insult the uniform, but he never got to the end of the sentence. He was too surprised when I grabbed his arm to stop him from hitting her. As I had hoped, he turned his attention to me.

"*Ah! Du bist der Starke!*"

Yes, I was the strong one. I released my hold on his wrist as I let out a breath I hadn't realized I was holding.

My eyes flicked at the whip in his hand, if only to avoid seeing the devil in his light blue eyes. He took a step closer and stared at me with a seething anger that I could feel in every ounce of my soul. His eyes penetrated mine like heat from a lightning rod. I was repelled and jerked back.

Then he stepped back, gave me a once-over, and flashed a menacing smile before grabbing my wrist and flinging me all the way around. His hand was cold and damp on my skin, and his breath came at me like fire. With utter rage in his eyes and a cynical smirk smeared across his lips, he shoved me toward the center of the room, giddy with anticipation over what he was about to do.

The man, this devil, came toward me with his whip, and I clenched my body to prepare for the pain. I was afraid it was going to be slow and agonizing, but never in my wildest dreams could I have anticipated such a gut-wrenching experience.

He grabbed me again, this time squeezing my arm tightly, and forcing me to lean over the chair as he beat me with the oxtail. The leather strap scorched my skin, stinging all the way to my bones and making my lungs constrict from the shock. When oxygen returned to my brain, the pain flooded my entire body. My pulse began racing, and I lost all my strength. A moment later, I was struck again, this time with a fiercer effort, and the pain this time sent shock waves through my entire body, triggering nerves everywhere. My screams shattered the air and echoed throughout the room. White spots appeared before my eyes, and with each crack of the whip, I only screamed and yelled more. The pain was excruciating, radiating from every fiber of my being. My only hope was that I would pass out. I wasn't that lucky.

Irenka stood with the other women, unable to do anything to help. She had tears in her eyes and an unrelenting guilt filling her soul. They were all bystanders to cruelty, witnesses to savagery. They stood like statues, knowing that, if any of them moved, they would be next.

Time seemed to stand in place, but the SS officer's strength was endless; stroke after stroke after stroke, he beat me, whipped me, almost killed me. The pain was unbearable, and there was no end in sight. It took many lashes, far more than I can or want to count, to fulfill that bastard's need to inflict pain.

Only after it was over, and I'd had time to recover—if that was ever even possible—did the other women tell me what had happened, that the SS officer enjoyed doing that to me. They said his eyes had gone from blood-boiling blue, filled with anger and hatred, to amusement and joy. My screams of agony had brought him satisfaction, my quivering body pleasure.

Finally, when it was all over, he dropped the whip on the chair, smiled at me, and laughed. Then he dismissed the group and walked out of the room, content with himself.

The other women tried helping me but were unable to. I could not straighten up, could not stand. The pain was so bad, I had been beaten so terribly, that my senses were no longer responding to commands. My rear end was swollen, welts were rising everywhere, and I could feel hot blood oozing from deep, open wounds. My face was soaked with a combination of sweat and tears that would not stop. I stared in horror as if looking through a windshield during a downpour. My eyes could barely focus, my ears unable to hear. Every fiber, every organ, every nerve in my body was on fire.

Irenka and the other women carried me to our already overcrowded cell and laid me down on a cot. I had to lie on my stomach because my backside was bleeding and burning. After several hours of compresses, I managed to finally fall asleep and end that long and horrible day.

It was months before the wounds healed and years before the scars, both physical and emotional, began to subside. But in all that time the pain has never completely gone away.

CHAPTER 27

THE FOLLOWING MORNING, we were awakened at dawn. Everyone was still tired, hungry, and afraid, not that the guards cared. They ordered us out of our cells before our eyes could open, before we could even think. They had an announcement to make, one we had to take very seriously.

"*Wenn-du-neicht-hörst!*" (If-you-do-not-listen!) Each word was enunciated harshly, so there would be no chance of misunderstanding. "*Wenn-du-neicht-kooperierst!*" (If-you-do-not-cooperate!) Again, each word came out carefully, and then there was a brief pause. "*Sie-wirst-der-nachste-sein!*" (You-will-be-next!)

Two other officers dragged a man in with his arms tied behind his back. They carried him to the center of the square and tied him between two posts, completely on display. Within a split second two large Doberman dogs with quivering lips, growling throats, and flaring nostrils materialized—barking, snarling, drooling, anticipating a feast.

Seconds later, they were released and attacked that man. The dog's teeth, sharp as razors, emerged from their jaws as they leapt into him, biting and chewing on his flesh. The man, whose crime I never knew, struggled to break free but had no chance. He stood there like a piece of cheese in a mouse trap. But he wasn't the bait; he was dinner, a victim of insanity. His blood-curdling screams pierced my ears, and everyone tried to look away but couldn't.

It lasted barely five minutes but was embossed in my memory forever and remains the most horrific sight I have ever witnessed. Those dogs tore through his skin and bones, devouring him alive. Pieces of him were flung in every direction, and blood spurted into the air.

Something happened to me in that moment that I have never been able to shake off. An electrical jolt surged through my body, and I bit my lip as I felt something snap inside me. Despite the heat, I was chilled to my core, and my legs had gone weak. A bitter, acidic bile moved upward from my gut and lodged at the back of my throat.

And then there was nothing but silence, the kind of silence that is undeniably painful. I was convinced that everyone could hear my every breath, my heart beating, my fear and repulsion. The dogs finished their meal, finished eating a man alive, and then were led away. The victim's body lay in front of us, chewed and bloody, and if we hadn't have seen him before the attack, we would never have known what it had been.

I closed my eyes, and as the blood was seeping into the ground, I forced myself not to vomit. I shook my head, trying to rid my mind of the horror. I had seen it, knew I had, but couldn't accept it was real. Not yet. Not ever.

I could not move, as if my limbs were paralyzed. My mind was not ready to process the lunacy. The uncomfortable silence continued, and as I looked away from the horror, I noticed that the German guard standing behind me was smirking. He found it entertaining. That vile, disgusting, inhumane act was humorous to these messengers from Satan.

The Nazis were very skillful at physical torture and had an aptitude for mental abuse. They were well versed in the art of injecting fear into the hearts and minds of their captives, and this was just another example. Forcing us to watch that horror was diabolical but very effective. I'd been through a lot already, suffered great pains and great loses, but had never been more repulsed or terrified before. It was too real to be a dream. The scene was too insane, the act too vicious. I couldn't understand how one human being could do these things to other human beings.

Several more silent moments passed, but the shock and devastation would not go away. Throughout my life, both before and after the horror of the Holocaust, I have always turned to humor to relieve tension and to help myself and others alleviate fear, hysteria, and panic.

This time I couldn't find any humor.

The silence was finally broken when the guard behind leaned in and whispered in my ear, in Polish, "*Ty jestes nastepny!*" (You're next!)

The words sent a shivering pulse down my spine, and how I said what I said next only God knows. I turned to look up at him and answered him. "Well, if I'm next, the dogs are going to have a picnic. After yesterday's beating, they won't have to chew very hard. One look at my ass, and they'll think they're being served chopped meat."

But I wasn't next, and there was no next. The Nazis had effectively delivered their message. It didn't matter what we did or what we wanted; one step out of line, and we would suffer as that man had suffered. Not too much later, we were taken back to our cells without another word or threat from the soldiers.

The other women in the cell talked almost all night about what had happened, but I couldn't. I hoped and prayed that it wasn't real, that none of this was real, but it was. Every time I tried closing my eyes, I saw that man's face, heard his screams, could feel those dogs. It's a vision that has haunted me more than any other throughout my entire life. Even now, some seventy-plus years later, I wake up sweating and shaking with tears streaming down my cheeks. I have never been able to look at a dog and not see those Dobermans, with their fangs hanging out.

CHAPTER 28

THE FOLLOWING COUPLE OF DAYS were spent under constant scrutiny and interrogation. The mental pressure of it was exhausting, while the physical beatings were brutal and debilitating.

On the morning of the third day, we were released from our cells. As we lined up in the same spots where we had watched a man eaten to death by dogs, I could not help but relive it. The body was gone, the blood had been washed away, and all that remained were the posts he'd been tied to, but the visions of it happening were still fresh—not to mention my rear end, which was in excruciating pain every time I moved with welts the size of quarters.

Unwilling or unable to do it themselves, the Nazis assigned several Jewish men to temporary police duty. Their job was to escort the female prisoners to another jail located in the Sosnowitz Ghetto. Knowing that during a transfer was likely the best time to escape, the Germans warned that, for every prisoner who attempted to do so, they would execute one hundred others at random.

Although the train ride was short, I was again hypnotized by the repetitious sound of the wheels. *Kchink-kchunk! Kchink-Kchunk! Kchink-Kchunk!* Mrs. Rosenberg! The Man-eating Dogs! The Whip! They were all interlaced in my memory and mixed with blood.

I woke in a panic. Once we arrived, I learned that our incarceration

LET'S ASK BETKA

in the Sosnowitz Prison would be under the supervision of Jews. It was a relief to be away from the Gestapo, and our anxiety subsided. There was less tension, and our nerves weren't as agitated, but we were still prisoners.

Barely moments after we settled into our new cells, we received our first visitor. Mr. Merin, the representative of the Jews in the Sosnowitz Ghetto, came to talk. Once the news reached him that women from Warsaw had been captured and were being interrogated by the Gestapo, he had begun making arrangements to have us transferred.

There was silence when he entered the jail with his entourage, and then he addressed all of us. "We have heard rumors of the atrocities that took place in Warsaw, and I am surprised that anyone managed to survive," he said quietly and with deep compassion in his voice.

Over the next several hours, he spoke with each of us individually and as a group, seeking to understand everything that had led us to that place. Each woman's story was the same but different, each at once a horror and a miracle.

As he was about to leave, Irenka approached him to ask whether he could find out if our cousin, Stanislav Wygdoski, was still alive, and whether he could get word to him. She wanted him to know that we had survived the Warsaw Ghetto and were now residing in Sosnowitz Prison.

Wygodski was a famous and highly respected author, known throughout all of Poland. Although Merin reacted with surprise, he immediately told her that he did in fact know the exact whereabouts of our famous cousin, and promised to contact him.

Stanislav worked at the Jewish City Hall in the nearby Bendjin Ghetto, and within the hour, the three of us were reunited. We huddled together in a corner of the cell and spoke of the events of the past year.

We even tried reminiscing about better times, and although it lightened the mood considerably, I knew I had to bring up a more serious topic. I was concerned that we would eventually be sent to Auschwitz.

The idea didn't surprise Stanislav, and he nodded in agreement. "Would it be possible to acquire two cyanide pills?" I asked him.

"I only have three pills—one for my wife, one for me, and one for my daughter." He spoke to us as if he was apologizing. "There aren't any more to be gotten at any cost."

There was a long pause, and I drifted into thought about what our fate would be. I pictured smoke stacks with black and gray smoke emerging, crematorium at Auschwitz. As long as we had each other, as long as I had someone to care for, as long as there was someone who still loved me, we would manage—together. The worst would be to be separated from my sister. Somehow, we had to get our hands on two cyanide pills.

Then he said, "I know about the Germans' threat to kill one hundred Jews for every person who escapes." He stopped, looked around, leaned in closer, so no one else could hear, and whispered, "I'm also aware that, at this very moment, Mr. Merin is negotiating the transfer of the entire group of women. If the negotiations succeed, you will be sent to a work camp."

"We had no idea that there were work camps for Jews," I said, the surprised expression on my face genuine. "We believed the only camps that existed were concentration camps with crematoriums."

By lunchtime the following day, everyone from Sosnowitz and the people from the adjoining town of Bendjin were buzzing with news about the Women of Warsaw. Prior to our arrival everyone had assumed that no one survived the Warsaw Uprising, and as such we became something like folk heroes.

Upon learning from Stanislav that Irenka and I were still alive, our father's cousins, Cesia and Lutek Krymulovski, arrived the following day with packages. They knew the Gestapo had seized all our belongings, and that we would need clothing and undergarments.

As prisoners under the authority of the appointed Jews, we received some food and water but stayed in our cells most of the time. Irenka and I got to know the other inmates. We spent time discussing our childhood stories and family backgrounds, learned the horror that each individual had lived through and how everyone had survived the past two years.

My buttock was still inflamed and throbbing from the beating I had received. It was best to remain still, to lie on my stomach without moving, but I found it too difficult to stay idle. My mind worked best when I was active, and despite the pain—the sores kept reopening and bleeding through my clothes—I kept myself busy. I was either cleaning something, straightening cots, folding blankets, sewing, or reading.

Although I never considered it a chore, I made sure everything I did was done to perfection. It's always been my nature, and I had an inexhaustible energy with which I pursued everything I did. Irenka confirmed to the others that that was how I had always been, even before the war began. She was used to it, but our new acquaintances were struck, not only by my constant movement, but by the efficiency with which I handled it all. What no one knew was that, if I didn't keep occupied, I probably wouldn't survive.

Before the war, there had been a Polish riddle about the popular comic strip character Betty Boop. The last line in the limerick was "Betty Boop—*roob chosh, roob chosh, roob*" (Betty Boop—do something, do something, do). The reference was to the fact that the caricature was constantly in motion. Betty Boop and I shared many physical characteristics. We were both petite and had the same hairdo, matching saucer-shaped eyes, and small noses with high cheekbones that were always rosy. Other than Irenka, who continued to call me Regusha, "Betka" became my nickname—an affectionate term that I was now known by.

In the middle of the horror of genocide, a new name blossomed where little else could.

LET'S ASK BETKA

CHAPTER 29

AFTER SEVERAL DAYS IN A NEW PRISON, a new cell, I developed an infection in my mouth and needed medical attention. Because I was one of the Women of Warsaw, and the woman who had showed no fear during the Gestapo interrogation in Zavierch, when I seized that officer's hand before he hit Irenka, I was considered a threat and required an escort to the dentist. Two Jewish police officers came with me, one who grilled me with questions about Warsaw the entire way. Like many others who hadn't been there before, Mr. Tzigler was curious about the Big City that had been known as a center of culture, education, and the arts, and then the place that the Nazis had turned into the largest of the ghettos, with the worst living conditions.

Never at a loss for words, I answered each of his questions, gave him intimate details, and spoke highly of what Warsaw had once been. I relayed horror stories of the death and destruction that the Nazis had brought with them. He listened with respect and appreciation of my candor, and at the end of our conversation, we both agreed that we'd love nothing more than to see Warsaw return to its former glory—if and when the Nazi regime fell.

On the day after I went to the dentist, things started happening in the Sosnowitz Ghetto. As he promised, Merin had traveled to the Gestapo Headquarters in Katowitz to discuss the women in the Sosnowitz Ghetto. He had met with SS Officer Parker to plead our case. We were all young and healthy, and Merin hoped to convince Parker to send us to work camps instead of Auschwitz.

He and his secretary, Mrs. Charna, who always traveled with him, never returned to the ghetto. Fear spread throughout the night that something devastating must have happened. Either they had been arrested for treason or killed.

With the knowledge that he had failed in his attempt, I decided exactly what to do. While others were panicking, I pulled Irenka aside and said very quietly, "With Mr. Merin gone, I'm afraid it will soon be the end of the Sosnowitz Ghetto. We must escape. The first chance we get, we run."

The following morning, everyone in the prison was startled out of their sleep by weapons being fired. Screaming and confusion followed, and before long we were all convinced that another selection was underway.

"Remember," I reminded Irenka, "the first chance we get," then looked directly at her. "Okay?"

She nodded.

Not knowing for sure what was going on was probably the hardest part. We imagined the worst, and it was easy to become alarmed and agitated. The Germans of the Third Reich were some of the best the world had ever known at psychological warfare; before they ever made a threat or raised a weapon, they had us afraid. It was their belief, and a good one, that havoc causes fear, and fear causes conflict.

It was late afternoon before the German soldiers entered the prison and began evacuating cells, but they had already established dominance and control. With their usual precision and order, they forced everyone to line up, forming a semicircle. The Women of Warsaw were stationed in front, with hundreds of others behind us. The man leading the charge this time, SS Officer Knoll, paced in front, enjoying the fact that he held life and death in his hands.

With his arms behind his back and a lethal glare in his eyes, he looked dangerous. He stood erect with wide shoulders, blond hair, and a large belly hanging over his pants. He didn't shy away from us either, making brazen eye contact and almost daring someone to say or do the wrong thing. We knew he was waiting for one of us to step out of line, to challenge his authority or disobey an order, and give him a reason to attack.

Standing on the front line, I had a better view (or worse, depending on your perspective) than most. I could see his cold eyes and feel his steps vibrating on the ground beneath my feet. He pulled out his whip, pointed it toward me, and I froze, feeling the need to grab my sister for security.

"*Du!*" he barked. "*Bewegst dich!*" He wanted me to move, but I couldn't. When he raised his whip, I took a step backwards, and luckily its tip only grazed me under my left eyebrow. But it was enough to pierce the skin, and blood began trickling out, slowly at first, and then more profusely.

From the sidelines, Tzigler—the Jewish police officer who had escorted me to the dentist a couple days before—stepped between me and Knoll and, in one motion, grabbed me under his arm and pulled me away. "I'm taking this prisoner to get patched up," he shouted as he sped up his pace.

The SS officer didn't seem to care, flipped his hand, and continued his selection process.

Tzigler brought me to Regina Scheftel, a nurse who stopped the bleeding, cleaned the wound, and bandaged it up.

When she finished, he spoke to me again. "Do not return to the group. Stay here and keep your hand over the bandage. You will be safe."

I nodded and, as he was about to leave, grabbed his arm. "Can you save my sister, too?" I pleaded.

"I'll try."

The selection continued while I stood there helpless, watching and listening. I later learned that Stanislav Wygodski and his family had been chosen for the transport to Auschwitz. As planned, he and his family swallowed their cyanide pills. His wife and daughter died on the train, but because the dosage Stanislav had taken was too weak to kill him, he suffered one burnt lung and destruction of the other, but he survived.

Upon learning that there was a famous Polish writer on the train, several young men from Bendjin kept him and his identity hidden. When the train reached the Auschwitz station, Stanislav was carried to a barrack and hidden; he eventually recuperated.

He survived the war and, in 1945, returned to Poland. He later remarried, had two more children, and became Secretary of Education. When anti-Semitism once again returned to Poland, disillusioned with communism, he fled with his family to Israel.

LET'S ASK BETKA

CHAPTER 30

THE SELECTION PROCESS CONTINUED as SS Officer Knoll pointed his whip and chose who would live and who would die. I sat on the sidelines, my hand pressed to the bandage, worrying about Irenka. As time passed and she did not join me, I grew concerned for her life. She was not just my sister but my best friend, my confidante, my safety net, the last connection to my family. I always believed we would stay together, no matter what happened or what the Germans did to us. We would survive the horror together, share our lives, take care of each other, and grow old together. That's what our mother had wanted and one of the last things she ever said to us: "Take care of each other."

Back on the train platform, the reality finally hit that I might never see my sister alive again. It sent me into an overwhelming panic, and I began searching the crowd, looking at everyone and wanting to scream her name. But she was nowhere to be found. Like Mama, and Vanda, the Germans had seized Irenka, too. I'd never get to see her again, hug her again, feel her comfort me, or allow me to comfort her ever again.

It shook my world, my very existence. So much had been taken from me, but I had my sister, I had Irenka—until I didn't.

With a bruised eye and my hands shaking uncontrollably, I watched the trains fade into oblivion, taking prisoners, women I knew—and my sister—to parts unknown. The nightmare had gotten worse, as bad as it could get, and then everything commenced to move in slow motion. There were voices and noises surrounding me, but they all became garbled together and I couldn't hear anything. I stood in the center of it, motionless, unable to control my thoughts. Tears began to flow, and despite standing among hundreds of others, I felt alone, utterly, completely alone, for the first time in my life.

I stared out in front of me but couldn't see anything. Through my teary eyes, all I could see was Irenka, young and strong, sitting at the piano and playing like a goddess. Her fingers were electric on the keyboard, her interpretations of the greats—Rachmaninov, Rubinstein, Chopin—were unique. She was gifted.

I've replayed those images, those memories, in my head so many times over the years, wishing I'd have one more chance to hear Irenka play, one more chance to hold her, to hug her, to tell her I love her.

As reality slowly returned that day, I found myself staring at the railroad tracks again long after the trains disappeared. Unfortunately, in the hell we were living, there was no time to grieve, no time to think about what could have been. Finally, I joined the others. Just as when Vanda was killed and I had had no closure, I had to deal with this last loss and concentrate on surviving.

I had no one to worry about anymore. Whatever happened, whatever decision I made, would be mine and affect me alone. The burdens were mine, the consequences—good or bad—mine as well. I no longer had feelings of guilt or a need to analyze, examine, or think about the future. It was just me left in the world, and I would live in the moment, survive in the moment, and deal with the rest as it came to me.

I had only one thought in my head as I stood there—the realization of how easily life happens. In a single instant, happiness and hope, those you love and who love you, can be washed away. One unguarded moment, and it's all gone. One by one, my family had been ripped out of my life. I felt like an orphan, alone and abandoned...and I was.

Years later, I learned Irenka's fate. She had been on one of those cars headed for Auschwitz, and her transport had been redirected straight to the crematorium. She had probably been dead before I stopped crying.

With her departure—my last connection to my old life—I began questioning all my past decisions and wondering what I could have done differently. Had my instincts failed me that badly? Had I misjudged Marmor? But there was no time for recrimination, no time for guilt, no time to grieve. I had no idea how I was going to endure a future without the people I loved.

But, I had to survive for them. My family was gone, and I had buried everything else that mattered to me, too. I had buried Regusha and Albina and everything that those names meant to me. I was Betka now—a new person in every sense of the word. My former self had feelings and concerns that I no longer had. The only thing I knew for certain was that I would survive, no matter what.

CHAPTER 31

THE GERMAN SOLDIERS KEPT THE REST OF US corralled outside for several hours after the trains left for Auschwitz. We stared at the tracks with no idea what was going on, what plans they had for us, even whether we were going to live to see another day.

There were so many people huddled together that it was difficult to breathe, let alone move without falling. Most of us stood silently, lost in thoughts and worries. Some prayed quietly while others were mumbling and crying. It was total chaos; chaos, I think, was the idea behind the whole process.

Finally, when we could hardly take the not-knowing any longer, our answer arrived. A dusty locomotive, with several wooden carts attached behind, rumbled to a stop on the tracks in front of us. It would be generous to say the things behind it were cars, because they weren't. There was no seating, no ventilation, and nothing that suggested it was suitable for humans. My guess is they were used primarily to transport cargo and sometimes livestock, but no living thing should have ever seen the inside of those crates.

The Germans didn't care. It was the cheapest, easiest, and cruelest way to move us from one place to another. Before anyone could object—not that any of us would, fearing the consequences—the hundreds of us left behind were shoved into those cattle cars. There was even less space inside than there had been standing on the platform, and once the door was closed, there was almost total darkness inside. A moment or two of silence passed before the bolts slammed shut, and with that sound, I felt the finality of my life close, too.

Slowly, my eyes adjusted to the dark, but not much else did. I was one of the lucky ones; I had been one of the first inside and was forced all the way against the wall. There was nowhere to sit down—and no room for it, except a few spots reserved for those who really needed it—and the air repulsive and stagnant.

However, there was a hairline crack in the wooden slats where I stood, letting in the tiniest amount of light and semi-fresh air.

That crack became my lifeline, the only thing that saved me. Inside, it was horrible, a claustrophobic, stench-infested cattle car with too many people and not enough oxygen, but I was able to keep my sanity pretending otherwise. When the smells—of wood, sweat, urine, and feces—became too much, or when I couldn't take listening to the moaning and tears from others, I would turn my back, press my eye to the small hole, and stare out at the world passing me by. I allowed my imagination to take over, and drifted away from reality.

The departure was abrupt and awful. We had been locked inside the over-stuffed train for several minutes before it took off without warning. People were flung backwards, some falling into others, and a lot couldn't keep from vomiting. As I was peeking through the hole, and imagining I was anywhere but where I was, I almost fell over many times. For all the wonderful amenities the boxcar offered, it was also unstable and constantly shaking back and forth. I was certain it would topple over at some point, killing us all.

Somehow, God willing, that never happened.

Within minutes, while trying to tolerate the heat, I was percolating.

Drops of sweat gathered on my forehead, and ripples of perspiration rolled down my back. The air in that wooden crate was filled with the intensity of a raging fire. Always preferring the cold winter climate, I realized that this trip was marked for me with perspiration, glazed eyes, and red, blazing cheeks—all from the sweltering heat.

With too much darkness to see my other senses morphed into high alert, I could hear everything being said, smell and distinguish each of those putrid odors, and used my hands as my eyes. Pressed against the back wall of the crate, hanging like a painting, silent, I could feel the sticky wear and tear of all the previous journeys it had made. It was disgusting—not only the dirt and grime, but a weird, sticky greenish fungus growing inside the layers of the wooden planks.

Throughout the trip, one thought continually overtook all the others: This is it; this is what the end must look like— dismal, gloomy, sinister.

The unbearable heat, the lack of air, and the smell of sulfur were intolerable on their own, but together they were almost lethal. We designated a small corner for relieving ourselves, and most of us either vomited or were forcing ourselves not to. Some women fainted. When I got close, and I did many times, I turned to the crack and sucked in whatever air I could to save myself. Standing with no relief was debilitating, but I refused to leave and give up my spot near the only source of outside life.

We rode all night and into the next day without food or water. There was very little talking, and the only sounds were cries or gasps for air. The repetitive churning of the train's wheels—*kchink-kchunk! Kchink-kchunk! Kchink-kchunk!*—were both migraine-inducing and mesmerizing. Slowly the energy drained from my body and I became exhausted, but my mind continued running at full speed.

Everything was overwhelming. In too little time, I had gone from

LET'S ASK BETKA

Warsaw to Zavierch to Sosnowitz to wherever the hell they were taking us now. I had changed my name from Regusha to Albina to Betka, lost my mother, my sisters, and almost my life, and I hoped that the devil would not find me. . .again.

As the night turned into another day, it was difficult standing. My legs were aching more than they ever had before, and combined with the heat and hunger, it was almost more than I could bear. For some women, sleep came easily in the cattle car, but I couldn't; any time I dozed off, I was jarred awake by the shaking of the car and that incessant noise of its wheel. The only progress was that, after more than thirty hours stuffed in there, I had finally adapted to the smell and no longer felt the need to vomit.

As I peeked through the crack again, I watched us pass town after town after town, wondering where we were and where we were going. The view outside for most of the trip was nothing but endless terrain. How far were we going? Where were they taking us? What the hell were they going to do with us when we got there?

I tried keeping track of the time, but that soon became impossible. And the truth was that time no longer mattered. Very little did. There was temporary relief whenever the train slowed, and when it did, I tried to figure out where we were or at least which direction we were heading in, but that made the sudden accelerations that much worse. Whenever the train jolted forward, the unstable boxcar only shook and bounced more, twisting and turning all of us in the wooden box. My spine felt as if it was bending in directions it wasn't supposed to, shooting pain up and down my nervous system. I wasn't sure I would be able to walk when we got out—if we got out.

At the end of the second day, June 23, 1943, the wheels slowed down, the rattling slowed, and the abrupt movement of the train ceased.

Moments later, the bolt on the door clicked, and then the door slid open. Fresh air infiltrated the cabin, triggering coughing fits among those whose systems were shocked after adapting to the putrid environment.

We were about to find out the next step of our journey, learn our destiny, but most of us were too sore and queasy to move. No one had laid a hand on us throughout the train ride, but I felt that I had been beaten down and abused—and as I said earlier, I was one of the luckier ones.

Leaving the train car and facing our fate was almost as terrifying as staying inside. The German soldiers were already shouting orders and looking for any excuse to punish those who dared defy them.

"*Raus!*" (Get Out!)

"*Raus!*"

"*Bewegung!* (Move!)

"*Raus!*"

"*Schnell!*" (Faster!)

It was impossible to move as quickly as the soldiers wanted us to. They hadn't been crammed into a tiny boxcar without room to move; their bodies and bones weren't aching with every movement, and they didn't have tingly sensations piercing every nerve. Those who had been sitting might have had it worse. Their legs wobbled weakly as they maneuvered out of the cattle car. Some women appeared like marionettes being controlled from above by strings or wires, and it was a challenge for them to simply stand up.

"*Raus!*"

"*Bewegung!*"

"*Schnell!*"

"*Raus!*"

I was in the same agony as everyone else but somehow managed to find the strength to push through stiff, sore muscles to move along with the crowd. Those who didn't move fast enough or were unlucky enough to be in the wrong place at the wrong time were whacked with clubs by the soldiers. They swung randomly, hitting whomever they pleased. Some people got it in the head, splitting open bloody wounds, while others took it in the ribs or torso. Those who were struck in the legs crumpled to the ground, which only caused them to receive further beatings for slowing down the line.

They marched us for what felt like miles, but in actuality it was less than two city blocks, and then loaded us into the backs of trucks. They were better than the train, but we still didn't know what was happening to us. Some believed it would have been better—and probably easier—if they had simply shot us the moment we left the train.

CHAPTER 32

A HUNDRED AND FIFTY WOMEN, ranging from ages as young as eleven all the way up to fifty-five, descended from those cattle cars and into the unknown. From there we were transported to an *arbeitslager* (forced work camp)—Gunterbricke by Breslaw. That trip was shorter, but just as terrifying.

The trucks shuddered to a halt and the women were told to get off. The soldiers outside ordered us to line up in rows of five for *appell* (roll call or inspection). Because I was small and petite, and still reeling from my earlier encounters with the SS officers and their whips, I hoped to go unnoticed. I stood in the back, trying to blend in and remain out of sight.

But anonymity was not something that was in the cards for me. The *lager fuhrerine* (camp leader) singled me out almost immediately. Frau Noigebauer was a tall, athletic, and beautiful woman with jet black hair, alabaster skin, and the chiseled features of a Greek goddess, whose presence equaled that of any soldier. I registered her frigidity, but there was an obvious underlying current of something else as well.

She began by introducing herself, her assistant, Frau Winter (another no-nonsense type with a rigid body and stern attitude), and three others who worked as liaisons between us and the German camp leaders. Hoodja Goldberg was the *Judisch fuhrerine* (Jewish leader), Paula Bradrian was her assistant, and Bena Post was their secretary.

Living in a German-controlled world for so long, I had been bound to pick up some of the language, but most of it remained a mystery. I could understand some words here and there but communicated mostly through hand signals and emotions. When Fran Noigebauer spoke, I concentrated, hoping to catch something and understand the gist, but failed.

Instead of continuing my futile efforts, I stopped listening and began looking around the area instead, taking it all in. A fence surrounded two barracks, an outhouse, and a mess hall. Beyond the gates were several warehouses, large enough that they could easily be mistaken for airport hangers.

What was in those buildings? Why had we been brought here? What did they want us to do for them now?

I was lost in thought, not listening to Frau Noigebauer speak, and didn't notice when she picked out someone specific in the audience.

"*Du. . .in den Rucken!*" she shouted, staring at the back of the crowd. No one responded.

"*Du! Mit der kleinen en Tasche,*" she went on, indicating the one with the "little red bag."

Most of those in the crowd, even the ones who struggled with the language, seemed to understand her, but not me.

"*Kommen sie hier!*" she demanded furiously, and I was startled back to reality when the woman next to me tapped me on the shoulder and whispered in Polish, "She's calling you to come up to her."

My first thought was of selection and that awful oxtail. "What the hell does she want with me?" I mumbled as I walked forward.

When I reached the front, I defended myself to Hoodja in Polish. "Is she angry because I have this red bag?" I asked, thinking maybe the German thought I was too arrogant in displaying it for everyone to see.

"No, not at all," Hoodja replied. "You and these other women have been chosen as foremen. The transport will be divided into five groups, and each group will be assigned a different work task. You will be responsible for one of the groups."

I almost laughed, then explained it was impossible because I could not speak German. She relayed my concerns to Frau Winters, who took a moment before reacting. Then she gave her decision, speaking every word if she were giving an official order: *"Du wirst es lernen!"* and even I understood she expected me to learn the language.

Early on, I had been taught that you get more with honey than vinegar, and I decided then and there that my best way to survive would be to treat leaders and bosses with kindness. So I offered my bag to Frau Winters.

She looked perplexed, so I turned to Hoodja and explained. "What do I need it for anymore? I don't see a date with a handsome prince in my near future, do you?"

Frau Winters appeared irritated at first, but when she took another look at the leather-and-ostrich feather billfold, a forced smile creased her lips, and she raised her eyes to look directly at mine, gave a curt nod in lieu of a thank-you, and accepted my gift.

It was striking that, of the dozens of women to choose from, the ones selected as foremen—Yasia Sachs, Hanka Levine, Rene Ofner, and myself—were also the most educated. Before the war, Yasia had been a bacteriologist; Hanka had a University diploma, and Rena and I were both high school graduates. Somehow, Noigebauer and Winters had recognized these leadership traits in each of us. It was obvious they were old hands at it.

Just before we were dismissed to take showers, the leaders assigned us our groups to supervise. I was given both ends of the spectrum in terms of age—all those under the age of sixteen, and everyone over the age of forty-five, were placed under my tutelage. Because it was the largest group any foreman was assigned, I was given an assistant, Nina Zondshein.

After taking showers in icy cold water, we were summoned again for *appell*. The air was crisp, a lot cooler than usual for that time of year. I guess our captors wanted to make sure that none of us decided to morph into polar bears and escape. We stood there shivering, our teeth chattering, while they slowly counted us off one by one.

I stared back at my kidnappers that night, and a deeper feeling of hatred developed inside of me. These weren't the same people who had come into my home and taken me and my family away. They were not the ones who had murdered my mother and sisters or who had beaten me within an inch of my life with an oxtail. But they were guilty nonetheless. They were kidnappers, even if not in the literal sense of the word. They had taken our lives, our dreams, our hopes, and crushed them for some pointless vendetta. They stood around looking at us as if they were better than us, as if we deserved to be there, inferior to them.

Then and there, I knew that, no matter what they did to me, I would come out on the other end stronger and better.

When roll call finally ended, we were assigned our living quarters. Each inmate was permitted to choose her own bunk inside the barracks, but the foremen were housed in a separate area inside, giving us a little more privacy. Other than the upgraded space, which wasn't much, and being allowed to keep an extra blouse, dress, or jacket, we weren't granted any special privileges. We all possessed the same items that the Germans gave us: a thin metal plate, a spoon, and a straw mattress to sleep on.

My first night as a member of the Gunterbricke Work Camp for Female Prisoners was not pleasant. Not only was the straw mattress thin and uncomfortable, but I was also visited by my usual nightmares, repeated images that kept waking me up, sometimes with a scream. The images were bright and luminous: The whip! Mrs. Rosenberg! The man-eating dogs and those blood-curdling screams! Blood, belonging to the children of Warsaw, dripping down the walls! They tormented me and refused to leave.

LET'S ASK BETKA

CHAPTER 33

THE NEXT MORNING, WE WERE AWAKENED, given breakfast or at least what they called a breakfast—a bitter black substance masquerading as coffee—and told that, if we wanted something to eat in the morning, we should save a portion of our bread from the previous evening. Then they escorted us to the *arbeitsplatz*, the workplace. The warehouse my team and I were sent to supplied the tools and equipment needed by soldiers fighting on the front line. Our job was to pack it up and ship it out.

The German supervisor assigned to me and my group was Herr Krieger. His job was to teach the assigned task to me, the foreman; I would in turn teach it to the others. But since I couldn't speak or understand German as Herr Krieger explained the details of my task, I simply shook my head in bewilderment.

When he finished, or at least stopped talking, I addressed the group in Polish. "Will someone tell him I have no idea what he's saying?"

Some of the women in camp, especially those who had a Yiddish background, could communicate in German and explained the problem. When Krieger openly wondered how a German-language illiterate had become a foreman, someone explained it had been the decision of the camp *lager fuhrerine* and her assistant.

It took longer than he would have liked, but Herr Krieger and I found common ground. Through exaggerated gestures and with the help of other inmates more familiar with the language than I was, I managed to understand the tasks being described. Then, I went to work running the warehouse and supervising my "staff."

I took to the job as I had to any other in my past and did it to the best of my abilities. As I had as a youngster, I functioned at a fast pace as a young adult. I believed every task should be completed as quickly, and as perfectly, as possible. It's part of who I am, the core of my DNA, and a quality that has served me well throughout life. Following my lead, the group developed a strong, quick work ethic.

But Krieger did not want the job to end too quickly. He had no idea where he would be transferred once our task was completed and was afraid he would be sent to fight on the front lines.

One day he came running in, yelling, "*Nein! Nein! Nein! Nicht schnell!*" He searched unsuccessfully for a prop to help translate, then repeated his orders. Using a broom he found in the warehouse storage closet and as the women inmates looked on, he showed me the speed he wanted them to work at when she approached. "*Wenn sie ansätze, schnell, schnell, schnell!*" he said, sweeping quickly. "*Und wenn sie geht, wirst du langsamer,*" he went on, slowing down.

I nodded in understanding, and we both smiled and laughed in agreement.

At night, we learned the Germans gave an entirely new meaning to the word "dinner." Each inmate, including foremen, were given a small piece of bread, of which we were supposed to save some for the morning, and a cup of nettle. For those who don't know what nettle is, it's an herbaceous plant with jagged leaves that secretes a stinging liquid. The Germans marinated this plant in water, disguising it as a sort of soup. One spoonful of that bitter water would cause anyone to gag. I only ate the bread, and many followed, tossing the green liquid into the toilet.

LET'S ASK BETKA

The younger girls in the group were famished and tried eating as much as they could. But whatever they swallowed came right back up. Diarrhea became rampant, and the adjacent outhouse was constantly filled to capacity.

One night, when Frau Noigebauer caught some of the women throwing away the soup, she became enraged. She immediately ordered all of us out of the barracks and lined up for *appell*.

She berated us for several minutes. The gist of the scolding was a warning: Anyone caught throwing out food would be severely punished.

The warehouse was hot and damp during the day, and the work hard and tiring. With mostly children and middle-age women to contend with, I set up my own schedule with two units. One group worked for an hour while the other rested, and then they switched. The younger girls took a liking to me and followed my lead, while the older women respected and trusted me. I quickly became an adviser and friend.

Soon the warehouse began to function well, and even Krieger was pleased. One morning, Frau Noigebauer made a surprise visit, and as she saw one group of prisoners working and one not, she turned and walked out without saying a word. I was concerned, but not overly so. . .until later.

That night as the prisoners were lined up to receive their meager portions of soup, our camp leader and assistant approached the crowd and demanded we line up for *appell*.

In a strong voice that echoed throughout the crowd, Frau Noigebauer berated us. *"Jeder hier ist gleich,"* she began. *"Es gibt keine Ausnahmen. Ich bin. . . ."* She was explaining that everyone was equal, and that there were no exceptions, but, having no idea what was being said and assuming we were being reprimanded for the new work schedule, I started to tune her voice out. Then, I caught a word I thought I understood, and another, and another. When I heard the word *"sitzen,"* I mistakenly thought the lecture was about the women sitting in the warehouse during Frau Noigebauer's surprise visit.

My rear end had not yet fully healed from my previous encounter with the whip, and despite being terrified of another one, I was not about to let any of my workers be punished for my choices. I knew I could communicate in Polish with Hoodja and approached her as Frau Noigebauer continued to berate the inmates.

"I am the one who should be punished," I pleaded. "The new system was my idea."

"What are you babbling about?" Hoodja asked, a look of confusion on her face.

I explained how I believed the schedule I had devised improved each worker's output. Eventually, she began to laugh, turned to Frau Noigebauer, and explained the situation. When she began to laugh too, I felt my blood turn cold with fear.

"Oh, this is just great. You're all hysterical, and I'm here shitting in my pants," I said, but the remark caused only more laughter which spread to my inmates.

To this day, I have not understood what was so funny or what was actually being said that night. Obviously, I had misinterpreted something and jumped to the wrong conclusions, fearing another beating. Thankfully, I didn't suffer at all for the warehouse schedule, received no punishment, but the language barrier caused many more moments of confusion.

Once, I was ordered to see Officer Kounart, the director of the warehouse at Luftwaffe by Breslau, who asked me to choose four girls from my group to clean the weeds by the railroad tracks. Confusing the word *"unkraut"* (weeds) with *"kraut"* (cabbage), I was afraid to tell him I didn't understand what he wanted. When I returned to the barracks and told the German supervisor that the following morning I was taking a few girls to clean the cabbage patch near the vegetable gardens, she thought it was odd and went to the director himself to verify the orders.

Later, I was called to Kounart's office and was met with an unpleasant greeting. He was annoyed but found humor in it as well and only laughed at me and the situation, calling me a *"dumm tomate"* (stupid tomato).

The next morning, four girls and I cleaned out the weeds near the railroad tracks as ordered. The story of my misunderstanding was retold throughout the camp by both inmates and Germans, and everyone had a good laugh at my expense. I didn't really mind being the brunt of a joke—and it was certainly better than being the victim of a whipping.

CHAPTER 34

MY LANGUAGE AND COMMUNICATION SKILLS improved as time passed, but they never reached a point where I understood everything, and I often gave the guards or other inmates something to chuckle about.

It was difficult to supervise my group while struggling myself. I often felt uneasy, but because of the concern for those working under me, I accepted the responsibilities. My enthusiasm and energy drew others to me, and whenever problems or concerns arose, the common phrase heard around the barracks was, "Let's ask Betka." The other women recognized my strength, and even the Germans appreciated me—in a way. Barely five feet tall, they referred to me as "Der kleine meister" (the little master). But to the inmates, I was a guiding light, an example of friendship, and a source of power and strength.

So much had changed for me in those twelve years, from the night Vanda first brought Stasiek home. I had gone from a warm, loving home environment to the darkest pits of hell, from the arms of a doting grandmother to the hands of the Germans. I had gone from my mother's gentle touch to the brutal beatings of the Gestapo. I had lost my entire family one by one and suffered through severe hardships. I had been beaten, tortured mentally and physically, and lost nearly all the hope that had once shone so brightly inside of my soul. I went from being cared for by a loving family to being responsible for fifty inmates, changed from Jew to Aryan and back to Jew. Somehow I had survived, but I would not escape the war without changing everything about who I was, and what I wanted.

The worst parts of the days were the nights when I closed my eyes and tried to sleep. Before I could drift off, so many images would flash before me, so many horrible experiences haunt me. My thoughts were disheartening and invariably accompanied by nightmares: every night the endless anguish, the screaming no one heard. The nightmares clung to me like cobwebs to my subconscious. A silent terror only I could hear was entwined in my memories. When I fell asleep, I would stumble into those gut-wrenching nightmares of Nazis chasing me with their whips and guns and the newest entrant to dreamland, those man-eating dogs, only this time it was me strapped to those poles.

Luckily, life in the Gunterbricke Work Camp during the day wasn't as terrible as it could have been or that I had lived through before. Most days passed quietly without much interference from the Germans. The guards were gentler, and random beatings and killings did not exist. There was always heat in the barracks when needed, prisoners always got their rations, and even our meals improved slightly. Breakfast was the same coffee, but for lunch we now received spinach soup (which usually had pieces of dirt or hair floating in it), and dinner was turnip soup with bread. The food was awful, but we devoured it and were still left unsatisfied. We were also given a treat twice a week, a sliver of marmalade on Wednesday or Thursday, and, on Sundays, a spoonful of chopped meat.

We were treated almost like humans. As a result, after the war, Rena Ofner composed a letter on behalf of all the inmates regarding Frau Noigebauer. We asked that she not be arrested or tried for any criminal offense. I'm not sure, however, what happened to her.

Despite these positive features at Gunterbricke, not everyone did well. The younger girls in camp became homesick and would often write letters to whatever family they had remaining on the outside. The only way to have them mailed was to pass them on to some of the friendlier soldiers and hope they followed through. Those who were caught were punished by having their heads shaved.

The Nazis were well-versed in torture, and they knew how people thought and what motivated them. They shaved the heads of all prisoners prior to entering the gas chambers, and did so to prevent the spread of lice or typhus as well. They also sometimes did it to set an example, to humiliate a female prisoner. Shaving off a woman's hair, one of her most seductive features, became common punishment for even the simplest of crimes.

When Basha Liebermann was caught trying to sneak out a letter with a guard's help, Frau Noigebauer called for the barber. To set an example, her hair was shaved in front of everyone. With a shamed face and clenched hands, Basha stood stiff as tears trickled down her face and her hair fell to the ground.

There weren't many incidents of these humiliations that I witnessed, and two months later the job at the warehouse was completed. All the supplies had been packed up and shipped off, and then we too were taken to another *arbeitslager*. This time we were not stuffed into cattle cars, and the trip between Gunterbricke and Klettendorf was much shorter. We rode in the back of military cargo trucks, and, though they bumped and jerked over the rough terrain, causing many of us to lose our balance and crack a few bones, being able to breathe fresh air made it a much easier ride.

We passed many farms along the way, and Polish farmers would stop their chores and stare. Sometimes they waved and sometimes they didn't, but there was always laughter and curses spewing from their lips. They hated us just like the Germans did, not simply because we were Jews but because they truly believed that we were the cause of their financial problems and personal troubles. They had no compassion or understanding for what was happening to us—and that was something I couldn't understand.

CHAPTER 35

WHEN WE REACHED OUR NEW DESTINATION on July 24, 1943, we were pleased to find out it was another work camp and not a concentration camp with a crematorium. When I jumped off the truck, I found that I was not as disoriented as I had been before. My muscles and bones ached, but my legs didn't feel like rubber, and though I was exhausted I didn't care.

There was a similarity between the Gunterbricke Work Camp and this new one, but it was much larger. There were higher fences, more warehouses, a lot more German officers, and more work to do. However, our task was the same—packing up supplies and shipping them off.

The Klettendorf Work Camp was under the jurisdiction of the German Air Force. Since it was a much larger *arbeitlager*, the workers from Gunterbricke were joined by an equal number of workers from another nearby camp, doubling the labor force.

Everyone arriving at Klettendorf was permitted to keep whatever garments they owned. I had a couple of dresses—the one my cousin had given me when I was in the Sosnowitz jail, which I wore as a nightgown, and the other, which I had been wearing the day the Gestapo caught us—and a spring coat.

During the week, the workers were given color-coordinated overalls to wear. The group that came from the nearby camp had black ones; ours were blue.

LET'S ASK BETKA

The menu at the new camp did not improve. The same disgusting coffee was served for breakfast, while turnip soup replaced spinach soup for lunch.

Dinner was another cup of some sort of rancid liquid, and we received the same ration of bread—with the same encouragement to save some for the morning.

Just as it had at Gunterbricke, the moment I tasted the putrid liquid my stomach gurgled, and I nearly gagged. "This must be the warm water they use for the laundry," I commented to no one in particular.

"And then they wash their feet in it," someone added.

Over the next several weeks and months, the women in that camp, nearly three hundred of us, spent every day together working side by side and trying to survive. We developed bonds that could not be broken. Without our families, we became each other's sisters, mothers, grandmothers, therapists, and confidantes. We ate together, slept together, and became a family.

The hierarchy of responsibility in Klettendorf remained the same for the inmates. Our direct supervisor changed—Herr Krieger became Herr Schell—but I continued as foreman and kept my girls together. The work was similar; we were packing and shipping supplies to the Germans on the battlefield, although this time they were machinery and tools. The iron was more difficult to handle, especially when the weather changed and the bitter cold arrived. A lot of girls got frostbite, their hands sticking to the metal. Sometimes their skin would tear and blister, causing bleeding and terrible pain. Those with the worst cases tried wrapping their hands in rags and homemade bandages, but those didn't help much; it was still horrifically painful, and the blood seeped through anyway.

There was talk of another warehouse shipping out gloves, and I knew getting some of them would save a lot of grief and pain. But I wasn't sure if the Germans would even consider it. They didn't care about us, and if or when we outlived our usefulness or were no longer able to do the work, I was certain they would kill us and bring in another round of Jewish girls. But, I figured, what would the harm be in trying? so I approached Herr Kounart—the high-ranking officer who had come with us from Gunterbricke. I spoke to him in broken German, using hand gestures to emphasize my point.

"*Ich rede mit dir,*" I said ("I am talk with you"), as he passed the warehouse entrance.

"*Sie sind zu kurz!*" he replied, barely giving me the time of day and dismissing me with a wave of his hand.

I couldn't imagine what my height had to do with anything— didn't understand the slang expression suggesting I was beneath him. I stepped in front of him, hopped up on the concrete slab holding the warehouse doors open, and, hands on my hips like Peter Pan ready for a new adventure, looked down at him and asked defiantly, "*Jetzt, genug gros?*" (And now, am I enough tall?")

He stared momentarily at me, then started to laugh, but I ignored that and pleaded my case. "*Nicht arbeiten!*" I insisted, pointing to the women working with their hands: They would not work.

He stopped laughing and demanded to know why, in a loud and irritated voice, "*Warum?*"

"*Kalt. Eison. Hand klebrig zusammen,*" I explained in my pidgin German: "Cold. Iron. Hand stick together," using exaggerated gestures and hoping he would comprehend.

Once I realized he was in fact understanding me, I went on, "*Handschuh—arbeit schnell!*" (Gloves—work fast.) My head darted up and down and my stare changed from daring to pleading.

He stared at me with an intense expression on his face, and then turned toward the warehouse. He glanced at everyone and everything, nodded a few times, took a pad out of his upper pocket, and scribbled a note.

Turning back to me he said, *"Du bist unvershamt!"* (You are brazen!), but he handed me written authorization for the gloves, clicked the heels of his boots together, and strode off.

I had no idea what he had said and didn't care. He could have called me anything he wanted, as long as I got those gloves. After he was out of sight, I smiled to myself and shrugged, only then realizing how daring I had been.

My confidence, sometimes too bold, sprang from a complete indifference to my own future and life. Getting whipped again scared me, but I had reached the point where I didn't care anymore whether I lived or died. After Irenka was taken away the last connection to my old life disappeared, I sometimes thought dying might have been better. Anyway, I would either survive or die trying, but I wasn't going to let what the Germans could do to me control my life and thought any longer.

Instead of dwelling on what I had lost, I found people who needed me. My inmates—my "girls"— looked up to me. I was astute and receptive to their needs, still am. My assertiveness, candor, and especially my knack of finding humor at bad times gained me the respect and adoration of my fellow inmates. Together, we would ride out the worst storm of our lives.

Music had been an important part of my life growing up, and hearing it played with precision and style brought a little bit of peace to an otherwise dreary, bleak, and monotonous existence. Sometimes, while we were busy in the warehouse, I would catch faint strains of classical piano music coming from the officers' club. After some research, I learned a

German soldier, Air Force Officer Farnhold, was performing, and it brought back a lot of wonderful and painful memories.

At times when loneliness was at its worst and depression about to consume me, his music saved me. It made me think of Irenka and miss her even more, but it also allowed her to live on in my mind and illuminate my heart.

Like the Sirens of Greek mythology who lured sailors with their irresistible singing, I was enticed by that music. The prisoners' bathroom was near the officers' club, and whenever I heard the music, I asked permission to go. Even if it was only for a few minutes, the sound of it gave me some relief from the pressures, responsibilities, and horrors of life in an *arbeitslager*. I could close my eyes and get lost in those melodies, pretending it was Irenka playing, and that my family was still alive, sharing warm moments with my father, remembering the love and comfort my mother had brought to every situation, memorable events with both my sisters, dreaming of concerts and ice cream parlors. They were wonderful memories of another place, another time, a better place, a better time. They helped me get through the others.

I couldn't stay in the bathroom forever, but after a few minutes I would leave feeling somewhat less gloomy. The music worked to brighten up my soul, at least for a little while. I would wipe the tears from my eyes—happy tears, sad tears, I wasn't sure which, and it didn't matter—and make my way back to the warehouse and the reality of what my life had become.

CHAPTER 36

THE MITTENS HELPED TREMENDOUSLY with the efficiency of the warehouse, and the work was being accomplished faster. The girls who spoke some German were assigned to do inventory and address the crates, but it was difficult for them to write while wearing mittens. I gave them frequent breaks to warm their hands in the corner by the stove, and the day came when those breaks almost got us all into trouble.

Officer Farnhold, the man who had created that beautiful music I enjoyed hearing, made an unannounced visit to the warehouse. He was tall in his pristine uniform and high, glossy black boots, and he took his military duties seriously. His long coat was draped over his shoulders with an air of authority.

He paused at the entrance of the warehouse but didn't enter, glanced around at the girls not working, and became irate. When I saw him, I must admit I was both intimidated and intrigued. He was scary—all German officers were scary—but also quite good looking. And I knew he was a genius on the piano. He shrieked, demanding to know who the foreman was, "*Wo ist der verarbeiter?*"

I could tell his blood pressure was up, and his deep voice echoed in the room.

As I made my way over to Officer Farnhold, he grabbed a pair of large wire-cutters and swung them as if he was going to attack me.

Everyone stopped working, and a loud gasp was heard, followed by absolute silence. My heartbeat soared as I tried exuding a self-assurance I did not have. Momentarily, I was rendered speechless but able to keep my fears to myself.

After that, everything happened in slow motion. He came at me with the metal shears aimed at my head. I swallowed hard and braced myself, ducking away in reaction. The blades came to a rest against my ear.

German was still a limited language to me, but I knew enough to make myself understood. My mouth was dry, my eyes on the shears. "*Wunderbar!*" I said drily. "*Jetzt werde ich eine zweite Van Gogh sein!*" (Great! Now I will be a second Van Gogh.)

My response so startled him that he stared at me in bewilderment. As he removed the blades from my ear without cutting me, I added in a broken German, "I knew that any man who could love and play Shubert so wonderfully could not perform such a brutal act."

He continued gazing, puzzled, into my eyes, not sure whether to be impressed or enraged. Everyone in the warehouse, especially me, held their breaths and did not dare to move. It seemed to last forever. Finally, he turned to leave. "*Jedes mal wenn ich hierher komme mochte ich alle Frauen sehen die arbeiten!*" he bellowed, warning me that, in future, he expected to see all the girls working when he showed up. His body stiffened then, and he added over his shoulder, in a quieter tone, "*Und. . .ich meine* alle *Frauen!*" ("I mean *all* the women).

As his words bounced off the walls I paused, brought my hands together in a prayer-like gesture, and lifted them to my lips. Only then did I begin to breathe normally again.

LET'S ASK BETKA

CHAPTER 37

EVERY FEW DAYS, A TRUCK CAME to pick up the tools and supplies. We were not only responsible for packaging and labeling the crates but for loading them into the trucks as well while the German officers did nothing but stand around watching. We would push the crates up a narrow ramp using a wheelbarrow, then place them on the truck. The crates were insanely heavy, and most of us suffered muscle spasms, pinched nerves, and terrible body aches.

I was injured on one of those loading days. One of the crates was heavier than the others, and several women were struggling to move it. Because I was stronger than most—much more than my frame suggested—I offered to help. I stood behind the wheelbarrow and pushed with all my strength. It was a hot day, and perspiration was pouring off my body. It dripped from my forehead and into my eyes. I couldn't let go of the wheelbarrow to wipe the salt from my eyes and continued pushing forward. As my muscles began to ache and constrict, I gave one final thrust with every bit of energy I had.

I lost my balance and fell off one side of the ramp while the crate toppled over the other. I was lucky that the crate didn't fall on top of me—I would have been killed if it had—but I landed hard on the large concrete stump below that held the door open to the warehouse. Excruciating pain surged through my body like a bolt of electricity, focusing most severely on my thigh and lower back. I tried keeping my breath even by inhaling and exhaling in quick gusts, knowing that, if I didn't force myself to stay alert, I would pass out. The spasms of pain were uncontrollable, and I was unable to control my body movements.

My last thoughts before losing consciousness were that I had been paralyzed. I closed my eyes, not sure if I would ever open them again.

Several of the other inmates—"my girls"—carried me to the nurse's office, where I was examined and treated. Nurse Scheftel, who had bandaged my eye during my encounter with the whip during selection in Sosnowitz, didn't find any specific injury or bone break, but said I needed to be wrapped tightly in a corset-like bandage.

When notified, Frau Noigebauer instructed Hoodja to cut up a bedsheet and use it as a bandage. I was wrapped so tight that I could barely breathe and slept that night on a cot in the infirmary. The slightest movement caused a shooting pain down my leg. Every gesture, the slightest stirring, caused knife-stabbing pain. I didn't know how or if I would ever recover.

After two days of rest, I began to walk again. I was determined to recover as quickly as possible out of fear of what happened to those who didn't. Anyone who was too sick or injured, and stayed in the infirmary too long, was eventually, sent to Auschwitz.

It was two weeks before I could stand up straight again. I would live with pain and spasms from that fall for the rest of my life.

CHAPTER 38

We spent a year in Klettendorf. It was better than some of the places I had been, but it's difficult to find positives in situations like that. As was true everywhere else, the bonds and friendships with the other inmates mattered most. Through the pain and misery, we endured. The Germans could take almost everything—our freedoms, our hopes, our families—but they could not take our spirits and, mostly, our memories.

Time dragged on slowly, with our lives passing us by. The mundane routines of working, marching, and shivering through the cold weather continued. As a group, we were constantly hungry, tired, and in pain but always hoping too and wondering when the torment would end.

A lot of people were struggling, but the children suffered the most. Many were unable to sleep at night because they were dry-heaving, which resulted in stomach and chest pains. There was plenty inside the camp and barracks to cause a person to vomit, but when there's nothing inside your stomach to throw up, it can be an awful sensation. The sounds of useless retching could be heard all throughout the barracks, but there was nothing I or anyone else could do for them.

The younger girls survived by giving up their childhood and morphing directly into adults. The transformations seemed to happen overnight. I watched the changes with both sorrow and awe. Some took it in stride while others nearly imploded. It shouldn't have been that way, not for them or any of us.

There was one girl I'll never forget. At the age of twelve, Felka Plovner came to camp as a skinny, emaciated little thing. She was quiet and timid when she first arrived, cautious about what she said and to whom. Within a few months, she had completely changed, becoming a fearless, streetwise girl. She would take on anybody in camp, wasn't afraid to speak her mind, and stood up for what she wanted. She became so sure of herself and so daring that it almost got her in serious trouble once.

Between the two barracks, where inmates slept, was a large bunker that stored food for the Germans, mostly potatoes and vegetables. Felka often asked permission to use the bathroom or get fresh air. Whenever she returned with a smile on her face, I knew immediately that she had stolen some food. She did it one time too many, though, and Frau Noigebauer caught her. It was after dark, but everyone was ordered to evacuate the barracks and line up in the usual rows of five—*appell*. I shuddered as the camp leader approached the crowd with a whip in her hand. Visions of my previous encounter with it flashed before me, and I could suddenly feel the pain it had inflicted on me vibrating throughout my body.

Frau Noigebauer summoned the team leaders to the front and handed Hoodja the whip, ordering her to use it on Felka five times. "*Bestrafen Sie Felka und geben sie ihre funf Winpern.*"

Hoodja handed the whip back and bowed her head. "*Frau Lagerleiter,*" she said, she could not whip one of her sisters: "*Ich werde nie eine meiner Schwestern peitschen.*"

Frau Noigebauer was stunned into silence, a silence that enveloped the crowd and hung in the air a bit too long. Then Hoodja continued, "Rather than beat her, I am ready to resign my position and join the others working in the warehouse."

As a Jewish Leader, Hoodja received certain privileges. She ate better, slept better, and was not forced to do manual labor. It could have been easy for her to turn her back on us, but she was still one of us and knew they would never see her as anything more than that either.

She glanced at Felka. "Her only crime is being a hungry child. I can't punish her for that."

Frau Noigebauer was annoyed but didn't force her to whip a "sister" nor did she accept the resignation. But Felka still needed to be made an example to the others. Face flushed with anger, she called for the barber. "*Rasiere ihren Kopf!*" she demanded, and, five minutes later, the entire camp of three hundred women watched as Felka's hair was shaved off her head. It left her bald and humiliated, but that was better than being beaten and bloody.

CHAPTER 39

It was a hot day in July 1944 when the entire camp of Klettendorf was awakened at dawn by a thunderous jolt. Without explanation, we were rushed out of the barracks, forced to line up in the usual precise five-row rule for a head count, and loaded onto cattle cars again. None of us knew what was happening or why, and we had no say in the matter.

It was a terrifying experience. Not until years later did I learn what had happened that summer day. The inmates at Klettendorf and likely all the other Jews being held in captivity were oblivious to the fact that the Allied Forces, led by the United States and England, were in the middle of an operation that would forever change the balance of power both in Nazi Germany and throughout the rest of the world.

I often wondered what was happening in the outside world, and whether anybody even knew what was going on with us, but I didn't dwell on it. I was too busy trying to survive the madness to care and suspected that whatever was happening wouldn't matter to me.

The D-Day invasion of Normandy had been scheduled for June 4, 1944, my twenty-third birthday, but didn't take place until two days later due to the weather. In the largest organized invasion in history, more than 150,000 troops stormed the beaches of France to drive Hitler and his Nazi forces out. While it was just another day in the most oppressive and brutal time of our lives for me and my fellow inmates, it was the beginning of the end of World War II.

In July, Germany also came under attack from Russia, whose forces were advancing into German territory in full force. The Nazis began retreating, cutting their loses and consolidating their power base. Prisoners had to be moved, and those of us at the Klettendorf Camp were among the first.

The cattle cars they crammed us into were more of the same we had all been through before—almost complete darkness, smelling putrid and without enough room or air. I don't know what anyone else was feeling that day, but I was neither nervous nor scared. In the past, my worries had always been for someone else—my mother, my sister, my friends or other inmates—never for me. I knew that, unless the Germans killed me, I was strong enough to handle whatever else they did, and that I could face whatever was coming.

We were off on another adventure to some unknown place, and the only thing I wondered about was how long the trip would take and what it would be like when we got there. Once again, I found a small crack in the back wall of the boxcar, and whatever minute amounts of air seeped through managed to dissipate my nausea and help me breathe.

I stared through the crack almost the entire way, looking with envy at the lush green hills and farmhouses that we passed. The scenes were strategically spaced to make a perfect landscape. At times, the smells of fresh hay and clean air from outside filled my nostrils, but that never lasted. The awful stenches of sweat, urine, and other odors I didn't care to identify came rushing back in their overpowering ways.

To avoid becoming overwhelmed, I tried getting lost in thought, reliving memories of the good times in my life before the Germans came.

But I couldn't stay hidden inside. The smells, the moans of other prisoners, and the constant churning of the—*kchink-kchunk! kchink-kchunk!*

kchink-kchunk!—were too much to overcome. Just as on the previous train, I had been stuffed into this one—bouncing, swaying, and rattling the whole way.

Cramped like sardines in a vault-like box, we traveled the entire day and night and into the next one. Most of us by then were on the verge of death, either from starvation or thirst, or from pure exhaustion and overwork, but not ready to give up yet. The worst for me was the lack of water. My mouth was cotton-dry, my lips on the brink of cracking, and I didn't have enough saliva to even wet my tongue.

When the following morning came, I peeked through the crack again, seeing sunny skies and beautiful weather. My imagination took over: a perfect day in a perfect world where freedom was guaranteed, where children could run and play in the streets, mothers could walk with their babies in the park—a wonderful day for a lover's stroll, and an artist could capture a picturesque landscape. I had all but given up on the idea of being free again but held onto the slightest bit of hope that, one day, I might be able to enjoy that kind of day again.

Inside that train, nothing was beautiful, nothing perfect. For the third time in two years, I was being taken to another place in the pit of hell and had no idea what to expect. What was next? Another *arbeit-slager*—or worse? Was this my final journey?

The cattle car left an indelible mark on my psyche. Fifty years after riding in those claustrophobic boxcars, I was invited to the opening of the Holocaust Museum in Washington D.C. On display was an actual cattle car. I froze, unable to get close, as my eyes began to water. The stench returned with a force stronger than I had remotely anticipated, and I immediately turned away, wanting to get as far away as possible.

In that horrible boxcar, we openly wondered about our destination, some fearing the worst. While there was a lot to be worried about, the biggest fear was Auschwitz. Anywhere else we still had a chance, but if the destination was Auschwitz, we were all as good as dead.

Adopting yet again a leader's role, I spoke up, hoping to alleviate fear and prevent panic: "Whatever's ahead of us, we will face it together." I wasn't sure what I believed, where we were headed, or whether we could survive, but it needed to be said.

Due to hunger, thirst, exhaustion, and conserving what little air the train had, no one spoke much during the trip. The monotonous sounds of those wheels, the moaning of prisoners, and the constant rattling of the boxcar were the only things making noise. The air was stagnant, I was unable to keep my eyes opened, and with the exhaustion came the usual horrible images jumping before me like flash cards. They came and went until they started to blend together.

Then, as quickly as the journey had begun, it ended. We awoke to the screeching sound of the brakes and the jolt of the stopping train. I was wedged against the back wall with my head resting against the wooden planks, and even though I hadn't been asleep long, I was momentarily disoriented. Rubbing my face with both hands, I tried wiping away the confusion from my mind. When, I wondered, will the day come when I can close my eyes and no longer relive those terrible visions?

Getting off the cattle car this time was even worse than the first one had been. My eyes took longer to adjust to the light, and my body felt awful. I had pain in every muscle, the most agonizing of it my lower back, hips, and legs; I was still feeling the lingering effects of the fall. After two days trapped inside, I felt close to death, as if I could keel over at any moment.

I wanted nothing more than a sip of water, something to ease the sandpaper texture the inside of my mouth had become. When I tried to speak, no word came out, only a harsh, grating sound. We were all thankful the trip was over, and eager for some relief, however minimal, but instead we were bombarded with loud, boisterous orders to line up and stop talking.

"*Ausrichten!*" (*Line up!*)

"*Ruhig!...nicht sprechen!*" (*Quiet! No talk!*)

I climbed off and landed on wobbly legs. Being outside with fresh air seeping into my lungs felt wonderful, but another foul odor quickly rushed in. It was unfamiliar and attacked my nostrils, crawling up my nose and lodging itself inside my mouth and throat. It irritated every part of me, burning my lungs, eyes and skin.

What the hell is that? I was wondering, just as more orders were given to line up quickly.

"*Schnell!*"

"*Ausrichten!*"

The soldiers continued screaming at us. There was a systematic precision to that madness, and they forced us to march along with them in military formation. Anyone who got out of line or didn't move fast enough was pushed along by the barrel of a rifle.

As we marched, I felt something on my cheek, and reaching to wipe it away, I realized it was a tear dripping from my eye. But, I wasn't crying.

Something else, something bad, was happening. Whatever was causing that horrible odor was affecting more than just our noses, but I still had no idea what it was.

"*Ruhig!...nicht sprechen!*"

The more we walked—somewhere, lost among deep and beautiful mountains—the stronger the stench became, and more people were reacting to it. Some began to cough and choke; others were sneezing and spitting. Whatever it was, it had the ability to overpower all our defenses and penetrate us from every orifice.

The soldiers marching along with us seemed to suffer no effect. Either they had been around it too long and developed an immunity towards it, or they had been immunized against it. Whichever was the case, I didn't like it.

Wherever they were marching us, it took a long time to get there. We didn't stop walking until almost dark, and then we were led in through a large gate and into another *arbeitslager*. An uncomfortable feeling came over me. I felt that all I had left in my future were work camps, one after the other. My old world of love and comfort had so rapidly disappeared. The world where my educational advantages afforded me the luxury of choices, from teacher to lawyer, had ceased to exist. The world where anything was possible was gone and *arbeitslageren* had become my future.

At least it wasn't Auschwitz; but something was different about this camp. I couldn't put it into words but continued to feel a sense of dread. The first thing that stood out was the number of guards. There were too many of them, almost more guards than prisoners, and there were too many dogs for my liking. Something was going on.

We were funneled into the center of the camp and surrounded on all sides by heavily armed guards hovering like hawks over us. They weren't the usual German prison guards either, but full-fledged, fully uniformed Nazi SS officers. Some had dogs at their sides, salivating and waiting to pounce at any moment. German Shepherds sniffed and snarled at my feet. The visions of those dogs devouring that man alive came raging back, chilling my skin and bones. I was in a conscious, panic-stricken state of mind. I found myself quivering in my shoes, biting my lip, and afraid to take another step.

Most of the prisoners were coughing, choking, sneezing, or spitting by then. I wanted to spit, to somehow get that awful, bitter taste out of my mouth, but lacked the moisture to do so.

CHAPTER 40

This new *Arbeitslager* was Ludwigsdorf, a Jewish prison camp in the mountains of Poland. It was under the jurisdiction of the Gross-Rosen extermination camp and, until our arrival, had been co-ed. Just before we arrived, all the men in Ludwigsdorf has been transferred to nearby work camps.

Other than the increased number of guards, the place at first appeared similar to any other I had been to. The barracks and warehouses looked the same, the gates surrounding the compound were familiar, and all the prisoners had been beaten down and humiliated but were still alive.

But it was odd for a lot of reasons. As I mentioned before, there were many more soldiers in full gear, with rifles, and many more vicious dogs. It was much dirtier than anywhere I'd been before, with some type of discolored soot covering every surface—the ground, the gates, the barracks—inside and out. If that wasn't bad enough, the air had a thickness to it, a mist that was painful to breathe.

Then, the strangest thing of all happened. Instead of orders and demands being shouted, we were lined up and fed. The Germans gave us each a cup full of that bitter liquid they called soup, something I was eagerly anticipating—not to eat, but to gargle with and wet my mouth.

We were then assigned barracks and told to go to sleep.

The air inside the barracks was just as uncomfortable as it was outside, with every inch of space coated in a layer of that disgusting soot. It wasn't a surprise, but I was too tired to care. I found my bunk, the lower half of a double-decker army cot, plopped my head down, and tried blocking out everything else. Sleep didn't come easily. If it wasn't the smells or sounds of others, it was the moments before exhaustion took over. There were scenic images dancing before me like marionettes on a string—Mama being dragged by the Nazis, selections, the whip with the blood, welts and pain brought on by the sinister SS officer. As usual, the images appeared, then disappeared, then reappeared: Mrs. Rosenberg deflating after being shot, the man-eating Dobermans with the flowing blood, all blending together. Eventually, I fell asleep, and then the nightmares took over.

That first night in the new camp, I was awakened after just two hours of a deep and unconscious sleep. Edzia Seidner, one of the Jewish foreman assigned to guide and help new inmates, shook my arms and shoulders until I opened my eyes.

"*Wstan!*" she whispered in my ear in Polish. I didn't know why she wanted me to get up; not wanting to wake the others, I opened my eyes but could not focus. It was too dark to see anything but her silhouette, and for a moment I thought I was dreaming.

"Come on!" she continued, shaking me again. "You have to get up and go to work," I heard through a fog.

"*What?* What time is it?" I asked, my voice hoarse.

"Midnight. Now, let's go!"

You have to be kidding me, I thought. My eyes slowly adjusted to being awake, and as I regained my bearings, I heard other inmates coughing and clearing their throats. I was both frightened and grateful—frightened because I was disoriented and not sure where I was, and grateful to be pulled out of a nightmare. I woke as I usually did, realizing that, either way, asleep or awake, I was in a living nightmare.

Although, considering the nightmare I had been having—and living—that might not have been the worst thing that could have happened. At least it would be over once and for all.

I pulled on my overalls and joined the group of women outside the barracks, composed of both prisoners who had already been at Ludwigsdorf, and some of us who had come from Klettendorf. There didn't seem to be any rhyme nor reason about who had been chosen.

As soon as we emerged, the voice of the Jewish foreman, a woman none of us from Klettendorf recognized, began shouting orders in Polish. "Line up!"

The newer inmates, like me, didn't realize that Ludwigsdorf lined people up differently from Klettendorf, in rows of three instead of five, and that we were out of place, causing disruption and angering the Jewish foreman. Her face turned red, and she started yelling again, her voice echoing in the distance: "Line up, I said!" To be honest, I was surprised she wasn't waking up everyone in the camp.

The younger girls were too tired and disoriented to know what was wanted of them, and the more the yelling continued, the more frightened and confused they became. Then, one young twelve-years-old girl named Figusha was singled out. "You!" the foreman screamed, pointing directly at her. "What is wrong with you?" she demanded in an annoyed and angry voice.

The bewildered little girl, who had once been under my supervision, started to break. She was so young, and had already been through enough to last ten lifetimes. Not knowing where to stand or what to do, and having the foreman scream at her, had finally done her in. Her frustration grew, and fear developed.

The foreman bellowed as she approached, "I said, Line up! Are you deaf?"

Shaken and exhausted, Figusha grew more uncertain where to stand. She vacillated from one spot to another. The more the foreman yelled, the more the child became disoriented.

To the shock of everyone, when the Jewish foreman did not receive a response, she raised her hand and slapped Figusha across the face. It was hard and loud, and every prisoner watching could feel the sting. The sharp blow struck her with great surprise. The little girl froze, fighting back tears, her cheek glistening under the blow.

She stared at the foreman with disbelief in her eyes, like a deer caught in the headlights, unable to understand such aggression from a Jewish leader. Violent attacks from the Germans were expected. Nazis were treacherous and enjoyed whipping, beating, and causing pain to Jewish people. Nazis were harsh, Nazis were brutal, Nazis were vicious. . .but a Jew physically attacking another Jew, when we were all in that horrible place together, was unheard of. A Jew acting that callously towards another was incomprehensible.

We were horrified over what happened, but no one dared move or say a word. I was working hard to contain myself, my anger, but internally, I was erupting. Finally, I couldn't take it any longer and approached the foreman with a stone-cold calm I had acquired but seldom used.

She was a tall woman who overpowered me in both height and bulk. I glared up at her, unafraid, yet refusing to show my anger either.

"May I ask your name?" I asked her in a quiet but authoritative voice.

"They call me Ostra," she replied, drawing in a loud and obnoxious breath, as if she were offended by the interruption.

"Okay, Ostra!" There was total silence as we stood face to face (we were never literally face to face, she was a head taller); I took a long pause for emphasis. "Now, listen to me," I said in a low but commanding manner, "and listen carefully." I wanted to make sure she knew I was not intimidated by her. "I was a foreman, just like you, and all these girls—" I pointed to a group huddled together with Figusha— "were under my care at Klettendorf, and I never raised a hand to them." I began speaking faster as the anger crept into my voice. "We are not used to this kind of treatment, especially from another Jew. Don't you lay a hand on one of my girls ever again. If there is a problem, I will deal with them, not you."

I walked away, but after a few steps, I turned around. "Ostra!" I called out, enunciating the syllables slowly, as if they left a bad taste in my mouth. "Your name fits you perfectly." (*Ostra* in Polish means "cruel," "sharp," and "harsh".)

She caught the irony of my comparison but didn't say anything and didn't respond to my warning. I could feel her eyes on me as I took Figusha by the arm and showed her where to line up. As the little girl began to calm herself, I felt a satisfaction I hadn't in a long time. I turned around and saw Ostra staring at me, unblinking. I stared back, but nothing further was said.

Finally, the foreman broke the silence, waving her hands to tell everyone to follow her. "March!" she commanded loudly, with anger seething in her voice.

The following day, word of the incident between Ostra and me worked its way through camp. Before long everyone had heard the whispers and asked for details, but I refused to discuss the matter. To this day, telling the story here, I have never spoke of it to anyone. To me there was nothing to discuss. I did what needed to be done—not for myself and not for pride or recognition, but because I needed to.

Some wondered whether I would be punished for it, but I didn't worry, and retribution never came. That was, however, the last time

Ostra ever raised her hand to another inmate, and the incident served as a warning to other foremen who felt the urge to strike one. Maybe things worked differently at Ludwigsdorf than "my girls" and I were used to, but perhaps all it took was someone, anyone, to stand up and make the foremen realize we were all fighting the same enemy.

LET'S ASK BETKA

CHAPTER 41

After everything that happened between Ostra and Figusha, and Ostra and me, that night, the selected group of women—some from each barrack—still had a job to do. We were marched into an underground facility built into the mountain, given orders, and forced to work all night.

When we returned at dawn, we were dirty and exhausted, and all of us were covered with powders of different colors. It was the same dirty, misty stuff that clogged the air and coated the grounds and walls of our barracks, the same soot that covered the benches, tables and cots.

I tried cleaning it off myself, washing and scrubbing my body and clothes with icy water—the only available—but wasn't very successful. I remained a little longer than I normally would have under the icy shower. It would take a lot more effort to wipe away the layers of dirt and sweat, and I didn't have the energy to do it. I wanted to lie down and close my eyes, but my inmates woke at first light and were concerned by my absence. Immediately upon entering the barracks, my roommates bombarded me with questions.

"Where were you all night?"

"What happened?"

"Why did they take you?"

"What's all that stuff all over you?"

It was too much, everyone speaking at once. "Please, girls, calm down," I said. "I'll tell you everything, but one question at a time."

They moved back to give me some room, and then we all surrounded the table to talk about what happened.

"They woke me and a bunch of others, and they took us to an ammunition factory that they built into the mountain—about three kilometers that way." I pointed towards the window. "There's an entire factory built underground and camouflaged." An aerial view would give you a false appearance and only show a large, forested area amid magnificent mountains. "And as for what's all over my clothes, it's dynamite powder."

"Dynamite powder?" several repeated in confusion.

"Yes. And I look good. You should have seen me before I cleaned up," I added, wanting to laugh, but not finding it funny. "Anyway, we were taken into this huge central room that had all these other rooms connected to it. Each room was set up for a different task, and there's all these machines. The odor that we've been smelling—it's so much worse up there. My eyes wouldn't stop burning. We were handling powders that came in three different colors: red, gray, and yellow."

"A dynamite installation!" someone remarked.

"Exactly! We were all shown how to weigh the powder and place the correct measurement into an opening in the wall. Behind the wall there's a machine that compresses it."

"Is this like a top-secret work camp?" someone asked, still surprised.

"Yeah, I think so. It's definitely a secret." I let that sink in before continuing. "The Germans are experimenting with dynamite. Something is going on, something big. The powder is what's causing us to sneeze and cough, and, as I said, it's definitely what we're smelling."

Because of everything I now knew, I suggested we keep the barracks as clean as possible. "At least we won't choke in here."

Despite being tired, I organized a cleaning party. Together, we spent the rest of the morning scrubbing, washing, and dusting every surface in the barracks. We stripped the blankets off the bed, shook out the mattresses, and attempted to make our space somewhat livable.

As soon as we were content with our cleaning and on the verge of complimenting ourselves on the good job, the first orders of the day were shouted, ordering us outside: *"Jedermann aubenseite! Jederemann aubenseite, jetzt!"*

The six hundred women in camp hurried out and lined up for *appell*. Standing on the other side, facing us, were men in work clothes, and behind them, the soldiers and SS officers guarding the camp. I realized at that moment that I had not been imagining what I saw when we were brought to the place. There were more soldiers than necessary, leading me to speculate that there was more than just dynamite testing going on.

One of the SS officers stepped forward and faced the group of prisoners. "We need volunteers for certain jobs. Is anyone a *klempner*?"

Two girls who knew plumbing raised their hands and stepped forward to join the first man in work clothes.

"Is anyone a *zimmermann*?

This time three girls who could do carpentry volunteered and walked away from the main group.

My German had improved considerably during my years in captivity, but there were still many words and expressions I didn't know. The words for the trades were still unfamiliar, but as the selection process continued, I knew I would have to volunteer for something—anything—or get stuck working in the factory. Anything would be better than that, preferably working outside in the brutal cold.

"Is anyone an *elektriker*?"

It was a relief to hear a job title I recognized, and one I believed I could handle. Immediately, I raised my hand and stepped forward with two other volunteers. They were both girls who had been with me in the ammunition factory the night before—Manka Zilberger was a tall, attractive brunette, and Bianka Gligsmann was a robust woman with an ample bosom and horn-rimmed glasses. The three of us followed the electrician, Herr Dietrich.

"Where did you get your experience and training in electricity?" he asked.

"I'm a high school graduate, and I learned about electricity in one of the science classes," I told him.

"Good enough!"

He asked the other girls about their qualifications and was satisfied with their answers as well. Then he told us what our jobs would involve. We would be responsible for all the electrical work around the camp, from mundane duties like changing light bulbs and moving electrical wires, to the main task of electrifying the fence that surrounded the camp. The orders were to arm every part of the fence with several hundred volts of electricity—either to prevent us from escaping or to keep outsiders from coming in, probably both.

When he finished, the Jewish foreman, Edja Seinder, approached our small group to explain that, since we had spent the night working in the factory, the three of us had the day off. She turned her attention to me and suggested I move into the same barracks as my new co-workers.

I had many concerns about this new camp, but I was somewhat enthusiastic that day. Moving into a new living space was fine with me, but not having to work in that mountain factory was a real relief—I loved the idea of spending most of my time outside.

Somehow, none of us were tired, not even after working all night in the factory. It was the adrenaline, I suppose. Instead of sleeping, we sat around the table talking, telling our life stories, getting to know one another, and comparing how we happened to be in the same melting pot.

I liked my new barrack-mates, but the place was just as filthy as the original one I had been assigned to. Despite having spent most of my morning cleaning the other one, I suggested we do the same. While the rest of the girls were out working, we spent the day scrubbing, washing, and disinfecting every inch of space. When the others returned, they were stunned by the clean and dust-free space. That night, I was voted the *stube alteste* (barrack leader).

A clean space was better to live in, but we were still prisoners, and we each hated every moment of our captivity. The Germans were good at subtle manipulation, too. They gave us blankets for our cots, but they were paper thin and barely provided any warmth. Though there was a warehouse in camp filled with extra clothes, taken from the condemned just before entering the gas chamber at Auschwitz, none of them were ever distributed. We were fed but never enough, always on the brink of starvation and willing to do almost anything for even the smallest morsel of food.

There was a stove for heat in the barracks—had been even in the previous camps. The Germans did not want any gap in the working schedule. If prisoners got sick, they might not fill the quota of items being shipped to the front. During the winter months, and only when the weather was unbearably cold, wood was distributed, and we took advantage of their kindness.

There were many women who had never been introduced to the whip. As a result, they were not as frightened as I was. I had no intention of doing anything that might cause a reunion with it. Some women brought back potato peels taken from the garbage near the German kitchen, while others managed to steal a small pot or two. We boiled the potato peels and made soup—far superior to the liquid the Germans called soup. It wasn't much, but it was a saving grace when we were exhausted and extremely hungry, especially for the younger girls.

The Germans kept us busy day and night—busy working, busy marching, busy coughing and sneezing. Each of us learned quickly that, even when you think you're too mentally and physically exhausted to go on, somehow you find the strength to do it. We found the support we needed in each other. We survived as best we could, despite everything the Nazis threw at us.

At night, the sounds in the barracks were depressing. People wrestling for comfort and warmth on their straw mattresses, the sobs and whimpering of children, and the gurgling sounds of unfulfilled stomachs filled the air. Every night I would lie down and close my eyes, praying for just one night of peaceful sleep.

It never came.

CHAPTER 42

LUDWIGSDORF WAS UNLIKE ANY CAMP I had been to before. It was bigger, imprisoned a larger workforce, and the guards were different, too, not just in their increased number and hulking presence, but in their duties as well. Many were posted along the perimeter of the camp day and night, while others' only responsibility was escorting workers to and from the underground factory.

Inside the camp, the six hundred or so female workers were under constant surveillance. The Germans watched everything we did. They were constantly on top of us, like ants at a picnic. We were divided into groups, each with a Jewish supervisor. After Osta slapped Figusha, there was no further physical violence from any supervisor, but some continued being mean and verbally abusing inmates. Were those women just cruel and did they enjoy causing pain to anyone "below" them? Were they fulfilling a need for power, or were they trying to make inroads with the Germans to save themselves? I didn't know and didn't care. They were just as much prisoners of that war as the rest of us, they just had a temporary title that could be stripped away at any time. I didn't know, didn't care, and it did not matter. It was unnecessary and degrading at a time when the women, especially the girls, needed the strength to go on, and were seeking understanding, compassion and help.

Winter came early in the mountains, bringing snow, crisp winds, and frigid temperatures. I thought, having lived in Warsaw, that I understood what cold was; but the elevation brought a new meaning to the word. It snowed a lot, and the temperatures were constantly below freezing, but it was the winds that caused the most havoc. They raced down from the mountaintops, piercing my face and skin with a sharpness I had never expected.

It was sometimes difficult to breathe in the high altitude, and I spent most of the time shivering, my teeth chattering, but I still considered myself fortunate. Anything was better than being in that warehouse with all those chemicals and explosives. The girls who were assigned there, the ones who hadn't volunteered or weren't qualified for the other tasks, suffered immensely. They breathed in the dynamite powder every day, and when they returned to the barracks at night the remnants covered their skin and hair. All of them complained of burning sensations in their mouths and throats, and their coughs were much worse than anyone else's. If they were lucky enough to survive the war, they would likely be dealing with burnt lungs the rest of their lives.

It took some time, but as the guards and soldiers had been when we first arrived, most of us grew resistant to the smells—whether that was good or bad was another story. My eyes stopped tearing after a few weeks, and though I still sometimes coughed and sneezed, it was nowhere near as often as it had been.

Ludwigsdorf was hell, no question, but on the days when I allowed myself a moment for my thoughts to escape reality, I appreciated the beauty of the surroundings. The village outside the prison camp was charming, set deep in the mountains with miles of spectacular views. When the snow covered the hills, it transformed them into a winter wonderland. The days the snow fell on the village was as if looking into a snow globe. There were times, however brief, when I could stare into the distance and imagine I was free. But it never lasted long—reality always came rushing back sooner than expected—but it gave me a momentary sliver of peace.

The cold was horrendous, though. Bianka and Manke were luckier than I was. Ludwigsdorf was their first camp since being taken from their homes, and they still had warm clothes. My journey had taken me the long way, through the Warsaw Ghetto and two previous work camps. Most of my belongings had been confiscated by the Gestapo, leaving me with barely enough clothing: a thin summer dress, and a spring jacket, to cover my tiny frame. Worn underneath my overalls, they hardly shielded me from the frigid mountain air and gusts of wind.

As I mentioned before, it was common knowledge among the prisoners that one of the warehouses was filled with clothing taken from those at Auschwitz, although none was ever offered to the inmates. No one dared to ask, fearing retribution—until one day when the cold became too much for me, and I saw the *lager fuhrerine* walking the yard.

I approached my supervisor hesitantly and requested his permission to ask for warmer clothing.

"They will not allow it," Deitrick informed me.

"Please. There is a warehouse full of clothing!" I pleaded. "I am freezing, and I don't know how I can continue. I just want something that will keep me warm."

Deitrick thought for a moment. "You are not allowed to ask, but I can ask on your behalf."

Frau Noigebauer stared at me while the request was being made, sizing me up. I stared back with desperation in my eyes, hoping she would agree to let me have something, anything, that would help.

After a brief consideration, she turned away and, with her back to me, spoke. "Come to the warehouse tomorrow morning." It was a direct command, nothing less.

The following morning, she rummaged through the clothes and chose a handmade wool cardigan woven with several different colored yarns and thick enough to keep me warm. As we were about to leave, I thanked her for her generosity and received a nod in response. Then she handed me a coat with a fur collar. I took it, thanked her again, and remember thinking that someone up above must be watching over me.

The first thing I did when I returned to the barracks was sew the required Star of David on the front and back of the sweater, which was sufficient to keep me warm with my other clothes. I was supposed to do the same to the coat but didn't, hiding it instead in the barrack loft and hoping that the opportunity to escape might one day present itself.

"I can't believe she gave you that sweater," Esta remarked.

I had first met Esta Malka Noiymark in Klettendorf, and we were sharing a bunk in Lugwigsdorf. She was tall and strong, but most of all fearless. We became good friends, a relationship that ended up lasting a lifetime. Esta was six inches taller and one of the few people who could keep up with me, and I admired her from the very beginning.

"I was shocked, too," I admitted.

"And that coat?" she continued with surprise in her voice.

"Would you believe she even chose it herself?"

Esta was lucky enough not to work in the factory, having volunteered for the carpentry unit. She was also lucky because she often worked in the German kitchen, replacing or fixing cabinets, shelves, or storage bins, where food was never in short supply and rarely guarded. Brazen, with no fear of being caught, she often slipped items into her pockets to bring back to the barracks, always sharing with me whatever she managed to steal.

As an electrician, I was in the kitchen a lot too, but had never dared to take anything. The times when Esta and I were there together, she would often push food in my direction, hinting for me to stuff it in my overalls, but I never did. Unlike her, I had been to Gestapo headquarters and savagely beaten with that unforgettable whip. The pain and the scars were still with me, and I believed that starving to death was a better alternative than going back there for stealing food.

At night, when we were safely back in the barracks, Esta would tell the story to the others. "What an idiot! She's in the kitchen, and I hand her food, and she doesn't take it!" She'd laugh without a hint of malice. I think deep down she understood, even back then, why I could share what she took but never take anything myself.

As the weeks and months passed, and life in camp continued on in its mundane routines, the friendships and bonds between inmates became sealed. Very little, other than the weather, changed. Everything else remained: We ate disgusting meals, we marched, we slept, we lined up for roll call, and we conducted our tedious work rain or shine. It was a worthless existence, but better than the alternative, a concentration camp with the crematoriums, or interrogation and torture by the Gestapo.

Most of the days were monotonous. I tried to wear myself out during the day, hoping I would be tired enough to sleep through the night, but the demons always returned to torture me. The nights lingered while the unspeakable nightmares still haunted me.

It didn't take long for the inmates to realize what was going on in the camp, why there were so many guards and so much secrecy. The scientists working behind the scenes were experimenting with different strengths of dynamite, developing stronger and stronger bombs. It wasn't until after the Liberation that I learned how close the scientists at Ludgwigsdorf had come to developing an atomic bomb. If they'd had another year, maybe even six months, everything that happened over the next several decades would have been vastly different.

Thank God they didn't have the time.

CHAPTER 43

When the winter snow melted and the leaves returned to the trees, the splendor of nature was visible through the barbed wire fence. In the other direction, the cruelty of mankind became even more clear. Here we were, six hundred women, surrounded by beautiful and lush landscapes, and we were trapped behind barbed-wire fences and treated like animals, or worse.

Along the front perimeter of the camp, set back a few hundred yards, were several homes that housed people from Ludwigsdorf. In one of the smaller farms bordering the camp lived two women, Lucy Casper and her mother. Their front yard was visible from inside the camp, and Lucy could often be seen on her way to the kitchen, dragging a wagon behind her. The Germans allowed her to rummage through the garbage for potato peels or leftover vegetables to feed her goat.

I saw her a lot when I was working on electrifying the fence, and we always said hello. Lucy was good about sharing any information she had learned from the radio about the war. One day around dusk, when the sun was disappearing behind the mountains and she was returning from one of her excursions, I was busy working and didn't notice her until she was almost on top of me, strolling slower and closer to the fence than she usually did. Not wanting to arouse suspicion from the guards while sharing her news, Lucy stared ahead as she whispered to me, "They're coming! They're coming! It will soon be over. Soon! Soon!"

The news spread throughout the camp faster than a locomotive, and before long many of the women were becoming excited about the possibility. I was not as excited, and not ready to accept it. I had been disappointed too many times. But I could not stop certain questions from creeping into my thoughts. Was it possible? Was someone coming to rescue us? Was freedom just around the corner?

It was impossible to know whether she was right, and even if she was, that didn't mean that whoever was coming to help us would be successful. The Germans were a well-trained and organized unit and had so far established dominance over a lot of people. But the thought of being rescued did allow a little bit of hope to enter my heart. I hadn't felt that in a long time, not since Irenka died, and even still, I was having a hard time letting go of my fear. But what was I afraid of? The Germans had already taken my family and done everything to me they possibly could short of kill me, and I had survived thus far. Why was I alarmed? Was I afraid that, after years in captivity, I'd no longer know how to live in society? Would all the emotions I had pent up over the years, like lightning in a bottle, suddenly explode the moment I was released and tasted my first breath of freedom?

A few days later, and weeks before the liberation came, muffled sounds could be heard echoing in the distance. Although you could tell they were miles away, the faint shots and explosions were clear and consistent. Someone was fighting back against the Nazis.

When the Germans realized the magnitude of the threat, they decided to prepare for a final showdown, stopping all work in the factory and ordering prisoners to remain in their barracks. With nothing to do but talk and gossip, rumors spread wildly. Every day, there was something new to talk about, and before long the atmosphere was filled with anxiety and tension.

It was then that I came to realize what I was so afraid of. I could not let myself hope for the freedom that I knew would never come. It was one thing to be imprisoned, tortured, and eventually killed. It was a rotten life, but there was a preconceived ending, and I could live with that, so to speak. But being led to the brink, letting us get close enough to taste freedom, only to have the floor ripped out from under us, was the worst form of cruelty. That I couldn't stomach, and so I couldn't let myself believe it.

There was no way the Germans could let us go. They had to kill us all to make sure that no one could tell the world about the atrocities they had committed. The people who had witnessed perhaps the most barbaric cruelties in the history of man all had to die to ensure the secrets of the Holocaust were never known.

When it became obvious that someone was coming, and that they were going to uncover what the Nazis had been doing, I knew death was imminent. I didn't know how, or when, but I was certain the Germans would kill all of us, all at once, somehow. If the past decade had taught me anything, it was that their evil was real, their threats were real, and their hatred was real.

CHAPTER 44

For their defense during the upcoming and inevitable warfare, the Germans planned to fortify the camp by digging a trench around the entire compound. Many of the girls, Esta, Bianka, Hanka Szancer and her sister, Esther, and me included, volunteered to help dig the ditch in return for more soup at lunch.

Things began escalating on May 6, 1945. Until our evening meal, it had been a day like any other. Then we finished eating, and the guards ordered us to return to the barracks and not leave them after ten o'clock. To emphasize the point, the guards screamed several times, "Whatever happens! Whatever you hear, stay in your barracks!"

Earlier in the day, I had learned that the curfew was being set because the Russians were closing in. The Ludwigsdorf camp was built adjacent to a railroad overpass, directly above the concrete road that led to the ammunition factory—the same road that prisoners walked every day to that factory, a road and a bridge that were much too close to the secret the Germans desperately wanted to keep hidden.

They couldn't let the Russians or anyone else get close enough to expose that secret, so they decided to blow it up themselves to keep it out of Russian hands. The railroad overpass was the main transport to Ludwigsdorf, Waldenburg, and other villages in the area, and blowing it up would ensure that no one could get in—or out.

As we returned to our barracks, the orders were repeated again and again. The Germans wanted us in our barracks by ten o'clock because they planned to bomb the bridge an hour later.

As soon as we learned our fate—that we would be trapped inside the barracks while a bridge not too far away was blown apart with dynamite—we worked to protect ourselves.

Every inmate stripped the straw mattress from her bed. There were enough mattresses for each two girls to hide under one, while we used the rest to cover the walls and windows—not that any of it provided any real protection; but it gave us something to do in order to keep our minds off the reality of the situation, off the fact that we might be blown up within the next few hours.

Sitting there under the mattress, listening to the wind and feeling every one of my heartbeats, I was scared out of my mind. I had no idea what was coming.

The barracks had been constructed as doubles, two units attached to each other by a thin wall giving the illusion of a mirror image. Genya Wyganska was an inmate in the barrack attached to mine. She had managed to smuggle in a watch when she first arrived. After roll call and just before we entered our barracks for the night, she and I agreed that, beginning at ten-thirty, she would tap on the wall every five minutes. Then, at ten-fifty-five, five minutes before the bombing, she would switch to one-minute intervals. We didn't want any surprises and preferred knowing the exact moment the explosions would start, and we would need to prepare ourselves.

The waiting caused anxiety to trickle long before the final countdown began. Inside the barracks there were a lot of conversations, but I have no idea what any were about. I do remember feeling the intensity of the moment, knowing that each of our lives was going to change—and possibly end—that night.

When the first knock on the wall came at half past ten, Esta and I were sitting together, huddled under a mattress and looking as silly as everyone else. It was the best we could do. The next five minutes dragged on longer than I could have imagined they would. We felt safer with the mattresses fortifying the room, but it made it hot, and clogged the air. Breathing was difficult, I began to perspire, and my mouth was dry.

Another five minutes passed, and Genya again knocked on the wall. It was ten-forty, twenty minutes before the explosion would come. It would either blow us all up and we would die—and we were prepared for that outcome—or we would manage to survive and figure out how to pick up the pieces of whatever was left. Some believed we would even be free when it was over, but I wouldn't let myself think about that yet at all.

The next five minutes of silence seemed longer than the first two, and I would have sworn we were hiding under those mattresses longer than I had been in captivity. The waiting, the unknown, the anxiety were becoming unbearable, and the suspense was killing me.

Five more excruciating minutes passed, and then we heard another knock on the wall. It was 10:45 p.m. Another came at 10:50 and again at 10:55. . .and the next few minutes would change everything and decide my fate: 10:56. 10:57. 10:58.

But the knock at 10:59 was different—louder, stronger, and more intense than any of the ones before. I felt it tear through my body, pulsating on every nerve. The strain stretched like a rubber band to its limit, and inside my head I began counting down from sixty. The last thirty seconds, I felt my body tense up, fold into a fetal position, and shut down my senses. I counted backwards until I reached zero, then closed my eyes and prayed.

LET'S ASK BETKA

At long last, 11:00 p.m. came...and nothing happened.

No explosions, no sounds outside, and no debris flying in the air.

Genya knocked on the wall again, signaling it was eleven o'clock. There was total silence inside the barracks, a tomb-like silence, with no one daring to move or even breathe. It was enough to drive a person mad.

A minute later, another knock came. We had passed the witching hour, and still nothing had happened. Maybe Genya's watch was off—maybe a little fast. Knocks on the wall came again at 11:02, and the silence continued as everyone stared at each other while still holding on to their mattresses. Three more knocks followed, and at the 11:05 sound, the silence ended, and the whispering began.

"Her watch must be fast."

"It has to be broken."

Then came 11:10, 11:15, and still nothing happened.

Maybe we were safe and the bridge wasn't going to blow up, but none of us were going to take that chance. We stayed in our barracks, huddled under the mattresses in near silence all night. Some of the girls fell asleep, but no one did for long periods. There was a lot of whispering, and many of us were scared. I felt confusion and curiosity and was unsure of what my fate, what all our fates, would be.

When the sunlight began pouring into the barracks, signaling the dawn of a new day, the first order was given: "We are evacuating the camp!" shouted a German officer into our barrack.

We soon learned that the plan to blow up the bridge and keep the Russians away had failed. The dynamite that had been planted to destroy it had been stolen by the men and women of the Underground. None of us knew what the Partisans planned to do with it, but it was better off in their hands than in the Germans'.

Then, after waiting all night to find out whether we would live or die, and then nothing, they told us we were marching to the Gross-Rosen Concentration camp in Silesia. Ludwigsdorf was one of sixty camps under the Gross-Rosen supervision, and it appeared the Germans would cut their losses and move on.

However, before the march, everything that had been distributed to the prisoners had to be returned. The Germans counted every spoon, every plate, and all the blankets. There seemed to be no reason for it—the stuff was nearly unusable—but the Germans were a precise and systematic bunch. I believe they took everything back to strip us of any potential weapons before the trip. I knew in my heart and soul that none of us would survive the march on the road to Gross-Rosen. I was sure we would never reach our destination. We were all going to be slaughtered along the way.

I gave back my meager belongings but kept the clothes I was wearing—including the coat that lacked the Star of David emblem. My only chance of survival was to escape, and I was going to try, even if I had no idea how.

The next morning, we were prepared to leave for the long march and likely be murdered, but the German police officer assigned to guard us defied his orders. He knew that the march was a death trap and proved me wrong about all Germans lacking souls. He would dutifully follow his orders...up to a point. Mass murder, killing of any kind, was not in his nature.

In the end, there was no march. There was no leaving Ludwigsdorf, and thus no reason for me to attempt an escape—yet! The officer told us to stay in our barracks and wait. It was the first order I was willing and happy to follow, as it meant living at least one more day.

Eventually, the decision not to march us to Gross-Rosen saved that officer's life. At a time when German officers were giving orders to execute as many Jews as possible out of fear of leaving witnesses, he acted humanely. As a result, after the war, many prisoners from Ludwigsdorf testified on his behalf, helping to spare his life the way he had spared ours.

CHAPTER 45

WE SPENT ANOTHER SILENT NIGHT in the barracks. We didn't know what was going on outside, but there were no explosions or other signs of violence. Daybreak came, and nothing happened; I decided that, as the barrack leader, it was up to me to find out what was going on.

With the sun casting its first shadows of the day, I creaked open the barrack door and poked my head out. The courtyard was empty, and there was total silence. I gambled a little more, stepping all the way out, and taking a good look around the entire compound. Nothing! A ghost town. The area immediately outside the fence was deserted, too. For a moment I froze, fearing that an ambush was imminent. But there wasn't one. There was nothing—no Germans, no soldiers, no orders, no noise of any kind. There were no birds chirping, no wind blowing, and the air was clean and fresh, as after a tornado, ready to re-build.

It was eerie. Was this a dream or the start of some new kind of nightmare? Would it, could it, be worse?

Esta, Bianka, and my other barrack-mates began following me out, and then all the other barrack doors started opening, too. With the same surprised and confused look as I had, they walked out into the courtyard and stared into emptiness. It was all happening in slow motion as the rest of the inmates, one by one, came out, looking for some semblance of understanding.

LET'S ASK BETKA

I was a little apprehensive, we all were, and everything kind of blended together. It was May 8, 1945, and the Germans who had dominated and controlled the Ludwigsdorf camp, and my life for the better part of a decade, were gone. They had simply disappeared overnight. I didn't understand any of it.

It was dawn, the start of a new day, the beginning of a new life. I glanced at the mountains, welcoming the sunrise above them, a sun I had not been able to welcome in years. It had been years since I felt that free and alive, and the landscape seemed to agree. The trees were bright and lush, and there wasn't a cloud in the sky. The Germans had left, taking their evil and hatred with them, and Ludwigsdorf woke up a better place.

The six hundred women who had been tortured, beaten, and deprived for years stood around in silence, taking it all in. Soon the whispers started, those doubting it could be true, that we could really be free. Before long, an anxious excitement began to circulate, and we all felt the change but were too afraid to say anything and jinx it all.

I stood motionless, looking out at the horizon. I wanted to relish the moment. I wanted to savor the sweet taste of freedom. I had earned the right to linger and enjoy it. We all had, and each handled the moment differently.

As we stood around trying to understand what had happened, how it had happened, and whether we were truly free, a faint sound in the distance caught our attention. Everyone's eyes darted toward a black-and-white dot racing towards camp.

Seconds later, the shape of a man on a bicycle, wearing black-and-white-striped pajama shirt with a yellow Star of David emblem sewn onto it, came into view. Was he a mirage? Was he wishful thinking? I was confused, and logic ceased momentarily to exist. I stared in disbelief as he approached. He was yelling something, but it was too difficult to make it out until he jumped off his bike and ran through the camp gates.

"It's over!" he shouted. "We-have-been-liberated!" Not wanting to be misunderstood, he enunciated each word slowly, clear and loud. "It's over!"

Mr. Goldwasser had been an inmate at Vister-Gersdorf, a nearby concentration camp, and knew that his wife, Sally, was imprisoned at Ludwigsdorf. "We're free! We've been liberated by the Russians!"

The moment I watched Sally run into her husband's arms was the moment reality hit me. It wasn't a dream, it wasn't a mirage. It was true. We were free.

The nightmare was over.

CHAPTER 46

Following Mr. Goldwasser were the Russian soldiers who officially liberated the camp. Their next task was to capture the Nazi soldiers who had escaped into the night. (With descriptions from the inmates and nowhere to run, many were caught within days.)

It took me longer than most to accept the reality, that the horror that the Germans had inflicted on us was over. I had been trapped behind those hellish gates, secluded from the world for so long, that chills of panic crept up my spine. I was free to go home, to live my life anyway and anywhere I wanted, and a smile almost creased my lips before I remembered that Warsaw was no longer my home. My entire family had been slaughtered, and I was the only one left standing. I had survived, but for what? What kind of life would I have without any of those whom I loved, and who loved me?

Feelings of confusion and apprehension overwhelmed me as I stood on the sidelines and watched others react. Many busted through the gates at their first chance, running to find the husbands, brothers, parents, and other loved ones they knew were in nearby camps.

I watched with sadness that I had nowhere, no one, to run to, but slowly the joys of freedom entered my soul. The horror was over. I didn't have to worry about being hungry or scared or beaten anymore. Maybe I didn't have my family, my mother and sisters, but I had my life. I had survived the worst and knew in my heart, even then, that I would build a life that my family could be proud of.

Since I spoke fluent Russian, I was designated as the intermediary between the inmates and the liberators. My priority was making sure that those who were sick, and in need of medical attention, received it. Even without the walls keeping us imprisoned, I still felt a duty toward those who had looked to me for support and guidance throughout the horror. It was the way my grandmother had taught me, what my mother would have done, and what would make my father proud of me. I had no doubt that helping those who needed it, those who were less fortunate than I, was the right thing to do.

Immediately, I sought out the Russian officer in charge, Captain Samuelowitz. "Many of us have decided to stay until things settle down," I told him. "A lot of the women here are sick and need treatment before they can travel. Getting them healthy will be our priority."

He nodded. "No problem." He began by ordering his soldiers to get whatever food was left in the German kitchen and transfer it to the camp kitchen. Then he made arrangements for the very ill to be transported to hospitals where they'd receive the care they needed.

For me, there was no time to think or reflect on the past. I was too busy trying to build a new world around myself and everyone else—the inmates who stayed because they chose or needed to—and Captain Samuelowitz and his soldiers relied on me. So had Irenka, and the Ojel family, and the women at Gunterbricke, Klettendorf, and Ludwigsdorf. For the time being, my calling in life was to help those who needed it when they needed it.

With the Liberation came a new foe—a different kind of cruel and vicious enemy had arrived, and I quickly learned that freedom was not free. Some of the men who had liberated us from the Germans felt justified in taking whatever they wanted. They were drinking, looting, and raping women—not only Jewish women, but anyone they wanted to, and quickly the chaos spread. It reminded me of the stories my mother had told about her life in Russia, and I began to understand why she had been so afraid to return.

I demanded that Samuelowitz arrange for protection, but he couldn't sacrifice any of his soldiers for the job. Instead, he gave me the suggestion and the tools—guns, rifles, ammunition, and such—to form a Jewish police force. I recruited every Jewish man who came to Ludwigsdorf looking for someone, to join that force. Most obliged, some staying on temporarily and others permanently. They would guard the compound and help make the transition from captivity to freedom a safer and smoother one.

Even with this police presence, it was still difficult to protect everyone from soldiers who wanted to act like savages. One method to keep them at bay was to frighten them. I remembered my mother telling me that most Russians were mortally afraid of disease. As a result, a sign appeared above the compound entrance that read *Bol'nuy* ("sick" in Russian) in bold letters. It gave the impression that the camp was quarantined, and after reading the sign, those soldiers who came to cause havoc instead fled in fear.

The day after the sign was posted, however, one solider insisted on entering the camp. The young men who were guarding the entrance held him back with their rifles, but because of the language barrier—they did not speak Russian—convincing him to leave was impossible. The guards sent for me.

Before reaching the gate, I began speaking in a voice that resonated with authority. "If you don't leave now," I warned him flatly, "I guarantee that you will face a firing squad first thing in the morning."

The soldier was intoxicated and slurring his words, insisted, "But I liberated you."

"That does not mean you own us. Leave this instant, or I will take the appropriate action."

He may have been drunk, but he knew who I was and that I had the captain's ear. My status in the camp was known to most, and what I lacked in stature I made up for with energy, guts, and tenacity. It's almost funny that those qualities only came out of hiding when I was protecting or helping someone else. I was never that brave for myself and preferred keeping a low profile whenever possible, but "Let's ask Betka" was being resurrected from within the walls of hell to flourish in the light of freedom.

My efforts proved worthwhile, too. There was no looting or raping of women at the Ludwigsdorf compound as there was at many others.

LET'S ASK BETKA

CHAPTER 47

IT DIDN'T HAPPEN OVERNIGHT, but the weak grew stronger and the sick became healthy. During that time, the people of Ludwigsdorf, and those of every other village, town, and city, formed a Jewish committee. Mindful of their responsibility towards the other survivors, the committee had two difficult undertakings. One was to educate, help defend, and make the transition from captivity to freedom easier. The profound fear was the risk of triggering an anti-Semitic reaction that would endanger us all.

The second function was to provide a way for loved ones to locate one another. Everyone was searching for a link to the past, and all Jews were asked to register. Survivor lists were created, and through those lists, and word of mouth, the news spread, and many families were reunited.

We had to be careful, though. The wounds of Germany's anti-Semitic regime remained fresh, and there were many out there who still believed the rhetoric. Prejudice is invisible, and no one wanted to stir that up again. The committees were to teach Jews how to move forward and defend themselves in a world where everything was questioned—both by themselves and outsiders. It was a dangerous slope, but if we were ever going to rebuild our culture it was up to us and no one else.

Men and women were making their way to the camp nearly every day, looking for someone they knew who had been imprisoned in Ludwigsdorf. No one ever came for me, but I was still happy to see families put back together after what the Nazis did to us.

Once order, and some semblance of normalcy, returned, I devoted more of my time to helping the committee—as well as continuing my duties as Captain Samuelowitz's official translator. Many of those who stayed in Ludwigsdorf remained living in camp, but others took residence in nearby homes.

Even though Lucy Casper and her mother lived outside the camp and had never been prisoners of Ludwigsdorf, or prisoners at all, they still feared the Russian soldiers. Two women living alone were unprotected against the looting and raping, and because of that fear, she sought me out. "Would you consider living with us at the house?" she pleaded.

I thought about it for a moment. "If you have the room for me and two other women, I will."

"There's plenty of room," Lucy said.

I asked Hanka Levine and Eva Weinstein to join me in the Casper home. It was the first time in years that any of us had slept on anything but a straw mattress, and the beds felt luxurious—soft and plush, with crisp sheets, fluffy pillows, and warm blankets. I felt I had died and gone to heaven.

But my nightmares followed me. It didn't matter where I slept or how comfortable I was, once I closed my eyes, those images, those reminders, forever torment me. I had spent every night with Mrs. Rosenberg, with the lost children of Warsaw, and then woken up with my heart racing, body drenched in sweat, as I relived the scene of the man-eating dogs, and felt the sensation that the Nazis were still chasing me. But it was still better than being in captivity.

Life in the Casper home wasn't perfect—it never would be again—but it was better than being Germany's prisoner.

LET'S ASK BETKA

During the day, I spent most of my time with the Jewish committee, helping people in ways I couldn't have before, and returned each night to the house I was sharing with four women. The Caspers were grateful for our protection and company, and Lucy and her mother cooked for us.

Whenever Captain Samuelowitz needed my assistance, he sent a horse and buggy to transport me to his headquarters. At one of our meetings, I expressed my concern for my safety and requested an official sign for the Casper household. Captain Samuelowitz authorized it, and the next day the sign went up on the front door. It read:

House Occupied
By Captain Samuelowitz's Interpreter

CHAPTER 48

I SPENT A LOT OF TIME WORKING beside Captain Samuelowitz, and learned more about him, the Russian military, and its government than I had ever imagined I would. Based on my family's history with Russian soldiers, and remembering how fearful my mother had been of them, I remained cautious, keeping them all at arm's length—including Samuelowitz, even though he was a Jew. He, however, proved himself to be an asset to all of those who remained in Ludwigsdorf.

Despite our political differences, he was an honest and compassionate man. He had orders to follow and a job to perform, but he took on the added responsibility of helping survivors, too. The world is a better place because of him.

During our many conversations, he relayed the story of how fate and circumstance had brought him and his men to Ludwigsdorf. They were engineers and had been assigned by the Russian government to dismantle the ammunition factory and send everything back to Russia. The Russians were aware of the research and advancements the Germans had made, especially their progress in developing an atom bomb.

Fancying that technology and armed with the knowledge that the Allied Forces of the West were on the brink of ending the war, the Russians struck at the most opportune time. Samuelowitz's orders were to clear out the ammunition factory and then guard the facility until the war ended. Afterwards, they were to liquidate everything in town, and make sure all German civilians returned to their home country.

I wasn't around to see the final stages, but it all eventually happened. Russia gained the technology it wanted, which, in the long run, probably wasn't the most ideal thing to have happened, and then they took apart the town.

During those early days after the Liberation, there was so much going on in such a short period of time that a lot of it has blended together in my memories. The biggest thing happening was the reuniting of families, of men and women coming in search of loved ones. More and more showed up every day, usually in groups because it was safer that way, especially for women. (It generally wasn't safe for women to travel without the accompaniment of men, which would leave them vulnerable to rogue Russian soldiers.)

There were two women I remember vividly, both because of the story of their travel, and because of how it eventually impacted my life. Thanks to the Jewish Committee's work, Manya Matjek heard that her sister and two aunts were in Ludwigsdorf. Not wanting to travel alone but having no male companions, she asked her friend Yadja Goldfinger to make the trip with her.

Together, they made their way to Ludwigsdorf, hoping to go unnoticed and arrive safely—and they had, for the most part. But on a vacant stretch of road, they encountered five unfamiliar men riding a horse and wagon—five young Jewish men, all close friends, who had relied on and helped each other during the worst moments of their lives, all survivors of Auschwitz-Birkenau.

Manya and Yadja had been frightened and unsure of what to do.

Immediately following the war, Jews were suspicious of all strangers. Many of them had taken an active part in the harassment and torture of

Jews. The Germans, Poles, and other Nazi sympathizers and collaborators naturally disavowed any knowledge of wrongdoing and tried to pass as ordinary citizens, or Swiss citizens, hiding their anti-Semitic feelings and continuing to kill Jews. As I've said before, prejudice is invisible, and we had to be extremely careful as we watched to guarantee that it would not touch us again.

Relief came immediately to Manya and Yadja, as soon as they heard one of the men yell out a question: *"Du bist amhul?"* (You are Jewish?). It put them at ease. *Amhul* was a slang word in the Jewish culture, a code word spread by word of mouth throughout the Jewish communities and used to test the identity of anyone claiming to be Jewish.

Manya and Yadja responded simultaneously with a nod and introduced themselves. Everyone relaxed, and the young men insisted that they not continue on the road alone. Though their destination was different, the young men altered their course and insisted on escorting the girls to Ludwigsdorf.

A short while later, the seven came across a young boy sitting on the side of the road who looked tired and dehydrated.

"Du bist amhul?" someone in the group inquired.

"Yes," he responded, nodding.

"You shouldn't be on the road alone. Where are you headed?"

"Nowhere special. I have swollen feet, and they hurt a lot. I can't walk anymore."

Rubin, one of the five men in the wagon, jumped down and ran an arm under the young boy's legs.

"Here. Put your hand around my neck," he insisted. "What's your name?" he asked as he lifted the boy into the wagon.

"Lutek Karp."

"Well, Lutek Karp, you are now one of us and part of our caravan to

Ludwigsdorf."

They arrived safely, and since the evacuations of Germans were underway, they had no trouble finding a place to stay. Once settled, Manya went off to find her family, while Yadja and part of the entourage—Zysek Adler, Monyek Rothstein, Henyek Usherowitz, and Monyek Zilbergold—registered themselves as survivors before checking out the town.

Rubin Eber, the man who eventually changed my life, stayed behind with Lutek, making sure the boy received the medical care he needed. Over the next several days, Rubin took care of the boy, helping him elevate his legs several minutes every hour, using compresses and massages to stimulate the release of excess fluid, and forcing Lutek to walk again. He continued the process for almost a week before the swelling was reduced and the pain subsided in Lutek's legs.

Shortly after Lutek's recovery, Rubin himself fell ill. He was exhausted and dehydrated, dizzy, spiked a high fever, and needed to be hospitalized.

One of the men who had traveled with him, Rubin's close friend Zysek, had been kept in the dark about his friend's condition. Due to his distrust of the doctors at the hospital, Zysek sought out the Jewish Committee's help. It was there that he learned of my connection with the Russian captain and begged me to intervene on his friend's behalf. "Please. My best friend is in the hospital, and I don't know what's wrong with him," he said, speaking very quickly. There was an uneasiness, a dread in his voice. "He's been quarantined, and they won't tell me anything. There's a group of us who are very concerned for his welfare, and we're afraid that, with all the doctors in the hospital being German, he won't get the care he deserves."

I immediately went to Captain Samuelowitz, who gave me permission to speak on his behalf and insisted that two of his soldiers, two of the bigger ones, go with me to make a stronger impression. I took Zysek with us to the hospital in Neurode, a small town near Ludwigsdorf, to check on Rubin.

With a soldier on each side, I approached the hospital receptionist and asked to see the doctor in charge. When she saw the two soldiers with rifles slung over their shoulders, her eyes darted back and forth between me and them, and she barely heard anything I said. She stood up without taking her eyes off the rifles and excused herself to find the doctor.

While we waited, Zysek took me to see his friend. Rubin was being kept in a glass-enclosed room, isolated from everyone else. Only the top half of the glass was clear, and since I stood four feet eleven inches, I was unable to see inside. The lower half was beveled glass painted white. Zysek had to describe what the inside of the room, and Rubin, looked like. "His complexion is gray, his eyes are closed, and there are tubes attached everywhere. He looks like death," Zysek said, almost in tears himself.

Having been surrounded by Germans for so many years in captivity, I was by then able to understand and speak the language. As the chief doctor approached—he, too, stared at the soldiers with their guns—I did not wait for an introduction. "*Herr Doktor!* What are you doing for the quarantined patient?" I asked in German, pointing to the glass enclosure.

He looked down at me but kept the corner of his eye fixed on the two men by my side. "We think he has typhoid."

Never one to mince words, I continued, "The war is over. We are all survivors, and that man—" I pointed again to the isolation room— "went through hell. If one hair falls out of his head, your head will roll."

I had made my point and felt no need to wait for a response. The doctor was left dumbstruck and couldn't respond even if he had wanted to. Zysek stared on in disbelief at the way I'd handled the situation, and I walked out with both soldiers following me.

Over the next several days, Rubin continued to struggle. He slept a lot and was tormented by nightmares and hallucinations.

When he finally woke up, he was alone, startled, and confused. As his eyes adjusted to the light, he realized he was in a hospital room, the walls sterile and white. There were tubes and needles protruding from his body, and machines beeping and making noises. *What's going on?* he questioned. *Why am I here? Where are my friends?*

He had a thousand questions racing through his mind, not sure what was real and what wasn't. Had the Jews been liberated, or had that just been a dream? Was he still in a concentration camp, or was this death? He tried looking around but was too tired and weak, and his fever was still high.

He was extremely tired and too weak to lift his head, and his fever had spiked.

A few minutes later, he was surrounded by strangers—doctors and nurses dressed in white. They explained the situation, his bout between life and death, and told him the details of his illness. He finally calmed down. He had been near death but managed to recover. It took him another two weeks before he left the hospital a healthy man.

Once he was released, he reunited with the friends with whom he had survived Auschwitz-Birkenau. Eventually, they all became members of the Polish Police Force, a voluntary unit that consisted of mostly Jewish men whose function was to keep law and order.

CHAPTER 49

THE FIRST TIME I ACTUALLY MET RUBIN was in the spring of 1945. At twenty-seven, he had already lived a challenging life. He was the youngest of four children, born on September 15, 1917, in Rowania, a small village in Poland near Rozniatow, close to the Austrian border. Today, he would have been ninety-nine years old, a great-grandfather enjoying his legacy, and we would have been married almost seventy years. To even think about that is astonishing.

At the age of three, he was scarred by the loss of his mother, leaving him with barely any memories of the woman most people considered one of the most beautiful for miles around. His father, Jacob, was constantly busy running his in-laws' bar and restaurant, and serving as the cantor of the local synagogue.

The Feinsteins, Rubin's grandparents, took on the responsibility of raising the children while Jacob ran the business. They were wonderful people, and Rubin loved them dearly, but they couldn't replace his own mother and father. Years later, Jacob married a woman who owned a grocery store, and he became its proprietor.

In the mid-1920s, Rubin's brother Leo, left Poland at the age of eighteen for Vienna, where the opportunities for work were better. He lived there with his father's sister, Devorah. Childless, Devorah Toback and her husband embraced him as their own.

LET'S ASK BETKA

In the years that followed, Leo's life changed a great deal. He eventually met and married a woman named Dora Berkstein, and together their life encountered a lot of turmoil. He ended up being one of the luckier ones, though. With the inevitability of war on the horizon, Nettie, Dora's mother, wrote to her cousins, the Hershbergs, in the United States, begging them to arrange legal paperwork for her entire family—herself, her husband Yakov, and their children, Dora and her husband Leo, Adele, and Max—to immigrate to America.

It didn't go exactly as planned. Before the papers arrived, Yakov, Dora's father, was taken prisoner by the Nazis and sent to Dachau—which, by the way, was the first prison camp in Germany. While Yakov was incarcerated, the immigration papers arrived, and the family liquidated their holdings but would not leave for the United States without the head of the family.

With both his and Yakov's American authorization papers in hand, Leo left Vienna and made the 275-mile train trip to Dachau, hoping he would not get stuck and drown in red tape or join his father-in-law as another number behind bars in a concentration camp.

But Leo managed, in the end, to secure Yakov's release, and the family eventually left Europe for America. So Leo and his wife's family were safe from Hitler and his minions. . .but it would be another thirty years before he was reunited with his brother, Rubin.

Rubin was never able to reunite with his other siblings either. His sister, Clara, had married and given birth to a child, but following the war, Rubin was unable to locate them or any knowledge of what had happened to them. Eventually, he accepted the fact that they had likely been murdered as had so many millions of other Jews.

His brother, Moishe, on the other hand, had a plan in place and was saving money to move to Palestine. He wanted to live and work on a *moshav*—an Israeli settlement grounded in the idea of a cooperative agricultural community of individually owned farms. From letters Clara wrote to Rubin, however, he learned that Moishe's dream of an *Aliyah* (moving to Palestine) never became a reality. Instead of going to Palestine, Moishe joined a resistance movement in the Underground. He worked behind the scenes with others to help defeat the German army—forging documents, producing anti-Nazi propaganda, sabotaging power plants and factories, and destroying communications facilities. The Underground worked hard to overthrow the Nazis. In the end, their strength was not great enough, and Moishe ended up dying for his ideals.

Rubin's own life took many twists and turns during his formative years. He attended both public and religious schools, although he never went to high school like many of his peers. Instead, he worked to help support his family, catching fish and lobsters in the river near his home. He was a strong swimmer, and he caught and sold enough to afford his family a more comfortable lifestyle.

When he was just seventeen, Rubin obtained a contract from the government that allowed him to lease a special section of the river along which he and only he could fish, and he sold the daily catch, mostly lobsters, to the local markets. The demand was strong, and he soon expanded and began shipping additional lobsters to the markets in Vienna as well.

Toward the end of the 1930s, Rubin was drafted into the Polish Army. With a love of horses, he was assigned to the cavalry. He enjoyed military life and the regimen and order that came with it. In his everyday life, he was decisive and determined; being in the military only enhanced those qualities. His unit was part of a cohesive group of men for whom discipline was an essential element.

However, he learned quickly that even the uniform couldn't protect him—or anyone else—from prejudice when anti-Semitism reared its ugly head. He hated what was becoming of his world, even more when it came from fellow officers.

One high-ranking Polish officer, a captain, abused his power, which grated on Rubin's nerves. He watched that officer take advantage of smaller, weaker Jewish soldiers by punishing them for no apparent reason, often with physical and verbal abuse. Rubin waited for the opportunity to stand up for himself and the others and extract some vengeance.

The chance finally came during a game the soldiers made up to keep occupied in the barracks. It was simple: One soldier would lie face down on a cot with his eyes closed while another hit him as hard as possible on his behind. The idea was to find out whether the one being struck could identify the one who had hit him. If he was successful, the two would switch places, and then another soldier would play. If he was wrong, he would lie back down and be hit again by the same soldier, over and over, until he figured it out.

When the Polish captain decided to join the game, Rubin knew he had his chance. He waited until it was the captain's turn to lie on the cot with his eyes closed and signaled the others in the room to stand back.

Tall and lean, Rubin did not outwardly project the herculean strength he possessed. He approached the unsuspecting captain and, with a quick motion like the crack of a whip, slapped him as hard as he could with his palm. The sound echoed in the room, and the captain winced in pain.

Within a second, he jumped to his feet and named one of the non-Jewish officers as his attacker, not believing any Jew was capable of such power. Jews weren't strong, they weren't fighters. They preferred reading and praying, and besides, a Jew wouldn't dare strike a captain. At least that's what this man thought.

He had to return to the cot, where Rubin struck him again. The process repeated itself. The captain winced in pain, then wrongly accused another non-Jew as his attacker. Over and over the attacks continued while Rubin cherished the pleasure he felt inflicting pain on the abusive captain.

Finally, the captain couldn't take it anymore. His heart was racing, his eyes were bulging, and his ass was on fire. He stood up from the cot, made one final incorrect guess, and then said, "I give up...I must know who hit me. I won't take revenge, but I must know."

To the shock of the captain, Rubin stepped forward and identified himself. From that day forward things changed. The weaker Jewish soldiers flocked to Rubin and came under his protection, while he had gained the respect of his captain.

CHAPTER 50

During Germany's invasion of Poland in the fall of 1939, Rubin's cavalry unit planned a full-scale combat operation. Their job was to strategically place cannons where they could protect and defend some of the smaller villages.

One afternoon, following a long day of moving heavy pieces of machinery and preparing for war, Rubin was exhausted. He had reached the point where his body couldn't perform anymore. Once he finished placing his last cannon at the edge of a small village, he found a spot atop a hill and covered himself with his leather bomber jacket for warmth. He tied his horse to a tree—for two reasons, to keep him from wandering off, and to prevent him from being stolen. It was common knowledge that cavalrymen valued their horses more than human life. Then, he fell into a deep, intoxicating sleep that lasted for hours.

Much later, he was startled awake by the nudging of his horse. He rubbed his eyes and tried focusing on the bright sun rising in front of him. *Is it morning?* he wondered. *How long have I been sleeping?*

He looked around at his surroundings, opening and closing his eyes several times, not believing he was awake. This had to be a dream—more of a nightmare, really. A wave of panic rushed over him, refusing to believe his eyes. He swept his hand over his face and through his hair, and rubbed his eyes again, trying to shake the confusion out of his head.

That's when it hit him—that it wasn't a dream or a hallucination. The area below the hill, where a healthy and vibrant little village had just stood—one he was trying to protect—was gone, destroyed. All that was left were piles of ash and thick clouds of black smoke rising in the air. There was no one and nothing around.

Another realization came to him, sending more chills down his spine. *Where's my unit?* It was quiet in every direction, nothing moving anywhere. Were they dead, or had they left, believing him to be a deserter?

Panicked by either option, he quickly collected his bearings, untied his horse, and made his way back down the hill to what had been the town's main road. It was even bleaker, standing in the middle of the rubble. He felt pain he hadn't experienced before. He was sad for the people who had lived there, and guilty that he had not protected them.

He took off walking, guiding his horse by hand, hoping to find his regiment and rejoin his unit. It was chilly, but he didn't feel it. He had walked for a while—an hour? Two? More?—when, out of nowhere, a German soldier with a rifle appeared, pointed the weapon at Rubin, and demanded his jacket.

Though unfamiliar with the German language, Rubin immediately knew what the soldier wanted and wasn't about to argue with a deadly weapon aimed at his gut. He began slowly removing the jacket, but the moment the soldier relaxed, Rubin attacked. In one quick movement, he seized the rifle and punched him on the side of the head with all his strength. The soldier winced and collapsed to the ground, either unconscious or, more likely, dead. Rubin didn't stick around to find out. *Looks like I've added murder to my resume,* he told himself. *I'm getting out of here.* He mounted his horse and raced down the road.

As luck would have it, he had chosen the correct path and soon rejoined his regiment. But the effort was futile, because a short time later the entire regiment was overpowered by a larger German force, captured, and became prisoners of war.

CHAPTER 51

THE YEARS RUBIN SPENT IN THE CAVALRY had taught him a great deal, but nothing could have prepared him for the horror he was about to endure. As a POW, he was treated differently from ordinary prisoners and taken immediately to the Gestapo prison in Lublin, Poland. At the time, Lublin housed the largest POW camp on Lipowa Street, known as Stalag 7, under German command.

Rubin spent weeks there being interrogated, beaten, and tortured. It went on for days the first time, the Nazis demanding information that Rubin either couldn't or wouldn't provide. Nothing he said would have stopped the Germans from harming him, and only when they realized the beatings were useless did they stop and change their tactics. They tied his hands together behind his back and hung him from the ceiling with a rope.

He didn't know how long they kept him dangling, but by the time they cut him down the damage had been done. His arms and wrists were badly bruised, his hands took on a bluish tint, and the pain was nothing short of agony, but the real injury occurred in his shoulders. The joints hadn't been dislocated, but he had permanent nerve damage that affected him the rest of his life.

Unable to break him that way, the Gestapo decided to use a different strategy on him—sleep deprivation. Sleep is a basic biological necessity, and the Nazis used it as torture. They kept him up for several days. Within the first day, he noticed his own lack of focus, and by the second or third he stopped fighting it and allowed the hallucinations to take over. It was the most difficult tactic he had to endure.

But that was not the end of Rubin's violent encounters with the Gestapo, though his time in Lublin was short. He was brought back to the interrogation room to be beaten and tortured twice more and then transferred to Majdanek, a forced-labor camp that later became a major concentration camp.

The Nazis were sadistic captors and killers, and they weren't playing by the rules. Despite being a captured military officer, Rubin was temporarily stripped of his POW status. As an ordinary prisoner, the Nazis felt they could do whatever they deemed necessary, although they didn't in fact care whether they violated the Geneva Conventions—since they believed themselves to be invincible, they had no one in the world to answer to.

After being tortured incessantly (the Germans were unable to extract any information from Rubin), the beating and starvation continued, but the Germans weren't killing any POWs...yet. They kept them alive in case they needed to extract information later. Rubin knew he was safe for the time being. But the Nazis were becoming more brazen and erratic by the day. They could wake up and decide, at any time, to murder everyone, POWs included. Rubin knew he had to get out of there.

But escaping was not easy. The Majdanek Camp had been erected entirely in open space. Anyone passing by had an unobstructed view of what was going on. He would have nowhere to run or hide even if he made it out alive—after he somehow climbed over the two barbed-wire fences, passed the attack dogs, and got out of range of the guards with rifles or the sharpshooters in the towers overlooking the camp. But it was all Rubin could think about. *And I know exactly what will be waiting for me*, he concluded, *if I try and fail.*

A tall chimney stood in the background, warning anyone to defy the leadership of the Third Reich. Smoke from the crematorium below puffed out day and night as Lublin Jews, and those from nearby towns, some as far away as Austria, were burned to ash.

Every scheme Rubin thought of was a bust, but he couldn't stop himself from hoping. The disastrous winter of 1942, with record cold and snowfall throughout the region, did nothing to help the situation. It also made working in camp unbearable. Rubin was one of the lucky ones. He was strong enough to withstand the beatings and the cold, and continue to do his work. Those who didn't, or who didn't do it fast enough, were killed on the spot by vicious SS officers.

Things began to change dramatically in March of that year, when the Nazis began using a different gas—Zyklan B—to murder prisoners. Majdanek then shifted from *arbeitslager* to an extermination facility. It began the fulfillment of Hitler's aspiration. He was implementing the dream of the Third Reich—the Final Solution, the annihilation of the Jewish race.

Rubin knew that he could endure hunger, beatings, inhuman accommodations, viciousness, and hard labor, but the combination of all five plus the savagery was unbearable. He knew the clock on his life was ticking. He had been led to believe that, if he remained useful, he wouldn't see the inside of a gas chamber, but he knew he couldn't trust them. He had to find a way to escape...and, finally, he came up with a slightly less than suicidal plan.

When volunteers were needed to repair a leaky roof on one of the buildings adjacent to the barbed wire fences, Rubin jumped at the opportunity. The roof was higher than the fence, and he knew that being on top of the building could give him a clear shot at freedom. For once, Rubin was thankful of being temporarily stripped of his POW status and given civilian clothes: He would look less conspicuous outside of camp. It was risky but better than the alternative of staying in an extermination camp forever.

While working on the roof with another inmate, Rubin confided his plan and asked if he wanted to come along.

"When?" the other asked.

"Now!" Rubin whispered.

He continued working and keeping an eye on the guards. He was waiting for the opportune moment when nobody's eyes were on him. He and his companion slowly and diligently moved toward the edge of the roof, and the moment the guard's eyes were elsewhere, they jumped over the fence and took off running.

They ran as fast as they could, making zig-zag patterns and dodging bullets, never looking back. Freedom was in front of them, and within minutes they had disappeared from the soldiers' view. A search party was quickly organized by the Germans, and Rubin and his fellow escapee could hear their footsteps and the barking dogs, but they never stopped.

Run—don't stop—run! He could hear the words as if someone was screaming them in his ear, and he listened. Despite the pounding of his heart, the shortness of breath, and the aches in his side, he continued running as hard as he could. *Run—don't look back!* He knew that looking behind him would slow him down. His legs moved so fast he couldn't feel the ground. His chest was heaving, his heart pounding, but the voice inside kept encouraging him.

He ran for miles, and eventually the sounds of the soldiers and their barking dogs began to fade. Only when he could no longer hear them anymore did he stop. His breathing was ragged, his body was trembling, and the burning sensation in his throat came from exertion and fear.

The two escapees hunched over to catch their breaths, both feeling a need to vomit. It took a long time for their heartbeats to return to normal, and then they set off again.

Danger was everywhere, but they had to risk it. They walked this time, for miles and miles, attempting to convey the image of two young civilians without a care in the world. They were both emotionally drained and physically exhausted.

Just when they thought they couldn't go on any farther, they came upon a farm. The Polish farmer was a godsend, giving them something to eat and a place to hide without any questions.

However, it wasn't long before one of the Nazi patrols searching for the escaped prisoners reached the farm, too. The patrol didn't have the dogs with them to sniff out the escapees, but it did scare the hell out of them. Rubin and his companion managed to make their way into the barn and hide inside the pile of hay in the loft, hoping it wouldn't be their final resting place.

When one of the soldiers entered the barn, the two men held their breaths, listening to the sounds of his boots scuffing along the wood surface of the barn. Each step was grating on Rubin's nerve, each a concern: Stay calm.

Every time the soldier stopped, it prolonged the inevitable. Rubin held his breath when he heard a creak as the soldier stepped onto the ladder leading to the hay loft and came up. Every rung made an irritating noise, sounding louder as he ascended. How does one stop breathing? How does one stop sweating profusely? How does one disappear? Rubin closed his eyes and heard the Nazi soldier jab something into the hay. He kept thrusting it in again and again. He would stop every few seconds to listen for any possible sounds and then continued thrusting.

Content at last that no one was hiding in the loft, the soldier climbed back down and left the barn, and that's when Rubin heard him yell, "No one here!"

Rubin listened to the soldier's footsteps dying away. He counted to twenty-five and slowly crept down the ladder. He ran to the barn door and squinted through a crack. There were no soldiers and no sound but the wind through the trees.

Everyone, the farmer included, was thankful when the soldiers left, but they all knew it was dangerous to stay in one place too long. People might get suspicious of strangers hanging around, and the last thing Rubin wanted was to expose the farmer to harm if he was caught.

After two weeks in the barn, hiding and resting, and with their stomachs filled with food, Rubin and his companion took to the road. The farmer gave them a change of clothes and a basket of fresh rolls for their journey. For his hospitality, Rubin gave the farmer some money and jewelry he had kept hidden.

The two men took the country road, passing one farm after another before being encountered by several Polish men in a field. "*Jude!*" one of them shrieked, pointing at them. The rest of the peasants looked up, and with rakes and sticks in hand, they came charging toward them.

"*Jude!*" they all yelled, this time with a hateful passion.

Because Rubin was stronger and faster than the peasant who charged him, he managed to sidestep the attack, take the peasant's rake, snap it in half, and whack him in his knees with it, shoving him to the ground. Facing the others, Rubin charged and attacked, punching one in the head with his fist, elbowing another in the chest, and lashing out with a crippling kick that sent another peasant flying. Soon all five were on the ground nursing their wounds. Rubin was pleased with himself momentarily, and then he saw his companion lying motionless on the ground.

He was dead.

Rubin's anger was at the boiling point. With the broken rake still in his hand, he confronted the peasants. "Is there a man among you willing to fight me alone, fair and square?" Staring at each one, he continued. "Otherwise, I promise I will kill all of you."

A husky six-footer with disheveled hair stepped forward. He approached like a trained professional, hands raised, fists held high, a boxer protecting his face. Though he had watched Rubin take on all the others, he was confident he could beat him in a one-on-one. A sinister smile crossed his lips, but before he could do anything Rubin attacked him. With one punch directly into the man's face, he sent him flying back onto the ground. As the brute stood up bleeding from his nose, staggering like a drunk after a vodka binge, Rubin slammed his fists into him again and again—a jab to the temple followed with an upper-cut into his throat. He knew it was not a gentleman's fight and felt no need to act as if it were. He pounced on top of the bruiser and continued beating him until he was nearly unconscious.

Then he rose in one quick movement and began to walk away from the bloody, confused peasant, turning his back on the rest of them. But knowing it wouldn't be good for him if unnecessary gossip about a Jew in the village spread, he turned back and called out, "By the way, I'm not a Jew," and laughed.

With the basket of rolls back in his hand, he strode off, leaving his companion dead in the road and his attackers gaping in disbelief.

CHAPTER 52

Now alone, Rubin felt terrible about losing the other man, but he had to go on. His survival depended on finding the partisans, those who believed in the cause of the Jewish people and were willing to fight for it, and that was the only thing on his mind.

He had been walking for hours when he noticed a German patrol car coming towards him. Not wanting to draw any suspicion, he kept loping steadily alone and avoided eye contact.

The car rolled to a stop in front of him with two German officers in it. "*Halt!*" one of them barked. "*Papieren!*"

Rubin never flinched. "I don't have my papers with me. They're at home," he said in Polish, pointing towards some village in the distance. "I'm bringing some rolls to my children," he added, holding the basket for them to see. "I'll take you there and show you my papers."

"No, I think we'll take you to our headquarters instead," one of them said as he grabbed a rifle, climbed out of the car, aimed the barrel at the side of Rubin's head, and led him off on foot.

Moments later, Rubin saw a buggy and two horses in the distance slowly making its way towards him and his captor. Although he had a barrel of a rifle trained on him, Rubin knew it was his only chance. Anything was better than going back to the Gestapo.

When the buggy reached them, the patrolman was momentarily distracted, and Rubin flung the basket of rolls at him, pushed the startled German to the ground, and took off into a ditch on the side of the road and the woods beyond.

They were dense and dark, but sunshine finding its way through a gap in the treetops threw down a misty diagonal of light that illuminated his path. He darted between trees, ducked at the sound of gunfire, and felt bullets whizzing by, too close for comfort.

He continued to run as panic rose in his throat. He was tracing different patterns, circling while dodging bullets. He ran for close to an hour, zigzagging like a football player avoiding a tackle. It was difficult to increase his speed. The ground was uneven. Raised tree roots protruded from the ground. The leaves were slippery, the trees were everywhere—and yet he managed to outrun the man chasing him. He hid behind a couple of trees to catch his breath, listening to the silence as he waited for his chest to stop heaving. Then came the sound of leaves crunching. With the German in pursuit, he took off again.

Only when he was sure he was no longer being followed did Rubin stop, collapsing under a tree to catch his breath. It was too dangerous to stay in one place long, though, and as soon as he felt ready, he rose and began to make his way out of the forest. He was totally disoriented. Every tree looked the same, every path identical. After a few attempts, reached a clearing, came out of the forest, and couldn't believe his eyes.

After all the running, all the twists and turns he had taken, having no idea where the hell he was, he ended up back in the same spot he and the German had encountered the man in the buggy. He laughed aloud. He'd circled a goodly portion of forest. But the patrol car and the officer were gone, and he was safe. . .for the time being.

Rubin remained in and around the forest for the next several weeks. He hid in several different places, never the same one twice, and did what he could to avoid the German patrols. When it felt safe, he would go to nearby farms and beg for food. He didn't need much—some bread and water to sustain him until he could catch up to the partisans. He roamed through the woods with very little sleep, with hardly any food except the crumbs given him by farmers, and found no Partisans. But he was determined. He had to find them and figured they too might be hiding amid the trees.

The hardest part for him was the lack of sleep. At night, the forest noises grated on his nerves. The wind sweeping through the trees and turning over leaves made him think someone was nearby. Animals scurrying for food kept him on constant alert. His exhaustion was greater than his hunger and anxiety.

Only when the exhaustion became too much for him to bear did he even think about closing his eyes, and it was not a deep or long sleep. He fell into an in-between sleep, not being awake but not fully sleeping either. And then there were the times he lost himself in thought, reliving the interrogations and beatings at the hands of the Gestapo. He could see the gas chambers at Majdanek, knowing they never stopped running and that one day his turn would come. He dreamed constantly of being chased by the Nazis, and as fatigue became more pronounced, it became difficult to know what was real and what was imagined.

Despite his best efforts, Rubin never did find the partisans. The Nazis found him instead.

He was sleeping under a tree when they came upon him, and again he was carted off to their headquarters to be interrogated. Rubin lied about who he was, claiming to be a farm worker. No one believed his story, and they spent hours questioning him, using mentally and physically abusive techniques.

But nothing worked to make him give up his identity, and eventually the interrogators gave up. They dragged him outside, tied his hands and feet together, and hung him upside down from a tree, dangling like a skewered pig ready for a feast. He was left that way for hours, exposed to the elements, and anyone who wanted to was welcome to harm him. Nazi soldiers passing by would kick or punch him, and before long Rubin was dizzy and nauseous. His limbs were stretched to their absolute limit, his shoulders were about to pop out of their sockets, and every part of his body was either seething in pain or numb due to limited blood circulation.

He was about to pass out when the ropes were cut, and he fell to the ground. Rubin never could remember being picked up or carried to a cell, but he was finally able then to get the long, uninterrupted sleep his body needed.

LET'S ASK BETKA

CHAPTER 53

ONCE AGAIN IN THE HANDS OF THE NAZIS, Rubin's nightmare continued. Three years before, he had been living in his father's house, planning to join the Polish army and protect his country. In the time that had passed, he had gone from soldier to POW to escapee roaming the streets and forests, trying to stay alive. He'd been through the Gestapo, two different Nazi prison camps, and finally landed in the hands of the SS—the most brutal Nazi killers of all.

Something about his appearance or demeanor told the SS officers that he was no ordinary man. They immediately suspected that he was, not only a Jew, but a Polish soldier as well, and demanded he admit it. He never did, but they sent him to Auschwitz-Birkenau as a POW anyway.

Auschwitz-Birkenau comprised two Nazi concentration camps adjacent to each other. Together, they made up the largest killing center of the Third Reich, and it was the death camp the Nazis were most proud of, the heart of their existence. In truth, it was a man-made hell hole. History books suggest that nearly one and a half million people perished there. Those who weren't killed in the gas chambers died from a variety of other causes—starvation, disease, forced labor, or failed medical experiments.

As soon as Rubin arrived, he was lined up to be branded with hundreds of other prisoners. Each inmate, male or female, was stamped with a number that became their identification, every other name taken away, every identity erased. Once you were branded like the animal they believed all Jews to be, you became a slave to the Nazis for life.

As a POW, at least a suspected one, Rubin's number was tattooed under his left bicep, which distinguished him from other prisoners. (Those who were "normal" prisoners received the branding on their forearms.) The Nazis were careful not to kill too many POWs, for the time being (again, in case they needed to extract information from them).

Since his POW status kept Rubin safe from extermination, he was sent to Birkenau to work in the coal mines. He solidified a friendship there with four men he was bound to thereafter for life. They developed an unspoken alliance, a pact of allegiance. It was a friendship built on support, responsibility, and encouragement during the worst years of their lives. In a place where there was a great deal of evil, something good blossomed.

Rubin was housed with a few hundred other prisoners in a wooden barrack originally designed to hold fifty horses, a waiting station for those who were condemned to eternal punishment. The conditions were horrendous. The roofs leaked, there were rats and other vermin running everywhere, and nothing was sanitary. The odors inside—of feces, urine, death and decay—were overpowering and offensive. No human being should ever have been subjected to such an environment.

Birkenau itself was a huge compound surrounded by an electrically charged fence and many guards. Escape was impossible, and for most it was simply a last stop before being murdered in the gas chambers. The Nazis might drag it out—interrogating, torturing, or worse—but eventually everyone knew they would get a chance to suck in those deadly fumes, which probably was a welcome relief for many.

Rubin was unlike the others, though. He preferred Birkenau to much of what he faced before, and definitely more desirable than Majdanek. For him the worst part was the unknown. He could handle the beatings, the interrogations, and the putrid smells and conditions of the barracks. He could withstand anything the Nazis did to him and could even face his own death if it came to that. But being alone, scared and unsure of what was out there, what was going to happen, terrified him more than anything else.

Rubin hated being disoriented by unfamiliar surroundings: trapped in the woods where creatures crawled on him at night, where everything looked the same, and where strange sounds grated on his nerves and chilled his soul. He hated going into villages that also looked alike and begging strangers for help, never knowing whom he could trust or who would betray him.

So, in a twisted way, he was somewhat relieved when the Nazis sent him to Auschwitz. There the days continued, one bleeding into the next. It was nothing short of horrible. The work was difficult, but nighttime in the barracks was worse. Everyone's body and muscles ached from being overworked and malnourished, and many found it impossible to sleep. The slabs they had for beds were outrageously uncomfortable, and it was hard to drown out the screams. Nightmares among prisoners were rampant, and the results echoed throughout the barracks. Even Rubin, as strong as he was physically, was unable to shut the horror of the world out when he closed his eyes, which he rarely did. His thoughts brought on his nightmares, his own special hell.

When tensions rapidly began to escalate in late 1944, the Nazis started feeling the pressures of the outside world. As the Allied Forces (led by American, French, and British forces) approached from the west, and the Soviets closed in from the east, the Germans realized they were trapped. Terrified of the world learning about the Holocaust and their intentions, they abandoned the concentration camps and decided to make a run for it.

In the final days, in hopes of destroying evidence and eliminating witnesses, thousands of innocent people were murdered. Those who were left at Auschwitz-Birkenau, some sixty thousand or so, were then marched away from the camps. They walked all day and night and into the next day, heavily guarded by armed SS officers, hour after hour, day after day, trudging through the freezing cold snow without the opportunity to rest or eat. Many didn't make it.

The SS officers were especially brutal during the march. The slightest mistake, the slightest struggle to keep up, was cause enough to shoot prisoners. The pace was grueling, and the snowy ground made traction nearly impossible. The worst part, however, was the icy wind slicing like razors across exposed skin.

Some prisoners managed to escape, to run away, but who knows if they made it somewhere safe with their lives intact or not? Most had trouble keeping pace and were either murdered or dropped dead in the street. It was sickening to watch SS officers shoot people for no reason and then be forced to step over their corpses and go on as if nothing had happened.

It took every ounce of strength and determination they had, but Rubin and his four friends made it. They walked all the way from Auschwitz-Birkenau to Czechoslovakia. Not wanting to give a Nazi soldier the provocation to shoot, Rubin offered to carry his backpack. He was hopeful that his life would be spared if he made it easier for the man. The backpacks were heavy, containing extra gear and food for the soldier, which made the difficult trek even more treacherous.

The five close friends survived. Not many were as lucky. Of the sixty thousand who began that death march, only two hundred or so made it to the end. (Not all had died—while there were tens of thousands of deaths along the way, some did escape, hopefully to freedom.)

Once inside the Czechoslovakian border, and supposedly out of reach of whoever was threatening the German empire, the remaining prisoners were led into the woods, where they were told they could sleep for the night. In the distance, Rubin and the others could hear the muffled sounds of explosions and gunfire: Someone's army was closing in. That might have been a reason to be optimistic, but lying in the woods on the cold ground, hungry and exhausted, no one was too concerned about what was happening somewhere else. Once they stopped walking almost everyone passed out.

When Rubin awoke the next morning, before dawn and before anyone else, everything seemed different. The noises they had been hearing in the distance were louder and closer, but the SS, officers and soldiers alike, were gone—no rifles pointed at his gut, no one barking orders or commands. They had disappeared into the nighttime woods.

It took a while for everyone to believe it, to realize they had survived the death march and were finally free. Many celebrated right there in the middle of the soil and trees, more excited and happy than they had been in years.

Rubin and his four friends, who had survived the worst together, left the woods that day with plans to return to Poland. They stopped first in a small village nearby, where they managed to scrounge up some food and trade their black-and-white pajamas for regular clothing. They needed transportation too and ended up stealing a horse and wagon from a nearby farm.

Finally, after years of captivity and torture, they set out to begin the next chapters of their lives, free of the Germans and the Nazi regime.

CHAPTER 54

The first time Rubin and I came face to face, he would probably tell you I scared the wits out of him. I might have been half his size, but I certainly made up for it in other ways. After spending the night on watch, he was returning to the villa he shared with his friends, while I had been reprimanded by Captain Samuelowitz. It was not exactly a recipe for a pleasant exchange.

The day before, the Russian captain had sent for me and explained that, since the German and Polish soldiers had been disposed of, they were going to start dismantling the warehouse.

"It is now our property," he said.

I appreciated being kept up to date on the situation in Ludwigsdorf, but I didn't have to be pulled away from my Jewish Committee obligations for it.

"What does this have to do with me?" I asked.

"The German scientists and their assistants, who had been working under the Nazis, will be dismantling everything under our supervision. I will need you as a translator."

It was nice to be needed, but the job would require my daily presence in and around the factory. Captain Samuelowitz also put me in charge of security, asking that I arrange for men from the Jewish police to guard the entrance. Those men would need to be there by seven in the morning and remain till nightfall. All the details—who would be posted, how long the shifts would be, and who the replacements would be—he left up to me.

"Authorized personnel will need special passes," he added. "The guards will need to check everyone thoroughly, entering and leaving the premises."

When I arrived at Captain Samuelowitz's office the next morning, he greeted me with a thunderous outburst. "What the hell is wrong with you?"

"What's wrong with me? You're the one who's screaming. What is the matter with you?"

He seemed not even to have heard me. "Do you know that no one showed up for sentry duty? I guess your friends are afraid of hard work!" In a lower tone, he snapped, "It seems they only like to work in an office."

My personality, the way I had been brought up, and the respect I had for myself wouldn't allow me to accept that type of mistreatment from him or anyone else anymore. When the Germans were around and had the guns and the whips, it was one thing, but now that we were free, no one would get to treat me like that again. "Oh, really? Is that what you think?" I asked, letting my emotions spill out. "Who are you? Do you prefer working in a factory, taking orders, and doing manual labor, or sitting behind a desk and giving orders to the soldiers?"

I was so upset I spoke louder and would not let him answer. "Well? Do you want to stand outside a factory all day holding a rifle and frisking those who come and go, or do you want to sit here in your comfortable office and tell others what to do?"

He tried staring me down, intimidating me with his cold eyes, but it didn't work. My heels were dug in. I had stood up to far more dangerous and menacing people than him.

The color returned to his face a moment later, and then he apologized. "But no one came this morning. No one showed up for sentry duty."

Then it was my turn to be angry. I stood up and stormed out of his office, growling over my shoulder, "I'll take care of it!"

I had gone straight to the Jewish Police headquarters and met with Lutek Karp. He was only nineteen but in charge of the whole force. He'd listened while I explained the situation, and he had promised to send two men to guard the warehouse in the morning.

I wanted to hear from him why he hadn't. I was angry enough to spit, and to make matters worse the horse and buggy that had brought me to the Captain's headquarters was no longer there, and I had to walk the three kilometers back to town on a very uneven terrain.

The entire way back I was fuming, replaying the conversation in my head. I had trusted Lutek to honor his word, and he had embarrassed me. Captain Samuelowitz was a compassionate man who'd put his career and rank on the line to help all of us. Most of all, he had put his faith in me. I had to make it right.

Halfway down the hill, I saw a man in a police uniform walking leisurely along, pushing a bicycle up the hill, as if he didn't have a care in the world. He might have been whistling in the morning air.

When I reached him, my blood was boiling, and my words spilled out fast and furious. "Are you one of the men who were scheduled to be on sentry duty at the warehouse this morning?" It was phrased as a question, but it was an accusation, and the man shook his head as I continued, "I spoke to your commander. He was supposed to arrange for two policemen to report at seven this morning. Do you have any idea how angry the captain is with me?"

The unfamiliar man stood there while I berated him, not saying a word—not that he could have with me yelling so—and studying me. He was not about to add anything to fuel the fire.

When I finally ended my tirade, I pointed down the hill. "I am not running down there again. You have a bicycle. Turn it around this minute, and go get two policemen, and send them to the factory."

The man, even though he did not know who I was or if I had any authority, did as he was told. He rode his bike down the hill to the police headquarters and charged into Lutek's office. "Are you out of your mind? The Russian captain asked for two men at the factory, you promised to supply them, and then you did nothing?" Rubin barked at Lutek, as I had screamed at him.

Lutek had no answer and quickly became frazzled and embarrassed. He rose, left his desk, summoned some officers, and immediately arranged for sentries to report to the warehouse.

Rubin, satisfied, headed for the exit. He had been on duty all night and was exhausted. All he wanted to do was lie down and close his eyes. But his thoughts stopped him before he got to the door. *That woman! Who is she?* "By the way," he asked, who's the firecracker with the big mouth that gave me orders?"

"Betka? She's the one that made sure you were well taken care of in the hospital. The doctors followed her orders, too."

"They could have used her on the front lines. The war would probably have ended a lot sooner."

By the time Rubin made his way back up the hill, I was gone. I wasn't sure if I would ever see him again, and to be honest, I didn't give it much thought. I had no idea that one day very soon I would marry that man and spend the rest of my life hopelessly in love with him.

CHAPTER 55

THERE WAS SO MUCH HAPPENING that the days seemed to be passing faster than ever. I was busier than ever. I loved being busy, and the busier I was, the less time I had to think about the past, the ones I had lost, or the future. I found myself involved in the present, and that was perfect for me. My responsibilities as Captain Samuelowitz's official translator were increasing by the day. I became the first female member of the Jewish Committee, and as had been the case everywhere I had been before, I became everyone's confidante and the voice of reason. "Let's ask Betka" was everyone's response when arguments needed to be settled, questions needed answers, or problems needed a solution.

It was an ordinary day of work at the Jewish Committee when Captain Samuelowitz sent a messenger for me asking for my immediate presence.

Oddly, I wasn't taken to his headquarters, but instead his home. It was a magnificent palace-like building overlooking the entire village. The messenger showed me to his office.

He was seated behind his desk waiting for me to arrive, invited me to sit in one of the luxurious chairs, and, as he walked around his desk, he greeted me. "We have a problem."

But he was too relaxed for it to be too big a problem, so I wasn't worried.

"For the past several nights, we've been noticing lights at the factory when no one's supposed to be there. Tonight, we're going to check it out and figure out what is going on."

"Okay! You have my permission," I said with a chuckle.

"Your sarcasm is amusing," he replied, smirking. "What I want is for you to come with us. I may need a translator."

The smile disappeared from my face. "Uh, I don't know about that. I'd like to help you out, but I've managed to survive this war so far without getting shot, and I don't intend to now. There could be some lunatic in there."

"There's no reason to be frightened. We'll protect you."

"Oh, really? How are you going to do that?"

"I'm taking a full squadron with me, and you won't go anywhere that's not safe. I promise you'll be okay."

After thinking about it for a moment, I nodded and promised to return at nightfall.

Leaving the Captain's home, I wasn't sure I had made the right decision. If he hadn't done so much to help me and all the others, I probably wouldn't have agreed to it, but I felt I owed him, at least that much.

However, the last thing I wanted to do was go all the way back to the Casper home to sit and think, and worry by myself, alone, and then trek back to Headquarters at night.

Luckily, there was a closer and better option. Directly adjacent to the captain's residence was a beautiful mansion that had once belonged to the chief German engineer; when the Germans were forced out of Ludwigsdorf, most of the homes had been taken over by surviving Jews. That house became the residence of my former bunkmate, the woman who may have saved me from starving to death, Esta.

A few weeks after we moved in with Lucy Casper and her mother, a man had shown up in Ludwigsdorf looking for her. His name was Yulek; he had met her at the Klenttendorf camp before it became female-only, and they had fallen in love. Esta was ecstatic to reunite with the man she loved. They quickly moved in together into that beautiful villa that was nothing short of spectacular. Because the place was too big for just the two of them, Esta and Yulek invited Rubin, Monyek, Lutek, his cousin Stasiek, and several others to join them.

After my meeting with the captain, I walked over to see Esta and couldn't help but admire the landscape of both mansions, with their diverse shrubbery, in the middle of bold, magnificent trees. There were beautiful flowers in strategic places on both properties. The two mansions stood high on a hill overlooking Ludwigsdorf. It was hard to believe that, for years, that beautiful little town had housed a cruel and uncivilized group of people, camouflaging the brutality of man.

The interior of the mansion was decorated in the extravagant opulence of its time. It was exquisite with many bedrooms, several bathrooms, and a tremendous kitchen with the latest appliances. The dishes and silverware were fit for a king. The rooms were furnished in quality woods with glittering crystal and magnificent silver scattered through the rooms that showed, not only good taste, but an abundance of money.

After she gave me a tour of the place, Esta and I sat at the kitchen table, drinking tea, while I told her about the conversation I'd had with the captain. She didn't think it was a good idea for me to go either but understood why I needed to. She agreed that I should stay with her until nightfall instead of making the long trip to and from the Casper home. "When it's time for you to go over to the headquarters, I'll have one of the boys take you."

"One of the boys" had become a common term for the men living in the house. I have no idea who started calling them that or why, but it had stuck, and the men didn't seem to mind, believing it to be a term of affection—which it was.

Though I had met most of the boys before, Esta reintroduced me—and I was stunned to recognize the man I had cornered and berated on the hill. "You're the guy with the bicycle," I said, feeling embarrassed. "I was angry, and I'm sorry I took it out on you."

"Yes, and you're the young lady who was influential in saving my life at the hospital." He bowed his head and extended his hand. "Rubin Eber—apology accepted."

None of us were strangers, but we didn't know each other too well and took the time that afternoon to get better acquainted. We talked until sundown, sharing stories about our lives before the war and the experiences we had gone through at the hands of the Germans.

I learned a great deal about the boys that day, but more about Rubin than I would have imagined possible. He was quiet, almost bordering on mute, but it was obvious he paid attention and heard every word spoken. He was the man the others counted on, the one they looked up to. He was stable, intelligent, and calm. He was a friend, confidante, and natural leader, and to some, like Lutek—eight years his junior—even a father figure. I sensed right away that he was someone I could rely on to be there when the chips were down.

Rubin was twenty-seven years old and handsome by any standard. An inch short of six feet, he had broad shoulders, thick palms, and ginormous fingers. He had the posture of a military officer, giving him the appearance, not only of being taller, but of having an aura of authority as well. He exuded strength and leadership.

Esta told me, "Rubin is loved and respected by everyone in the house. He's a paragon of calm and common sense. He's also the bread winner."

I was intrigued. Had anyone noticed I kept staring at this man? Had

Rubin himself picked up on it? *I must stop.*

Blushing and thinking everyone was reading my mind, I kept turning away from Rubin and back to Esta and the others. Inevitably, though, my eyes would drift back to him. At one point, our eyes met, and it felt as if they were holding onto each other a moment longer than necessary.

Did it happen? Did I imagine it?

Rubin reminded me a lot of my father, a man of pride and sincerity, a man who made me feel safe.

Later, he walked with me to meet Captain Samuelowitz and his men, and before I left him, I turned back to thank him for the escort. When his eyes met mine, I felt a shiver up my spine and knew instantly that I could trust him, and that made me feel better about my mission. "If I don't return within the hour, get some of your friends and come looking for me."

"I will," he said, and smiled at me. There was a lot behind those eyes and that smile that Rubin wouldn't let the world see. Although in constant pain from a slipped disc which he had acquired in Auschwitz at the hands of the Nazis, there had been no time to stop and worry about it. He had had to forge through the pain to survive.

The world was changing quickly, and he joined in the process. He not only hid his physical pain but his emotional suffering as well, masking it with the strength and determination to rebuild what the Germans had taken from him, from all of us. He was incredibly strong, incredibly intense, but there was something warm and gentle too about him. The combination was almost irresistible.

CHAPTER 56

The raid of the warehouse went more smoothly than I expected. Surrounded by Captain Samuelowitz and twenty commandos with rifles, we slowly made our way there. I was the first to speak. "Captain, the light is coming from the building that houses the chemical laboratory."

Five of the soldiers remained outside with me, hiding behind several large trees, while the rest went with the captain and approached the front entrance. Other than the rustling of leaves on the ground, all was silent. I watched him signal to the others with a nod, and then two soldiers rammed their way through the door, followed by the others with their rifles extended.

That's when I thought all hell would break loose, but it didn't—no yelling, no shooting. The entire raid took less than five seconds. It was totally silent again, and moments later Captain Samuelowitz yelled for the rest of us to come inside. "It's safe," he insisted.

Entering the building, I was still nervous, but not nearly as nervous as the pale, fragile man shaking in the corner. His hands were raised in the air, and he was trembling. "Herr Krolik? What are you doing here?" I asked.

"I was s-stirring—no, no, I was m-m-mixing ch-chemicals." He was petrified by the guns pointed at him. "I was m-making s-soap to sell to m-make m-money." He swallowed hard and repeated his explanation, which I translated.

Herr Krolik had been a chemist working for the Germans during the war. When I finished translating, Samuelowitz began yelling at the man as if he were hard of hearing. "First, let me inform you that you are under arrest," he said, and, after a long pause, added, "Now, since you are an expert at making soap, you will continue manufacturing it, but we are going to sell it."

The laboratory again fell quiet while I translated. The captain stared at Krolik, letting his orders sink in.

Then he, and a couple of his men escorted me back to the villa, and, on the way, he asked if I knew anyone who would be interested in buying the soap. I told him I would think about it but already had an inkling of an idea in my mind.

Back at the mansion, I sat around the table once again with Esta and the boys, and explained what had happened in the warehouse. They found parts of the story amusing and weren't surprised the Russians wanted to benefit from the chemist's soap. That's when I told them my idea.

The next day, I introduced Rubin to Captain Samuelowitz and suggested a business relationship that could benefit both parties.

LET'S ASK BETKA

CHAPTER 57

As TIME WENT BY, it became obvious to everyone that we needed to stop focusing on what had befallen us and start living the rest of our lives. We couldn't grieve forever. But before we moved away from our past, we first had to say goodbye to it, and as such, in June 1944, Zygmund Turkow of Warsaw, Weiner Linkowski of Chrzanow. and I organized a formal remembrance ceremony.

Mass grave of Jewish slaves murdered in Ludwigsdorf, Petersvaldaw, and Langebilaw concentration camp, after Libration in 1945. Betty is fifth from the left, front row.

The Nazis weren't exactly known for their care of Jewish people's remains, and many of the corpses had been buried in mass graves. One of those sites was in a field adjacent to the Ludwigsdorf Camp, and those inmates who worked inside the factory passed it every day. Prisoners from Ludwigsdorf and two other local camps who were murdered had been thrown into that pit and buried as one.

It was there we held our memorial. A monument was erected, and with tears in our eyes we said *kaddish*—the Jewish prayer recited by mourners. *Kaddish* is a prayer for the souls of the departed and an expression of love for our personal loss of family and friends. We cried for all the lives that had been snuffed out because a maniac craved world domination and racial superiority.

Flowers were laid to let them know that they would always live in our hearts. A Star of David symbolized the Jewish souls buried there, and when we finished the ceremony, a ribbon was placed as a symbol of a promise made by the survivors to each other and to those who had perished to never forget and never let it happen again.

It was time for new dreams, for new lives, to be fulfilled. We could finally start moving on and forge the future that had once seemed so bleak. Together, we could make it happen; together we could make it through anything. After the years of imprisonment and torture, we all wanted warmth and compassion, friendship and love. We wanted to take back those things that had been stolen from us.

Some were better at adapting than others, quickly moving on. Esta had already reunited with the man of her dreams, Yulek Schwebel, and moved out of the house. Bianka, the be-speckled girl who worked as an electrician with me, had taken up with Zisek Adler, Rubin's friend. They had moved into an apartment together and were planning to get married. Hanka Levin met Dr. Rosenberg, and Yadja fell in love with Monyek Zilbergold, one of Rubin's friends from Auschwitz; both couples planned to marry and start their lives together.

LET'S ASK BETKA

Many others had similar stories and plans, but not me. There was no time for me to worry about myself. I was still caught in the middle, drifting between being the little girl who had lost her entire family and the feisty, take-no-bullshit leader of the barracks. I felt that I still had a job to do in protecting my girls, and I would move on with my own life when the time was right.

My responsibilities continued to grow. I was the connection between the survivors and the Russians who had liberated us, the liaison between the Russians and the Jewish committee, between the Russians and the Jewish police, between the Russians and the German scientists and chemists. My relationship with all these groups was the link that held them all together.

My job as Captain Samuelowitz's translator kept me as busy as ever, which didn't help if I was ready to move on and search for someone special in my life. Because I was so busy with the captain and often at his headquarters, Esta suggested I move into the villa next door and take her place. Yulek Schwebel had been assigned to head the Jewish police in the nearby town of Waldenburg, and she was leaving with him to become his wife. It worked out because, with Hanka gone from the Casper home, it felt too vulnerable for Eva and me.

The day the two of us moved into the mansion, I called a meeting with all the tenants. "It's time you boys stopped living like pigs."

There was silence as everyone around the table stared at me, not sure what to say. Rubin had told them all about his initial meeting with me on the hill, and since no one was interested in a similar verbal lashing, they just listened.

"I insist that we hire a maid to clean the villa and keep everything in order. Since we all live together, we should also pick a designated time to eat dinner every day, *together*." No one disagreed.

As I walked up to my bedroom that night, I saw the mansion for what it truly was, a museum. Beautiful, expensive paintings hung on the walls, the chandeliers were crystal, and the stonework throughout the house was of the highest quality. I had goose down pillows and a comfortable bed in a room reserved strictly for me. It had been years since I slept in a room alone and had the luxury of privacy: my own room where the plush rug felt like heaven under my bare feet. A desk and chair sat in the corner, a closet with a chest of drawers ran along the far wall, and I had two lamps to illuminate my surroundings, all set up for comfort. I have never been materialistic and didn't *need* such things to feel good, but it was very nice indeed to *enjoy* them.

Over all, the house lacked a homey feel, those finishing touches that would make it a home. In an attempt, to bring beauty in from the outside, to liven up the place, I picked flowers from the garden and filled the empty vases. Then I sewed and hung curtains in the kitchen, and decorated the living room. It was not *home*, and would never be perfect, but it was better.

CHAPTER 58

IT WAS DIFFICULT TO REBUILD OUR LIVES, and every one of us faced serious challenges, but it was a price we gladly paid for our freedom. Most people became merchants of some kind, selling whatever they could to make a profit. Every sale—of clothing, home goods, or jewelry—pushed us one step closer to normalcy. Thankfully, in the days after the war, the demand for products and services was increasing, and business began to boom.

Rubin was working with the Russians, selling the soap Herr Krolik was producing and splitting the profits. He and I soon became friends, and when he returned to the villa after work, we would spend the evening talking. He shared the details of his day and what he hoped for the future but rarely talked about his past. It was difficult for him to relive it, but eventually he told me the stories and shared his feelings.

Sometimes a group of us, those who remained in Ludwigsdorf, would meet at the local tavern after work. We would have a few drinks, talk, laugh, and try to feel normal again. The tavern was run by one of the survivors of Ludwigsdorf, Bela Lefkowitz, and her father and brother. They had reunited shortly after the war and taken over the operations of the tavern. It was in the heart of the village and became our regular nightly hang out.

One night, if I remember correctly on a warm September evening, most of us were at the tavern enjoying ourselves. The only noticeably absent member was Rubin, who was tied up with work. But we had the pleasure of meeting a handsome stranger, a traveling merchant passing through. He stopped in for dinner but ended up leaving with a lot more than that.

The man was funny, charming, and the life of the party. He managed to capture everyone's attention, and we were all drawn in. His attention, however, was fixed on only one of us. Her name was Margot—a tall, attractive blonde of nineteen. She was swept away by the man's charms, and the two shared flirtatious moments most of the night.

It wouldn't have bothered any of us, if Margot hadn't already been attached to someone. In fact, just days before this evening, Eva and I had been in the middle of planning a wedding reception for Margot and Rubin—the night's only missing guest.

Was she simply engaged in a little last-minute flirting? Or was something serious going on?

The following day, Margot met the handsome stranger again, and again they talked and flirted. He even brought her gifts this time, including jewelry—which isn't something you do for an engaged woman. Margot was overwhelmed and began falling for him and his promises. Young and impressionable, she had a lot of dreams for the future.

This prince charming swept her off her feet with promises that he'd take care of her and support her while she attended Warsaw University. She fell under his spell, mesmerized by dreams of a better life and the promise of wealth and dignity. The years of suffering had raised her thirst for a more prosperous future, and she made her decision.

The following afternoon, she came to the villa in search of Rubin. She began tearing up upon seeing him and couldn't even look him in the eyes. He sensed that something was wrong.

"I met a man last night," she confessed. "I am in love."

The admission shook Rubin to his core. This was the woman he planned to marry and spend the rest of his life with. His entire future, everything he dreamed about, was suddenly in doubt. She had discarded him and everything they meant to each other—or rather discarded what he *thought* they meant to each other. She got rid of him as one gets rid of the trash. He couldn't speak, a throbbing headache pounding inside his skull.

"I'm leaving with him and going to Warsaw. I am sorry, Rubin."

A simple apology was not enough, would never be enough. He couldn't understand how a woman who had claimed he meant everything to her just days earlier could so easily leave him. She returned all the gifts and jewelry he had given her and then walked out of the mansion and out of his life.

When I returned to the villa that evening, Monyek Rothstein brought me up to speed on what had been going on. Rubin had been hiding in his bedroom ever since, not speaking to anyone.

On my way upstairs, he warned, "He's a mess!"

I wasn't sure what I could do or even say. All I knew was that Rubin was a friend, had been hurt badly, and needed someone to talk to.

At the top of the stairs I turned and, as I approached his room, I figured I would lay it out and see what happened. I knocked on the door. There was no response.

"Rubin?" I called out, and knocked again. Still, there was nothing.

"Rubin, I'm coming in." He didn't answer, but I didn't care. I twisted the knob, pushed on the door, and entered his room.

I guess I shouldn't have been surprised, but I was. Rubin was a meticulous man, but I hadn't expected that room to be so immaculate. It was spotless—nothing out of order, not one speck of dust anywhere. The bedsheets were folded neatly and tucked under the mattress, and Rubin lay on top of them, staring at the ceiling, with his arms folded across his forehead.

"Rubin, talk to me," I said, nudging him in his side.

He removed his hand from his head, glanced at me, and slowly rose. He was proud of his insight into people, believing he could easily judge their character. He was bothered by Margot leaving him, but even more by his inability to see it coming. *Was the need to be with someone and have a future to share together so overpowering that he* wanted *it to be true more than it was? Had he been blinded by her beauty? Or was he just blind?*

With a million questions racing though his mind, none of which he or I could answer, Rubin began endlessly pacing the room. His heart and ego were both damaged badly. "I thought my future with her was set," he said. "How could I have been so wrong?"

I thought about telling him what I was thinking, that he was better off without someone who could drop him so easily, but didn't. He was angry, mostly at himself, and needed to express it. He finally sat down on the bed again, looked at his hands, and began rubbing them together, as if he were washing them. He spent over an hour pacing back and forth, ranting, berating himself, and trying to make himself feel worse. I let him. I listened for as long as I could tolerate it, and when he finally stopped, I opened my mouth. "What the hell is the *matter* with you?" I asked. I wasn't yelling, but there was no mistaking my tone. "She wants to go, let her go."

Rubin's head snapped around, and he stared at me in disbelief—I'm not sure if it was the words or the way I spoke them.

"You've been through worse. You lost your entire family and managed to overcome that. You've survived everything the Nazis have done to you. Did you lose your mind?" I asked but didn't wait for a response. "No, you didn't." I was angry now, too. "I lost my family and everyone I cared about all at once, and *I* didn't lose *my* mind. You can't lose yours over some girl who's too immature and too foolish or too stupid to see what's right in front of her."

Rubin's expression began to change, and I could see the words were slowly beginning to register. Underneath his anger and humiliation, I think he knew—even before Margot told him she was leaving—that what I was saying was the truth.

"After everything we've been through," I went on, "after all the Germans did to us, there is nothing we cannot survive. Don't let some girl destroy your life."

I didn't wait for a response and headed for the door. Just before I closed it, I turned back around and ended my tirade with three words, spoken in a harsh tone that bounced off the walls. "Get *over* it!"

CHAPTER 59

That same evening, Margot packed up all her belongings, however meager, and eagerly awaited the arrival of her savior. She sat in the tavern all night waiting for him, the hope and anticipation slowly corroding into fear and dread. Finally, reality set in and Margot came to understand that the handsome stranger who had arrived out of nowhere and promised her the world wasn't coming. She was devastated.

The following day, she returned to the villa, heart in hand, and begged Rubin to take her back. With tears streaming down her cheeks, she apologized for being stupid and selfish, and promised to love him forever. Rubin allowed her to say what she needed to, listened to every word, but nothing she could say could sway him. Rubin was a man of honor, a man of pride and self-respect, a man whose word was his bond and who followed the straight and narrow. He could see that she was truly remorseful and did want him back, but he was too badly hurt to accept. When she had finished, he said, "You walked away from me—now just keep on walking."

Not long afterwards, she left Ludwigsdorf and returned to her home before the war, Berlin. He never sought her out and never heard from her again.

It took Rubin some time to move past his pain over the Margot situation, but he eventually did. When she walked out of his life, he fell into a tailspin of disbelief and denial that deepened into depression. The hardest part wasn't that she had left him but that he could have been so wrong about her and their relationship. He was no longer sure he could trust his own judgment.

He came, then, to realize that I had been right, and that the woman who would share in his future was still out there.

At the time, I had no idea that woman would be me. We were just friends and didn't think of each other in any other way. But things slowly changed. We confided in one another, spent a lot of time talking, and were there for each other. At every crucial juncture, we were together, and I soon came to understand Rubin even better than he understood himself.

From the very beginning, fate intervened in our relationship. It seemed as if I had always been around and come between him and adversity. I had been influential in making sure he had the best treatment at the hospital. At every uncertainty, every crossroad, he had turned to me for confirmation—with Captain Samuelowitz and the business, and with Margot.

He said he admired my compassion and was in awe of my vitality. A serious man, he found comfort in my ability to laugh in the face of hardship and misfortune. I could sense what he needed and wanted even before he did, and it became clear that he cared for me more than he knew or was ready to say.

Often, Rubin would check in with me to make sure I was home in the evening, so we could talk, and he was disappointed when I had to work with the Jewish Committee or Samuelowitz.

As our friendship grew, he began to realize that I was the woman he wanted to take care of and protect, the one he wanted to be there when he came home. But uncertain thoughts fluttered through his mind: *Is she the woman I love? How does she feel about me? Can we be more than just friends?*

Eventually, I learned from him the turmoil he was going through, and his thoughts about us being together.

I was having strong feelings, too. I cared for Rubin and at the time could not imagine my life without him in it—somewhere. *But as life partners? As husband and wife?* I didn't know whether our friendship was fated for that, or we were just meant to be friends.

The past several years, had taught us both a great deal about life. . . when it came to anything but ourselves. In fact, we had each other in our thoughts, wondering how the other felt, and could not see a future without one another. Together we could fulfill our dreams and meet every challenge. Together we could carve out a happy and wonderful life. But, for the time being, we hid these feelings. We were friends and not about to jeopardize what we had. We were both leaders, people others came to for advice, and yet we didn't realize what was staring us in the face.

CHAPTER 60

Change was constant in our house, people coming and going from the villa all the time. Daily, men and women continued arriving in Ludwigsdorf, either for business or in search of family and friends. When Hanka Levin got married and Esta and Yulek moved after their wedding, they were replaced by Henyek Zimberknopf and by Zigmund Watash and his wife, Tzesha.

I was still busy working as Captain Samuelowitz's translator while Rubin formed a partnership with Watash and his cousin Monyek Zilbergold. The three became merchants. Together, they built a business that sold soap and other goods, which generated a decent profit. Rubin continued to be the breadwinner of our villa, making enough money to supply us all with food and necessities.

Constantly searching for ways to enlarge the business and increase the profits, he went to the next village to talk to Yulek Schwebel about contacts to spruce up the business. Although it was a short walk, the ditches on either side of the road made it difficult to maneuver.

It was already past 9:00 p.m. when I began to worry, because I expected Rubin home before nightfall. It was dangerous at night on the road. There had been several killings. The situation was ominous.

A little over an hour later, I was frantic. Scared but determined, I went to find him. A dense fog had rolled in, and as usual in the mountains of Ludwigsdorf, it was impenetrable. It was treacherous avoiding the ditches, unable to see one foot in front of me. I was familiar with the nocturnal sounds—the hoot of an owl, the chirping of crickets, the hiss of a snake. But the next sound I heard through the fog left me unwilling and unable to move. At that very moment, I felt the slightest brush against my arm as the hair at the back of my neck stood at attention. *What had touched me? A creature of the night, or someone with cruelty on their mind?* Simultaneously, I felt something and heard the click of a gun.

"Stop! I'll shoot!"

I recognized the voice before he finished speaking. I managed to croak, "Ru-Rubin!" He recognized my stammer in the nick of time.

"Where in heaven's name were you going?" he asked as he grabbed me under the arm, and we started back. He nearly shot me that night, and I gained a few additional gray hairs.

CHAPTER 61

THINGS WERE GOING WELL, but as autumn replaced the heat of summer, Ludwigsdorf went through new changes. The most dramatic shift was a change in politics that shifted the supervision of law enforcement, including the temporary Polish police, to an upper level Russian government agency—Encavude, much like the FBI.

These changes affected us very little at first; we went about our daily lives without much intrusion. Then, one evening, it came right to our front door. Rubin had spent the previous few days accumulating enough merchandise to be sold, but when he met Monyek that night, they learned the Russians had already loaded it all on their truck and confiscated it. They claimed it was *theirs*, that *they* were going to sell it.

At the villa, we were unaware that something had gone wrong, but when Rubin failed to return on time, we all began to worry. Too much had happened to us in the past not to immediately think the worst. As the minutes and hours ticked away, my fear grew.

When, after midnight, there still was no sign of Rubin, who should have been home before nine, when I watched the clock, the hours crawled as they always did. I was scared out of my mind, worrying and feeling things I never had before. The blood slowly draining from my face, my stomach was in knots, and my throat felt raw. I had lost a lot of people in my life, God knew I had, but it had never felt like *this*. I jumped at every sound, flinched at every movement.

Where was Rubin? Why was it bothering me so much?

Finally, he walked in the door shortly before 1:00 a.m. He apologized for worrying everyone and explained what happened. "I only came to let you know that I'm safe," he said. "I doubt they'll return our truck, but I'm going to try to at least get our merchandise back." After an exasperated sigh, he continued, "I'm a police officer, at least a temporary one, and maybe they'll be reasonable. If not, I can try to bribe them."

"I'm coming with you," I said with the same conviction I had the day we met on the hill. "I'll stay back with Yadja—" (Monyek's wife)—"and I'll be close by, and you won't have to trek all the way back just to tell me you're okay." He wasn't going to tangle with me.

I knew he hated the idea of me coming and possibly being in danger, but he liked that I cared enough about him to want to be there.

That was the night everything changed for us. Rubin was unable to get back his truck or merchandise, no matter what he tried. He reasoned, pleaded, and offered bribes, but nothing worked. The Russians were intent on keeping the goods for themselves, and Rubin returned a dejected man. He felt like a failure for having lost so much money on the venture and knew everyone in the villa would suffer because of it. No one blamed him, but he felt guilty nonetheless.

We returned to the villa at dawn, tired and hungry. Everyone else had fallen asleep earlier, but not before finishing off the entire roast I had made for dinner before we left.

Looking inside the nearly empty pan, I remarked with annoyance. "At least they left us some sauce at the bottom—how generous!"

"That's the best part," Rubin responded. "I'll get the bread, so we can start dunking."

At that moment, we were the only two people in the world, and I realized something that I cared more about him than I knew and in a way I hadn't expected to. We shared a comfort level with each other that I hadn't known could exist. Looking at him gave me butterflies in my stomach and made my heart beat faster. When he was missing earlier that night, I had felt *helpless*, and knew that I couldn't lose him, too. That feeling existed every day and lasted a lifetime. *I needed him.* We needed each other.

For a man who preferred not to say much, especially about himself, he let out a long sigh and began talking about his life. He had spoken to me about personal things before, but not in such detail. He spoke about his past, his life growing up in Poland, and losing his mother at such an early age. He talked about his older siblings, how he missed those who had died, and wondered if Leo had made it safely to the United States or not. He told me about the times leading up to the war, and his experiences in the Polish Army. He spoke about surviving the Auschwitz death march, but not much else about his imprisonment. It was too hard for him, and most of it was buried too deep in his psyche to retrieve, usually only showing up in nightmares tormenting his sleep.

When the first rays of sunshine crept in through the windows, Rubin finished his story. I had listened to every word he said, saying very little myself. I had known who he was before that night, but after listening to him tell it, I gained a deeper appreciation for the man he had become.

A silence fell over the kitchen, and as I was about to stand up to clear the dishes, he stopped me. He placed his hands in mine and looked in my eyes. It made my heart flutter in a way it still does every time I think about him.

"If you marry me, you'll make me the happiest man in the world." The surroundings were not romantic, but he was, and his sentiment and warmth illuminated the kitchen.

I had been aware of my feelings for Rubin for weeks but, until that night, chosen to deny them—at least that's what I think I did. I was too busy being supportive to my friends and engaged with my responsibilities for Captain Samuelowitz and the Jewish Committee to even think about my own future.

Besides, even if I couldn't consciously admit it, I did feel abandoned by my family and was afraid of getting close to someone and risk losing them again. The pain was too intense, and I didn't want to hurt that way ever again.

Irenka's death had been the last straw. I'd given up on myself and planned to spend my life alone—safe from love and affection, and the eventual heartbreak that followed.

Then Rubin had come along, a man I hadn't counted on meeting who by his sheer existence in my life wiped away any fears I had and opened my heart to love again. Even before I knew that I knew, I *knew*. . .and hoped he did, too.

I looked up at him, yet again felt my heartbeat flicker, and said, "Yes, Rubin. I will marry you, and you should know that, right this minute, I'm the happiest woman in the world."

CHAPTER 62

WE TOLD EVERYONE LATER THAT MORNING, when they came down to breakfast, but no one was surprised. They all knew what had taken Rubin and me weeks to realize—that our relationship was special, and they had only wondered what took us so long to realize it. It felt wonderful for both of us to have our friends' approval. They spoke about the way I would gaze at him when he came into the room, or how his voice changed when he talked about me. They recognized that our relationship had been built from the ground up on mutual respect, friendship, and adoration. We were totally devoted to each other, a devotion that has lasted to this very day, long after Rubin's death.

Two weeks later, on the tenth of November, Rubin and I went to Waldenburg, the closest city to Ludwigsdorf, to legalize our union and become husband and wife. We knew of two orthodox Jews who, despite not being official rabbis, conducted marriage ceremonies. We got married by the laws of Moses, which are legal in the eyes of God.

We left early on a Sunday morning, traveling by train. I had no white dress and no veil, just the clothes I had owned since my liberation. I wore my Sunday best—a vest, a sweater jacket, and a coat. They were the items that Frau Noigebauer had chosen for me at the warehouse, the clothes that saved me from freezing to death.

Rubin, dressed in a jacket and tie, looking very handsome as we walked hand-in-hand together to the railroad station. Waiting for the train, I glanced at him and knew that my home would be wherever he was, and I would feel safe and protected in his arms. Together, we would spend our lives building a life filled with happiness and joy, a life that the world would envy.

We boarded the train for Waldenburg and set off. It was the happiest day of my life, but not one without painful memories. This time the train had fresh air, comfortable seating, and food to eat, and I tried not to relive my experiences of the past, but the wounds were still raw. The sounds of the wheels churning, and watching the Polish countryside pass through the window, triggered painful memories. I missed my family and thought about them the entire way. I ached for my father's presence, wishing he could give me away. I longed for my mother's wisdom, needing to hear what she would tell me on my wedding day, and I wanted my sisters by my side to share in and witness my joy.

We reached Mr. Davidowitz's home—he was one of the men who performed wedding ceremonies—before noon and explained that we had come to receive the blessings of marriage. He guided us into the living room and summoned his wife to witness our vows. We said our hellos to one another, and when I removed my coat, Mrs. Davidowitz turned white as a ghost and inhaled sharply with a loud gasp of emotion.

"*Gott in Himmel!*" she exclaimed in Yiddish, grabbing hold of a chair to keep from falling over.

Her husband ran towards her, taking her in his arms. "What happened?" he said. "What's the matter?"

Rubin and I looked at each other, confused, and watched Mrs. Davidowitz begin to cry, struggling to breathe. Her husband fetched her a glass of water, and after a few minutes her trembling subsided, and the color returned to her face. She apologized for scaring everyone and turned to address me. "You are wearing the sweater my mother crocheted when we were in the Lodz Ghetto." Tears welled up in her eyes again as she continued, "Watching her crochet that sweater is my last memory of her. She made it from small remnants of used wool left over from other sweaters and scarfs that women were crocheting."

The room fell silent, and an eerie emotional presence overtook it. When Mr. Davidowitz understood his wife was all right physically, he tried helping her cope with the shock of seeing the sweater. So many memories came back to her, and for a few minutes she was mesmerized by them.

Once Mrs. Davidowitz began to calm down, she added, "If you don't mind, may I see the inside of the sweater? I remember that Mama lined it with a brocade fabric."

Everything happened in slow motion. As I unbuttoned the sweater, my hands began to tremble. It took extra effort and concentration, and the moment I saw the brocade pattern I gasped, feeling tingles up and down my spine. I felt awful for causing that woman pain. At the same time, I knew I was wearing something special and felt an instant connection to Mrs. Davidowitz. Without hesitation, I took the garment off and offered it to her. "This belongs to you."

She shook her head. "Too many painful memories. I would rather remember my mother as she was the last time I saw her, sitting near the window knitting that sweater."

Tears flooded my eyes when Mrs. Davidowitz whispered, "My mother went to Auschwitz wearing that sweater."

That statement caused me to remember the circumstance that had brought me to possess that sweater. It was from the warehouse in Ludwigsdorf, the one where the Germans stored the clothing that belonged to the victims exterminated in Auschwitz. I thought back to Frau Noigebauer specifically choosing that sweater for me during the winter of 1944, neither of us ever thinking about whom it had belonged to before. I was speechless, tears streaking down my face.

Moments later, with dry eyes, I grabbed hold of Rubin's hand and stared at Mrs. Davidowitz while her husband officiated our wedding ceremony. Rubin and I made a commitment before God, taking vows of love and friendship, honor and devotion, vows that were never broken.

I thought about that sweater all the way back to Ludwigsdorf. It had traveled a great journey in only a few years, from the loving hands of a mother in the Lodz Ghetto, through the extermination camp of Auschwitz, and finally into the hands of another prisoner, one who survived the horror—me.

That sweater jacket became very sacred to me. The day of my wedding was the last time I wore it, but I have never forgotten its meaning or the history behind it. It has traveled with me from Poland to Germany to Israel and finally to the United States of America.

That evening when Rubin and I returned home we were happier than either of us ever remembered being, but more exhausted than we expected. We were married and ready to live the rest of our lives as husband and wife. There was no honeymoon, just a small celebration with our friends. But that was enough.

Having friends, being able to get married and think about the future, had been all but impossible only a short time before.

Betty and Rubin on their wedding day, November 1945

CHAPTER 63

Shifting into married life wasn't difficult. The hurdles that often plague young married couples didn't exist for us; Rubin and I simply fit together. We made each other whole, sealed the wounds of the last decade, and brought out the best in one another. There was a special comfort waking up next to him each morning, one I hadn't felt in ten years.

Life was good again, and Rubin made it worth living. We moved out of the villa and into an apartment of our own, and despite the huge changes to our lives, we continued our routines as usual. I continued working for the committee while also taking care of our home, and Rubin continued his business dealings and making sure we had enough money to eat and pay our bills.

Getting married provided me with comfort and security, and helped give me the courage and necessary push to confront my past—my demons. It wasn't long after we recited our vows and began settling into married life that I decided to return to Warsaw.

With Rubin by my side, I felt safe making the trip. None of my immediate family had survived, but I wanted to register myself in case anyone was looking for me, and I wanted closure with people I knew. We didn't go near the house I had grown up in, the school where I spent my formative years, or any of the places that possessed significance. The city where my father paid an exorbitant amount of money, when his five-year-old daughter, his precious Regusha, called in a false alarm because she loved watching the fire engines with their loud sirens, was gone. The city known as the center of Polish culture was gone. Warsaw, for me, was the past, and I had no interest in seeing the remnants of a once great life and reliving all the horrible things that had happened.

The city I loved, the place I first felt happiness and security, was gone. The streets were filled with strangers, while the stores I shopped in with my mother and grandmother had been burned to the ground and destroyed. It was all different; people living there weren't connected to me or the Warsaw I remembered.

I was instead watching an active place rebuild itself and bring normalcy back to its life.

Instead, Rubin and I made our way to the Jewish Committee. I wanted to search through the directory of those who already had. The names were listed alphabetically, so I immediately flipped to the back and began scanning the "W" section. . .U–V–W.

My heart stopped when I reach the "W"s, and then I read the names off in rapid succession: Wasserman, Werner, Wiszna, Wizerman, Woldman, Woraski, Wynik, Wysocka. No Wygodski. *None!* No one else in my family had survived—a large and prominent family, *gone!*

I had known it was a long shot and hadn't really expected to find anyone else alive but couldn't help hoping. As the revelation of being truly alone in the world came crashing down, my legs weakened, my stomach rumbled, and I wanted to cry.

I took a deep breath, swallowed hard, and continued searching through the directory, hoping to find a name, any name, that was familiar. Page after page after page, and I found nothing. . .but just as I was about to give up, something struck a nerve. *Marmor. Halinka Briskin Marmor.*

I froze and looked up at Rubin. "Halinka survived. She married that Nazi SS officer I told you about."

The image of Director Marmor was still vivid and real. I remembered all he had done for us—the German officer who had helped Irenka and me escape the ghetto, who had come between us and disaster more times than I cared to remember, who had changed my destiny. I was, and will eternally be, grateful for all he did for me and the others, but I had never understood how Halinka could fall in love with an SS officer. For all the good things he did, I had to keep him at a distance, a certain level of distrust; he was, after all, loyal to the Third Reich, a political juggernaut that wanted us all dead.

Next to Halinka's name appeared the words "Marmor Furs" and an address. That they were in the fur business was not surprising. Marmor had been a furrier before the war and the head of the Tobbens Fur Factory in the Warsaw Ghetto, and Halinka's family had been in the business, too. A joint venture made sense.

I remembered every street and alley in Warsaw, and could find my way anywhere blindfolded. We were about a block away from the store when its signage came into view. We hurried across the street and entered the front door. A bell rang, alerting the owners of our arrival.

There they were, both Halinka and Director Marmor, seated behind the counter. They recognized me immediately, and their stunned expressions quickly creased into smiles. Halinka leapt from her chair and came around to hug me, while Director Marmor glanced past me toward the door. I knew what, or rather who, he was looking for.

"Did she. . .survive?" he asked in barely more than a whisper, and even getting that out seemed to be a struggle.

"No." I shook my head. Then I introduced Rubin and told them the story of Irenka's fate at Auschwitz. "And the two of you?"

Marmor looked around the store, making sure we were alone before speaking. "When the Russians entered Warsaw, I destroyed my German identification papers, burned my uniform, and joined Halinka in the village I had kept her hidden in for years."

"Director Marmor, I will be forever grateful for everything you did for me and my sister, but I must ask—*why*? You risked your own life. You stood between us and death many times. I would never presume to question you, but why would you risk everything to save us again and again? Especially Irenka."

"...Irenka reminded me of my own sister. She was as beautiful and refined as her. It was uncanny how much they looked alike." Tears welled up in his eyes as he paused, remembering her. "My sister was also exterminated at Auschwitz."

I couldn't even speak.

He nodded. "When the Germans came, I managed to steal one of their uniforms, hoping that it would help me survive somehow. Since I spoke the language fluently, I masqueraded as an SS officer. My family had been in the fur business, and I was able to secure the position at the Tobbens Factory, and then...."

As I listened, I also thought back to everything that had passed between us. The compassionate man who gave me the pass I needed for my sister, the man who grabbed Irenka during *selection* to save her life, the man who arranged for our escape from the Warsaw Ghetto: I had been thankful for him at the time but could not understand how an SS officer could have done the things he did. He had turned a blind eye to so much and managed to help two Jewish girls survive.

As he continued speaking my attention returned. Tears were now filling my eyes, and I felt the chills of reality crawl up my spine with Director Marmor's last five words: "Yes, I am a Jew!"

CHAPTER 64

THE WINTER OF 1945 GAVE WAY to the warmer weather of spring, and with it came a lot of changes. Rubin and I had been through so much together already, but when Ludwigsdorf officially became a territory of Poland, life for everyone changed.

In the months that followed there was an exodus of people from Ludwigsdorf and the surrounding towns. Everyone wanted to go somewhere—America, Palestine, England, Australia, Canada, South America, anywhere they had family or friends and could live freely, any place where neighbors were friendly and fear was no longer around the corner. Because Germany had come under American jurisdiction following the war, it became a haven, a place that was easier to migrate from.

Rubin and I watched many of our friends leave one by one, and then it was our turn. In April 1946, a year after our liberation, we began making plans to leave Ludwigsdorf with Yadja and Monyek Zilbergold. So far nothing about our lives had been easy, and that wasn't about to change.

"You understand that, because of the quotas, we're going to have to smuggle ourselves into Germany," Rubin explained, holding me close. "I will ask around. There are plenty of men willing to smuggle Jews into Germany for the right amount of money." His confidence reassured me, and his arms around my shoulders made me feel safe.

Less than two weeks later, he had made all the arrangements. Our plan to escape to Germany was solidified. Our entire estate consisted of two overstuffed suitcases and one greater-than-average pocketbook. We left Ludwigsdorf in the back of a rickety wagon pulled by a horse. We rode out of town escorted by two handsomely paid smugglers and began a new chapter of our life. We made it to the Polish border.

Then things got worse.

When told our next step on the journey was going to be a trip across the river in a rowboat, I felt a shiver of panic. It was darker than dark, almost total blackness, and since I couldn't swim, the idea of being in open water was terrifying.

We climbed into the boat with several other Jews, all on an illegal journey into Germany. Most of us carried bags or suitcases, and each clung to his or hers tightly. Rubin carried the two heavy pieces of luggage, leaving me with only my oversized pocketbook. However, my bag was probably the most important one, containing our valuable assets—jewelry and American currency sewn into the lining, money that we planned to use to start a new life somewhere else.

"Don't you worry about anything except holding onto that bag," he said after we stepped into the boat. "Our entire future is in your hands."

I assured him about the safety of the bag but in that moment was more concerned with the uneasiness in my stomach. The water was calm, almost to the point of complete stillness, and yet my insides were rumbling, and I could taste the bile climbing up my throat.

Is it possible to get seasick without the motion of the sea to cause it? I feel nauseous. Breathe deep! Don't let me vomit on this boat. Take deep breaths! The evening was cool, and I breathed in several long breaths, somewhat quelling the unpleasant rumblings in my gut.

The trip across the river only took fifteen minutes or so, and once on the other side, I happily climbed out of the boat and found a place to sit on the ground. We had to wait while the boat and our handlers made another trip across the river to pick up more Jews hoping to illegally enter

Germany.

Once the entire group made it safely across the river we began our walk toward the border and freedom. Monyek and Rubin walked together, carrying the heaviest luggage and still outpacing Yadja and me by several steps.

The trek started off uneventfully, but my nerves had been shot since getting on the boat, and I was a wreck, unsure I would be able to make it all the way. When Yadja stopped to adjust her bags, I took a break with her, taking a moment to gather my bearings.

Yadja looked at me. "Betka, where's your pocketbook?"

Panic instantly swallowed me up, goosebumps engulfed my skin, and I could literally feel my heart pounding inside my chest. Instinctively, my hands reached for the strap that should have been on my shoulder, but I knew it wasn't there even before feeling it missing.

"Oh, my god!" Busy talking and engrossed in conversation, I had never realized that I was without my bag. "I must have left it at the riverbank!" I exclaimed, feeling my stomach drop like an elevator plunge from the thirty-eighth floor.

My throat was dry and constricted, but I managed to yell loudly enough for Rubin to hear. He came quickly, recognizing the panic in my voice. "The pocketbook!" I struggled to get it out. "I think I left it at the riverbank."

He didn't say a thing and didn't panic; he dropped his bags on the ground and took off running into the darkness as if he was competing in the hundred-meter dash at the Olympics. Our entire future, everything of importance that we owned, was in the lining of that large pocketbook. *He had to find it and make his way back safely.*

Fortunately, we hadn't walked too far—maybe a quarter of a mile from the riverbank. Shaking nervously and biting my lip, I looked down at the ground I saw my pocketbook among Yadja's bags. She must have picked it up with her luggage when we started walking.

"*Rubin!*" I yelled, this time with a moist and confident throat. "*Rubin, I found it!*"

He made it back to the caravan a moment later, stared at me a little longer than usual, then shook his head, picked up the bags, and started walking again. He never said a word about it, never blamed or chastised me. That's the type of man he was.

The remainder of our trip was uneventful, and crossing the border, although dangerous enough, was a success.

CHAPTER 65

I WAS AND WILL ALWAYS REMAIN GRATEFUL to the Russians for liberating us, but history has proven they can't be trusted. My mother believed that to the core of her soul, and for that reason alone, I was thankful the Americans had secured governing power in Germany after the war. Even though it was to be a temporary stop, it helped me feel safer and sleep better.

The first stop on our journey was Bergen-Belsen, a former Nazi concentration camp that had become one of the largest displaced-persons camps for Jews in Germany. Since it was under British rule, we planned on resting there overnight before continuing our journey, and it was there we parted ways with our traveling companions. Monyek had friends in Bergen-Belsen, and they planned to stay with them, while Rubin and I were hoping to find lodging for the night. We had no intention of staying long.

We were walking around the camp when a familiar voice called to us from above. Manya—the young girl Rubin and his four friends had saved from possible danger when they encountered her and Yadja on the road, and accompanied them—had spotted us from her second-floor window. She came rushing down and, with zealous enthusiasm, practically jumped into Rubin's arms and embraced him. She credited him and the others with saving her life, and she eventually married one of them, Henyek Usherowitz, Rubin's closest friend.

Manya invited us into her apartment and offered to let us stay with them while we searched for housing of our own. It was a tiny one-room apartment, with barely enough space for the two single beds, table, and chairs it contained. Down the hall, there was a communal bathroom and, on the first floor, a shared kitchen. Rubin and I moving in, even temporarily, would make their already tight living situation nearly impossible, but we accepted their invitation. It was difficult, but we made the best of it. We were four friends, we were young, together, and most importantly, *free*.

Rubin and I had reached Bergen-Belsen just as *Pesach* (Passover) began. The ancient holiday celebrates the freedoms won by Hebrew slaves from an Egyptian pharaoh centuries ago, and it was both fitting and ironic.

Our first Passover as a married couple and liberated people went off without a hitch. We had a traditional *Seder* (Passover feast), celebrating both the freedoms won by our ancestors and our own. Wine was poured, candles were lit, and the Seder began as Henyek and Rubin prayed. All was done to commemorate the redemption of the children of Israel from Egypt, and to bring the events and miracles of freedom from bondage into present-day reality. Although the holiday brought back memories of loved ones who had perished in the war, it was a nice evening, and comforting to spend it with Rubin and our friends.

CHAPTER 66

SEVERAL DAYS PASSED, and the crammed living situation became too burdensome for any of us to bear any longer, so Rubin and I ramped up efforts to find our own place. While he went searching for work and ways to make money in Germany, I began scouring the Bergen-Belsen camp, looking for housing. As luck would have it, I bumped into Mr. Londner—one of the members of the Jewish Committee in Ludwigsdorf. In Poland, he had been responsible for registering survivors; at his new home in Bergen-Belsen, he'd become an administrator whose duties included helping displaced Jews organize and plan their futures.

We stopped to talk, reminiscing about the past and updating each other on our current lives. Londner explained his role in the camp, and barely a few minutes into the conversation, he promised to arrange housing for Rubin and me.

The following day, Rubin and I walked up a flight of stairs and into an apartment of our own. It was tiny, similar in size to Manya's, and had the same features. However, the unit felt abandoned, filled with dust and cobwebs, and was overpowered by a musty odor. That, combined with the scents of disinfectant from the common bathroom and leftover aromas of whatever someone had been cooking in the kitchen, made it practically unbreathable.

The first things I did were to open the window for fresh air, roll up my sleeves, and begin cleaning and scrubbing everything in sight. It might only have been a temporary stopover on our journey, our life, but I had to make it the best it could be. I had done it everywhere I had been before—every camp, every barrack, every hellhole, and that wouldn't change now that I was free to enjoy it. I cleaned the apartment, sewed curtains for the windows, embroidered a tablecloth, and added creative touches. I turned that dingy apartment into a home that Rubin and I could be proud of.

Living in Bergen-Belsen was never boring. People were always around, always talking and gossiping. The war was over, but there was still so much uncertainty. *Who survived, and who didn't? Where was the best place to settle? Which country offered the best haven?* There were so many questions to ask, answers to digest, and we did it in a place where everybody shared a strong and common bond.

On one occasion, while a bunch of us were sitting around talking, Rubin learned that a friend of his from Auschwitz, Nathan Shapelski, was alive and well and living in Munchberg, Germany. They had been close in Auschwitz, helping each other survive. Rubin hadn't seen him since the death march out of Auschwitz, when Nathan had managed to escape either to freedom or to his death.

He'd made it to freedom eventually, landing in a town adjacent to Ludwigsdorf. Like the rest of us, he had been liberated by the Russians, migrated to Germany, and soon become the head of the Jewish community in Munchberg.

With so many people wanting to migrate into Germany, there were strict quotas, and many different rules imposed by the Americans. Since Rubin and I, like so many others, had snuck across the border to Germany, we lacked proper documentation. When Rubin learned that his friend held an official position, an idea came to him. The next night he invited Manya and Henyek Usherowitz to our apartment to discuss leaving Bergen-Belsen for Munchberg.

"Do you remember Nathan Shapelski?"

As Henyek was nodding his acknowledgment, Rubin continued, "He's head of the Jewish community in Munchberg and might be able to get us the proper paperwork we need." After a hesitation, he continued. "At least it's worth a trip."

Henyek looked to his wife first, then turned to Rubin. "The sooner we leave, the better."

Days later, I learned I was pregnant. It was a blessing, and both Rubin and I were excited, but it meant that I couldn't go with him to Munchberg. The trip would be far too stressful, the train ride long and treacherous. It was decided that Rubin and Henyek would make the trip alone, leaving Manya and me behind to keep each other company and worry.

While Rubin was away, I had difficulty sleeping. With him next to me, the nightmares didn't come as often, and when I did wake up sweating and trembling, he was there to comfort me. Without him, I had no safety net. The nightmares somehow knew that and began terrorizing me worse than ever. Rubin was only gone a few days, but it felt much longer. I felt much safer and more secure when he was home by my side, especially at night.

Whenever I closed my eyes, those images haunted me. *The Gestapo! Mama! The Man-eating Dogs! The whip! Mrs. Rosenberg! Irenka! The cattle car!* It was all the same, all horrible, except this time Rubin appeared in my nightmares. His stories somehow merged into my memories. As I watched the man I loved being chased by the Nazis and experiencing the horrible details he had told me about Majdanek, I screamed in my sleep

Rubin enjoyed his trip to Munchberg about as much as I enjoyed being without him. The train ride was slow, lasted several hours, and they didn't reach Munchberg until long after nightfall. The trains were overcrowded with passengers crammed in like sardines, and Rubin and Henyek had little interest in stuffing themselves inside a compartment. Instead they decided to "train surf," riding the entire way on top of the train car.

LET'S ASK BETKA

When Rubin returned and told me about his adventure, train surfing was fun and gave him an amazing view of the passing landscape, I was angry that he had put his life in jeopardy that way. However, the joy his return brought me overpowered the other emotions, and I forgave him.

He returned with good news. "Nathan will be able to procure the necessary papers for the four of us," he said, embracing me tightly in his arms.

From there, things happened quickly. Nathan began putting together the paperwork, and within the week, the four of us prepared to travel to Munchberg.

But when we arrived at the railroad station, we were disappointed to learn we were just four people among hundreds looking to board. Rubin's concern for me—because of my condition—escalated, and he was worried something would happen to the baby.

I tried to quell his fears, pointing out one of the cars that was filled with soldiers. "I know you're worried. I am too, but I'll be fine. You go with Manya and Henyek, and I'll go *there*," I said, pointing to a compartment filled with soldiers.

Rubin wanted to stop me, reaching for my arm as I turned away, but I wouldn't let him. I grabbed my pocketbook, this time holding it more securely than before, and headed toward the car filled with soldiers. I moved slowly, my hand on my lower back as I thrust my belly forward to exaggerate my condition. I avoided eye contact with any of the soldiers until two of them stepped outside and offered me a place in their compartment.

As two soldiers took my hand and helped me up the train steps, I glanced at Rubin, who was shaking his head in disbelief. It was an expression I had seen before and would many times again. It was obvious what he was thinking. Then he joined our friends in the luggage compartment, while I traveled to Munchberg like a lady, pampered by soldiers.

CHAPTER 67

THE DAY WE ARRIVED IN MUNCHBERG was warm and sunny, perhaps a sign that our futures were bright—and we believed they were. The war had been over for less than a year, but we had already accomplished so much, the best being Rubin and me falling in love with each other, marrying, and conceiving a child. Life was almost *normal* again, and our journey was taking us to a place we could eventually call *home*.

Our first stop in Munchberg was the building that housed the Jewish Committee. Rubin introduced us to Nathan, who had arranged for the four of us to stay at his sister Sala's home our first night in town. The permanent lodging set up for us wouldn't be ready until the following day. Nathan helped us register and promised our papers would be completed as soon as possible.

Once we settled in, living in Munchberg was everything we hoped it would be. With old friends around us, we settled in and felt stable and secure and, with the addition of new friends, formed a large, inseparable group. We all had our stories, our horrors, but we had survived the Nazi regime—and, which is something that no outsider can ever truly comprehend, it unified us.

Although Rubin and I considered Munchberg another temporary stopover, we felt during our time there as if it was home. We came with only a few bags, my infamous pocketbook included, and some memories of another time, another life, and too many nightmares, but soon created something new and special. We never allowed ourselves to forget the millions who had perished while we survived.

Not long after arriving in Munchberg, Rubin and I attended another ceremony at a mass grave site in the nearby town of Helmbrechts. This time the prayers were conducted by a Rabbi Shapiro, a chaplain in the U.S. Army.

The Munchberg community flourished, and the building that housed the Jewish Committee was constantly busy registering new arrivals, holding wedding ceremonies, and naming new babies; there was always something going on.

Individuals and groups gathered to pray, conduct business, but mostly to sit down, talk, and get to know one another. It was a resurgence of our lives with people who remained our life-long friends, and we wanted to enjoy every moment of it.

Just like everywhere else I had been, I found myself thrust into the center of everything. Even today, I'm not sure what others see or sense in me, but so many have flocked to me for leadership and guidance—"Let's ask Betka." It happened with my family, in Nazi prison camps, and after our liberation, too. I don't know why, but I've never not been willing to help when I could.

Frieda Rabinowitz, a woman who would become one of my closest and dearest friends for the next fifty years, refused to have her baby without me. She was eighteen years old, and though I was seven months pregnant myself, she insisted I remain by her side when she delivered her child.

Three months afterwards, on the morning of December 28, 1946, I gave birth to my only child, Jacob (named for his paternal grandfather). The delivery was long and difficult, but in the end it was all worth it. The first time I held my baby in my arms, counting his fingers and toes, I felt exhilaration, as if I had been fulfilled as a woman.

Jacob, equal parts of Rubin and myself, born out of our love and an extension of both our families, was a symbol of hope. The moment I looked in his eyes and he in mine, all the questions about why I survived were answered; everything made sense. My life had been spared for Jacob. Through his sheer existence, he represented the future, something none of us could have hoped for not long before.

Roughly six million Jews died at the hands of the Germans over the course of a decade, with only a pitiful few surviving. However, those of us who did survive were determined to make it count. We were going to produce a second generation of survivors who knew our strength and built upon it.

To Rubin, the birth of a son meant everything—the continuation of the Eber name and the rebuilding of the family he had lost. It was a cliché, but Rubin and I felt the sun rose and set on Jacob, although we consciously tried keeping those feelings from him, not wanting to put any undue pressures on our son.

Today, I am proud to say that third and fourth generations of survivors have been added to my family tree. Jacob has blessed me with two wonderful grandchildren, who have in turn blessed me with two extraordinary great-grandchildren. They will all live on and continue the heritage that Hitler tried to destroy.

LET'S ASK BETKA

CHAPTER 68

WHEN THE NAZIS INVADED POLAND, I was a young, naïve, and inexperienced teenager. In the years afterwards, during the hellish days of war, I observed, listened, and learned from the world's greatest teacher, life. Like most survivors, I was in a whirlpool—it was sink or swim for me—and I had to bury many of my feelings and memories in order to have the energy to rebuild my life.

The war was over, but the world was still struggling to piece itself back together. The economy flourished in the first three years after the war. There was demand for products and employment, and Rubin—being young, smart, and aggressive—seized the opportunity. He partnered with his two friends, Henyek and Monyek, and went into business. Together, they ran the canteen at the Jewish community complex.

The three of them took turns traveling between Munchberg and Munich to gather supplies to stock the canteen. They returned with candy, cigarettes, liquor, and anything else they could lay their hands on. Every transaction was conducted in an underground market where there were no price controls, which meant higher profits.

Since Munchberg was a textile city with factories throughout the area, they decided to expand their business. They bought a variety of piece goods, sold them at a considerable profit on the black market in Munich, and returned with lucrative merchandise that could be sold at the concession in Munchberg. They added a fourth partner and began selling merchandise in both Munich and Munchberg.

While waiting for our papers to be processed so that we might migrate to America, we settled into a comfortable life. We were careful with our money, saving as much as we could for the future. I became a housewife, caring for our son while Rubin worked. On his days off, he played ball, went to friends' soccer games, and spent time with Jacob and me. I often gathered with friends, playing cards, talking, and shopping. Nights were still the most difficult, but together Rubin and I managed to help each other through them.

Within two years, Rubin and his partners had made a good deal of money, and life was good. We were thriving, Jacob was growing and learning, I was submerged with the unconditional love of a devoted husband—and yet I couldn't shake the feeling that a gray cloud of desolation still hung over my head. I wanted out of Germany, away from the place that had given birth to the Third Reich, away from everything that had made me who I was. There were too many bad memories both there and in nearby Poland, and too much anti-Semitism still lurking.

At that point, I was certain that nearly everyone else in my family, both immediate and extended, had perished. The only two who survived the war were my father's cousin Stanislav Wygodski and my mother's cousin Yakov Tennenbam, who had escaped with his family to Palestine.

If only Mama had chosen to go.

Rubin was the only member of his family who went through the Holocaust and survived. He held out hope that his eldest brother, Leo, might have avoided the war altogether. While Rubin was still in the cavalry, his final communication had been a letter from his sister, Clara. In it, she'd said that Leo and his family had left Vienna for England, with America being their final destination. (Leo had hoped to join two of their uncles who had immigrated to America in the 1920s and were living in New York.)

LET'S ASK BETKA

In hope of finding something out, we placed an advertisement in the *Jewish Forward*, a daily newspaper in New York City:

Rubin Eber from Rownia
searching for brother
Leo Eber

Rubin and I knew that, every day, people all over the world were reading personal columns in newspapers, hoping to find someone—a family member, a friend, or anyone else they knew who had survived and made their way to safety. After placing our advertisement, we could do nothing but hope and wait.

In New York, a neighbor of Rubin's aunt Sara recognized the name and immediately informed her. She in turn contacted Leo with the news. That same day, Leo wrote to his brother. Several weeks after placing the ad, we finally received a letter —and an enormous amount of relief—and a steady correspondence began.

If possible, Rubin and I became even more eager to join his family and our friends in America. He wanted more than anything to reunite with his brother. . .but as fate would have it, it wasn't going to be easy. We were once again tested, both mentally and physically.

CHAPTER 69

Soon, it was early 1949, and another year was emerging; Jacob had recently turned two, and Rubin's business continued to prosper. However, we were still waiting for the paperwork that would allow us to come to America. We believed it was only a short time away; and then I received a devastating phone call from the Jewish Committee that nearly shattered my world: "Rubin has been in a terrible accident, and he's in the hospital at Bayreuth," the caller said.

It had been his turn to make the Munich supply run, and he'd hitched a ride with Monyek's cousin Gelbart, who was driving a few others to Munich. The transactions on the black market had gone smoothly, and the group were on their way back to Munchberg. Since traffic was light on both the highways and winding roads of the country, Gelbart was driving with a heavy foot on the gas pedal.

From the passenger seat, Rubin asked, "What's the rush? Are we in a race?"

"I just want to get home," Gelbart replied, accelerating even more and swerving between and around any vehicles that got in his way.

He continued burning up the roadways. The scenery out the window became a blur. Although Rubin was uncomfortable, he wasn't scared—and then a screech, a spin, a bang, and a crash.

A quiet countryside road was suddenly swarming with emergency vehicles. The cargo truck Rubin and the others were riding in was on its side, nearly crushed. Rubin, despite being badly bruised and in immense pain, climbed out on his own accord; none of the other passengers were able to. Fortunately, no one died, but at the time I hadn't know what had happened.

I left Jacob with a friend and, together with the spouses of the other passengers involved, rushed to the hospital in Bayreuth. I had no idea the extent of Rubin's injuries, only that he was alive, and for that alone I was thankful. The entire way my heart was pounding, my head throbbing, and my stomach twisting and turning.

He'll be all right. He must be all right! We didn't come this far for me to lose him. Scarred or crippled, I would take him home and love him as I always had. He was my husband, my other half, my life partner, and no matter what had happened to him, he would be the same man.

I was lost in my thoughts and prayers when I heard a voice calling to me from inside the car. "We're here."

I literally ran from the car to the hospital to find Rubin, and the moment I saw him, I felt better. He was badly injured, and it was obvious the pain was intense, but he was standing on his own two feet waiting for me. He placed his arm on my shoulder, and the touch felt magical. My headache subsided, my breathing normal, and my heartbeat returned.

"Let's go home," he said.

When we returned to Munchberg, he checked himself into the hospital to get treatment and recover. For the next several days, things were looking positive, and I began to relax. Then word spread that the police were looking for him. The contraband goods in the back of the truck had been found, and now Rubin was a wanted man. He couldn't stay in the hospital or he would be arrested, but since the police knew he was in the hospital, the only option was to escape.

Most of what we owned, other than furniture, had already been packed for our imminent move to Munich (where we would travel once our paperwork came through) for our eventual trip to America. While I finished packing the remainder of our belongings, several of our friends came visiting—actually, it was for a meeting. They came to help and to discuss how to get Rubin out of the hospital, save him from prison, and solidify our future. Not everyone was sure we had a future anymore.

"You can forget about going to America."

"He'll need a new name," someone else suggested.

Everyone was tossing around ideas.

"What about Palestine?"

"That's perfect, but it's Israel now. In May the State of Israel was established, and no papers are needed—*all Jews are welcome!*"

Listening, I realized that Israel was our only option. Rubin would be safe from prosecution, and we could have the new beginning we had been planning. Not knowing what we would find in a new country, especially one in the middle of the desert surrounded by Arabs, I began making mental notes of what I needed to pack and bring.

While I was thinking about Israel, someone in the room asked an important question. "How do we get him out of the hospital?"

"Rubin's room faces the back of the hospital," Peter Gershenowicz said. "His toilet has a window. I'll wait for him in my car. If he can make it outside the hospital, I'll drive him to Munich."

I often wondered how friendships and bonds could form so tightly so quickly. We had known each other for less than two years, and yet people were willing to share everything, willing to incur any risk or danger. Our friends were proof that there was still good in the world, and that, while Hitler tried to destroy us, he had failed to *break* us. We were bonded for life, and whenever one of us needed help, the others were there without being asked.

I didn't ask, yet they were there for me, for Rubin, and for our future without question, without hesitation. Peter stepped up without any thought of the danger he was putting himself in. "We have to arrange a time," he said.

"There isn't much," someone else pointed out. "It has to happen soon, very soon."

Two days later, everything was ready to be shipped to Munich, the starting point for destinations all over the world— and then, if everything went according to plan, Israel.

A few other families—Sonia and Avram Hurman, and their little girl, Manya, and Eni and Aaron Topiol—decided to join us. Eni had been with me throughout my incarceration, and she and Aaron decided that wherever Rubin and I made our home, they would, too. We were friends; we were family.

The conversation in the room continued; suggestions were made, and ideas were discussed.

"The Jewish committee in Munich will help them."

"I'll take Rubin to the hospital first," Peter said.

"No! Rubin needs a new identity. He can't travel anywhere under his own name, or he'll be arrested."

"My cousin, Pinek Potok, is already in Israel, and I have papers in his name," Jerry Posluszni suggested. "Rubin can use them."

Slowly, everything was being arranged. A time late in the evening was chosen, when most patients were asleep in their rooms and there were fewer nurses on duty. Rubin gathered his clothes, went into the bathroom, dressed, and squeezed himself through the window. He leapt the ten or so feet to the ground, then took off running. Peter, waiting in his car as promised, saw him and honked the horn. Rubin darted toward the car and freedom. He climbed in the passenger seat, took a deep breath, and closed his eyes as Peter revved the engine and sped away.

Rubin was now a fugitive from justice.

CHAPTER 70

Peter and Rubin drove straight from the hospital to Munich, arriving safely a few hours later and before daybreak. Rubin checked into a hospital and registered under the name of Pinek Potok. He had the proper papers, and no one was any the wiser. Over the next few days, he received intensive treatment and care for his injuries.

I arrived in Munich with Jacob later that day and stayed at the home of a friend I knew from Ludwigsdorf. It was a relief that Rubin was safe from the law, but we were both eager to leave Munich as soon as possible.

Fortunately, Rubin healed quickly, and it wasn't long before he was strong enough to travel.

While our dream of immigrating to America was on hold, perhaps permanently, the thought of moving to Israel was uplifting. Of course, he was disappointed not being able to reunite with his brother and other relatives, but starting over in a new country had its advantages. After everything we both had been through, being among the first settlers in a country built for and by Jews, and having a part in creating that community from the ground up, was very appealing.

I hoped that starting over somewhere else would obliterate my past, or at least help me forget it. I let myself believe that, if I got far enough away from the horrors and found a place where safety and happiness existed, my nightmares would stop. I missed my family, my home, and my childhood; that had all been taken from me too soon and too fast, but

I was ready to move on and forget about everything. All I cared about was Rubin, our son, and the future we would share together. . .be it in Israel or America.

In many of the cities throughout Germany, there was an Israeli office set up with delegates representing and recruiting Jews. I informed the office in Munich that our plans were to immigrate to Israel, and requested their assistance in locating my cousins, the Tennenbaums.

The office was efficient; two days later, I had an address.

It was only another day or so before Rubin was discharged from the hospital, healthy and ready to travel to Israel. We weren't going alone. The Hurmans and the Topiols joined us as we boarded the train to Marseille. We arrived in time to connect with the ship heading to Israel.

Rubin was out of Germany and safe from prosecution. He left Pinek Potok in Marseille, boarding the ship as Rubin Eber. His ordeal was over—but mine was just beginning. I was about to wage a battle against the sea.

The sun was shining, but it was cold and windy. Hundreds of people—men, women, children, people of all ages—swarmed the docks, preparing to board the ship that would take us all *home*. We were Jewish citizens from all over Europe, survivors of the Holocaust and ready to start over in the Jewish homeland.

Everyone was talking, yelling, laughing, and crying; the noise was thunderous, a cacophony of sounds, but nobody seemed to mind. They were the sounds of happiness, of joy, of *freedom*.

As we boarded the ship's main entrance, the sound of men shouting in several languages could be heard echoing inside. They were seamen, addressing the crowds and giving instructions. Each was speaking a different European tongue—Polish, German, Romanian, and so on— all saying the same thing: "Women and children to the upper cabins, men to steerage."

By the time Jacob and I reached our cabin, I was already feeling dizzy. Moments after the ship left the dock, and the swaying motion of the water took effect, I became nauseous, with the uncontrollable urge to vomit quickly following.

And that wouldn't stop until we reached Israel and I was able to step back onto solid ground.

Each morning, Rubin came up from steerage to care for Jacob and me. He made sure our son was okay, then tried comforting me—not that it did much. I couldn't eat or even look at food without throwing up, whatever went down my throat came up just as fast, but the dry heaves were worse. The only thing I managed to keep down was dry, stale bread, and that was difficult. I lived on day-old bread supplied by a steward Rubin had befriended.

The dizziness faded when I closed my eyes; the nausea never left. My head and stomach felt awful, but the burning and aching in my throat was much worse. After two days of hell, I was begging to be put out of my misery. *How crazy is that?* I'd been through so many horrors at the hands of the Nazis, been beaten, starved, worked to the brink of death many times, but I had never prayed for it before; I had been through a horrendous childbirth during a time when drugs weren't so readily available, yet I'd never reached the point of wanting to die—until we were on that ship.

But I thought of Rubin and Jacob, and knew I *had* to live.

At least Jacob wasn't affected by the sea. At the age of two, he was a free spirit, running all over the ship, playing, eating, and laughing, while telling anyone who would listen, "*Mami spuken! Mami, spuken!*" an abbreviated way of telling them I was "spitting up."

Several days into the voyage, on February 12 to be exact—on one of the rare occasions that I was sleeping soundly, I was awakened late in the afternoon by the sounds of laughing and cheering. An announcement came over the ship's speaker system, repeated in several languages, but I couldn't make it out. However, the laughter and cheering continued to grow louder until the racket sounded as if it was right outside my door.

I was about to go and find out what the hell was going on when my cabin door opened, and Rubin stepped in carrying Jacob and smiling. He told me the good news everyone else had already heard: "An armistice agreement was signed between Israel and its neighboring countries. The United Nations was involved and outlined their commitment to maintain peace and stability in the region!"

The rest of the night was spent celebrating with most of the ship's passengers. There was drinking, dancing, and partying. Almost everyone was having a good time. However, as ecstatic as I was about the news, I did not join in the festivities.

As a matter of fact, I only left the cabin once during the entire ten days we were at sea. It was after I had eaten the stale bread, and my complexion brightened. Up till then, I had been pale and chalky, and Rubin was worried about how sick I truly was. Once he realized I was going to survive, he suggested we take a walk on the deck. He thought the fresh air might help.

He was wrong. The moment I stepped on the deck and looked out at the waves, I felt the bile rumbling in my stomach, and within two seconds it was all over the deck floor.

Jacob found the entire scene amusing, again telling anyone and everyone, "*Mami spuken!*"

Ten days feels like an eternity when you're seasick and trapped on a boat. Even today, decades later, I still can't look at the ocean waves without feeling queasy or remembering that horrible trip. The only thing that got me through it was knowing that, on the other end, were freedom and our future.

CHAPTER 71

I VENTURED UP TO THE DECK ONCE MORE, but only after the ship docked in Haifa. It would take time before we could disembark, and most of the passengers came out to see the city we had journeyed to. Built in the shadows of Mount Carmel, Haifa was an up-and-coming town with unlimited potential.

I was taking it all in when my eyes caught a glimpse of the Israeli flag, and I froze in place. Seeing the Star of David, the six-pointed figure that had once represented nothing but hatred and pain, gave me goosebumps and sent a chill up my spine. The Germans had used that symbol to identify us, to treat us as less than human, to know whom to attack, beat, torture, and humiliate. Now, hanging high above the city and swaying freely in the wind, the Star of David had come to mean so much more. It was now a symbol of hope and freedom that had the power to unify an entire nation.

The disembarkation was slow but efficient. Once my feet touched land, my nausea and dizziness disappeared. I felt better both physically and mentally. In that one moment, all my fears faded away. Standing on the soil of the homeland of the Jewish people, I sensed I was safer and more secure than I had in a long time.

But the cost of achieving that feeling was significant, and it would never become lost on me. In a world where more than six million people, mostly Jews, paid heavily with their lives for this land and its—from their ashes rose the State of Israel—I was one of the lucky ones. I'd survived and gotten to see the rainbow at the end of the storm.

LET'S ASK BETKA

The newly formed Israeli government—or what constituted a government at the time—had set up a temporary refugee camp, or *mahanot olim* (absorption camp), essentially a series of tents to provide immediate accommodations for the influx of Jewish refugees arriving daily.

Rubin and I took a tent near the Hurmans and Topiols. It wasn't much, but after what most of us had been used to, it was a godsend. No one living in the tents dared to unpack their belongings—doing so would have suggested that the camp was something more than a temporary stop—only taking out what we needed.

The day after we settled into the camp, I left Rubin and Jacob to fend for themselves and went off on my own. With the address I had received from the Israeli office in Munich in hand, I took a bus from Haifa to Tel Aviv, hoping to reunite with my cousins. Ten years had passed, and there was no way they could have known I survived. I wasn't sure what type of reception I would receive.

I made it to their house with ease and knocked on the door. Anxiety flooded over me, and I was overwhelmed with memories, none stronger than the night Yakov had begged my mother to join him and his family on their voyage to Palestine.

Ola, Yakov's wife, opened the door and stared at me for a moment.

My mouth was dry, and the three words I uttered in Polish came out raspy. "*Ya yestem Regusha!*" (I am Regusha!)

The confused look on her face was replaced with instant shock, followed by joy, as the realization that Sonia's youngest child had survived. Then the tears started for both of us.

I spent the rest of the day in the home of my cousins, talking and sharing stories about the horrors I had lived through. After an exhausting but exhilarating day, I took the bus back to Haifa, to Rubin and Jacob, and I had good news to share with them. Not only were my mother's cousin thrilled I had survived, but Yakov's sister, Vanda, had offered to put us up in her home.

Rubin and I moved out of the refugee camp several days later. Our friends who had traveled from Munich with us both found housing as well. Sonia Hurman had a brother living in Hertzlia, and they secured an apartment of their own nearby, while the Topiols stayed in camp for about a month before finding an apartment.

Once we were settled in Tel Aviv, it did not take Rubin and me long to find our own place. Through Yakob, I learned that his older brother, David, who had immigrated to Palestine ten years earlier, was arranging an apartment for us. He had a friend who worked for the housing authority at the *iriya*, the city hall. He, too, was shocked to see me alive and happily arranged housing for us.

Rubin and I ended up sharing a four-room apartment with another family, the Levis. Susan and Marco were nice people, and Marco's mother was a Turkish woman who cooked like a chef. In time, they became more than just neighbors and friends, and we considered each other family. Jacob even took to calling Marco's mother *Savta* (Grandma).

The apartment was just outside Tel Aviv, in a town called Sheh Mones, adjacent to the Yarkon River. It was a quaint village with dirt roads, a single telephone line for everyone to share, and a bus that came once a day from Tel Aviv. Our apartment was above the local grocery store and situated on a hill.

Inside, there were four rooms—two for us, one for the Levis—and we shared a bathroom, a kitchen, and the main entrance-sitting room, to which all the other rooms connected.

Within a short time, Rubin built *Savta* a room of her own and a separate kitchen for us. Our apartment had two large windows overlooking the village and, in the distance, a view of the Mediterranean.

For the next seven and a half years we shared, not only the same dwelling, but our lives. It was home, and the Levis were our family. Even after we left for America, the bond remained strong. For the next fifty years, letters criss-crossed the Atlantic Ocean several times a year, and our friendship never withered.

LET'S ASK BETKA

CHAPTER 72

THE TRANSITION TO LIFE in a new country went more smoothly than we expected. Rubin and I adapted to the customs quickly, and picked up the language, too. When Ola Tennenbaum learned that Rubin owned a bicycle that he had brought with him from Germany, she immediately arranged a position for him as a delivery man at a dry-cleaning establishment.

It was tough work trekking back and forth to Tel Aviv several times a day on a bicycle, but a job's a job, and Rubin needed one. Besides, it wasn't long before he came home one night and announced he had found a new one.

After completing his deliveries for the day and on his way home, he had come across Zysek Adler, one of the five friends who survived Auschwitz together. They had once promised eternal allegiance and friendship to each other, and Zysek had married Bianka, one of my closest friends from Ludwigsdorf.

Zysek worked for a construction company that was hiring strong, able-bodied men to build roads and sidewalks. It was a steady job with good pay and came at a time when the country was on the rise and construction was booming. A few days later, I was reunited with Bianka, Zysek, and their son, David.

A short time following our reunion, I heard from Esta and Yulek. Upon learning that Rubin and I were immigrating to Israel, they made plans to join us. It did not take long for the Schwebels and their son,

Yosi, to reunite with us. I was elated that my two dearest friends were going to be close to me, and soon our sons became friends. Watching the three of them play together and get to know each other made everything we suffered for worth it. They were the next generation, the generation we survived for.

Things were progressing well, but before we could even reach a level of comfort, Zysek approached us. "Rubin, do you have any money saved?"

"Why are you asking?"

"I want to go into business with you," he said. "I want to buy two horses and a wagon and become partners as contractors."

"Contractors?" Rubin asked, surprised.

"Yes! We would continue to work for the construction company, and they would contract our horses and wagon."

Rubin and I didn't have a lot saved, and we weren't what you'd call risk-takers, but Rubin never hesitated. We were living at a unique time in a country with a government that was in a hurry to make a home for its citizens and more incoming refugees. Most of all, Rubin couldn't deny the excitement in Zysek's voice, and he wanted a part of that.

Rubin used most of what we had saved to rent a barn, pay his share of the horses, and, just like that, we were all in business together.

The weeks and months that followed proved Zysek's initiative sound. Because of the influx of survivors—hundreds coming daily from all over Europe—cities were being built all over Israel amid the rocks and sand. Buildings were going up, roads were being laid, and all of it was happening with alacrity. Apartment buildings, schools, movie theaters, and office buildings were not being built fast enough for the growing population. Rubin and Zysek flourished.

After a short time, word came that the government was requesting bids from companies to build the main highway from Tel Aviv to Haifa. It was a big job, and for a country with limited resources, they insisted the job be completed by a certain date or they would suspend all financing, and any costs incurred for the remainder of the job would be the contractor's responsibility.

Not many companies bid on that project, fearing they wouldn't finish on time, but Rubin insisted on it. Zysek was apprehensive, but when they won the bid and finished the road on schedule, he was thankful Rubin had pushed for it. Their reputation as contractors grew, and with the government's backing, their business began to thrive.

That main road, although wider and more developed today, still exists and still connects those two cities.

CHAPTER 73

Life in Israel, for the most part, was pleasant. We were surrounded by a new enemy—the Arab world—which posed significant threats to our way of life and newfound homeland, but I felt strangely free from danger. With a means of support, a place to live, and supportive neighbors, friends, and family nearby, I was content.

I no longer looked over my shoulder, worrying about what might be lurking behind every corner. For more than a decade, I had carried an oppressive burden—from the first time I saw, on store windows, *"Don't Buy From Jews!"*, *"Dirty Jews!"*, *"No Jews Allowed!"*—to the moment I stepped off the boat in Haifa. I felt an enormous pressure lifted from my soul.

Rubin and I were proud to be part of the beginning of something special, the creation of a homeland. As survivors we were elated to be a part of the planning, seed planting, and growth of the State of Israel. Every day was a constant struggle to establish our foundation in that small part of the world where anti-Semitism had ceased to exist.

I hoped that, in time, I would be free of anxiety too, and that my nighttime visitors would leave me forever. For the time being, they remained, and I often woke up from a deep sleep in a cold sweat and shrieking. The images were as clear in my dreams as they had been the day I witnessed them, unrelenting, frightening, trapped inside, every scene dripping with blood. The images didn't come as often as they had, but they still came far too often.

Because of the newness of nation and the ever-lurking threat from the Arab world, the State of Israel demanded its citizens form a protective military force. Every man and woman who came of age was required to serve in the army, and all able-bodied men under the age of fifty-five had to enroll in the reserves. Being a cavalryman, Rubin didn't mind; he enjoyed returning to his life as a soldier for two weeks every year, going away for updated training, while I added the chore of caring for our two horses, Rifka and Felka.

Slowly, Rubin and I fell into a routine. He spent six days a week working to support us while I stayed home cooking, cleaning, washing, and caring for Jacob. I made friends, sewed curtains, washed, cooked, and trimmed tablecloths. I was an ordinary housewife with a comfortable life, but I wanted *more*. I wanted roots, a sense of *permanence*, but that wasn't to be for a while longer.

The days and weeks passed quickly, and before we realized it six and a half years had gone by since we first set foot on Israeli soil. We had a good life and probably could have been happy living there the rest of our lives. But Rubin dearly missed his family and was still aching to reunite with his brother in America. We often wrote letters, but words on a page weren't the same thing as being together.

There was also the issue of Rubin's health. He was a strong and sturdy man, but the years in captivity, in the camps, and the hard labor working in construction had done a number on his body. The weather was against him, too—too hot, too humid, too wet, too damp, too everything, too bad. He was constantly in pain, and thanks to the slipped disc he had suffered during his incarceration at Auschwitz, the excruciating pain had extended from his back into his neck, shoulders, and arms. The slightest movement—bending to hug his son, a cough, even a sneeze—could trigger severe muscle spasms.

None of the doctors could help him. All of them, even Dr. Goldberg, the man who treated me as a child in Warsaw, offered the same advice: "Change your profession, and get the hell out of this climate."

Israel had a lot to offer us, but my husband needed to go somewhere that was less taxing on him physically. We didn't have a plan, or a place to go to right away, but the obvious choice was staring us in the face: America, as we had originally planned to go to years before. It was still the most desirable place on Earth, and Rubin had family he desperately wanted to reunite with.

We began preparations to leave Israel for good. Rubin's brother, Leo, already an established citizen in the United States, signed all the paperwork and agreed to sponsor us.

Everything was finalized for Rubin to immigrate to America in February of 1955. He boarded a ship heading for New York while Jacob and I stayed behind. The plan was for Rubin to establish himself in the United States, to start laying the foundation of our new lives, and to get his green card, while I went to work liquidating our belongings and helping prepare Jacob for a move across the ocean when the time was right.

It would be seven months before we were together again.

CHAPTER 74

Rubin's journey to America was long and tiring. He was traveling with thousands of others, but without Jacob and me he felt alone. During his fourteen days crossing the Atlantic Ocean, doubts crept in. Aware that he was leaving a happy life, a thriving business, and cherished friends, he could not help but wonder what was waiting for him in a new land.

It was a bitter-cold, rainy day with a biting wind when the ship docked in New York. Since it was late, Leo had to return to work and left his two sons, Martin, thirteen, and Lenny, three and a half years younger, waiting on the pier for over ten hours.

They escorted their uncle to their home on the Lower East Side of Manhattan. Even though it had been more than three decades since they last laid eyes on each other, when Leo came home, there was instant recognition on both sides. As Rubin and Leo embraced, the years apart vanished; they were brothers, they were together, and that was all that mattered.

A couple of weeks later, I received word of Rubin's safe arrival in America and the details of his reunion with his brother and family. In his letter, Rubin described feelings of euphoria upon seeing Leo again, and wrote about his brother's wife. From Leo's previous letters, we knew Dora was ill, but not to the extent Rubin found her. He expected a sick woman, but also one who was vibrant and energetic. Instead Dora was barely clinging to life; she had lost a significant amount of weight, her complexion was gray, and she was bedridden in a hospital.

Once Rubin arrived in America, he spent time with his sister-in-law and became a pseudo-guardian of his nephews. Leo owned a luncheonette in the Bronx, leaving daily before dawn and not returning until nightfall.

Rubin's brother was struggling more than he could have imagined, and life in America was not as picture-perfect as we thought. Early on, Rubin's doubts about leaving Israel grew stronger. He ended his first letter with a shocking revelation:

> *I think I should return to Israel and forget all about the 'American Dream'. If my older brother, the one who was supposed to be the smart one, the capable one, is living like this in the land of opportunity, then there is no hope for us here.*

Unable to contact Rubin right away and find out what was going on, I began to worry. Before he showed up back on our doorstep in Israel, another letter came in the mail, this one saying he wasn't returning—yet. Things were not much better for Leo, but he spoke highly of his aunt Sara, the woman who had married his uncle Hyman, and who'd somehow managed to convince him to stay in America for the time being.

Sara was a special person in the history of the Eber family. Despite never finishing high school or having much formal education, she had good instincts about life and people, and cared greatly for her family. She had been widowed at an early age (Hyman died tragically of typhus at thirty-eight) and been left to raise five children on her own. Those five people —Max, Rae, Kalman (Tom), Jack, and Fred—would go on to play dramatic roles in establishing the Eber family's foundation in America for years to come.

When Rubin phoned Sara, his heart was set on returning to Israel. Life in America was too uncertain, and he couldn't risk doing that to his family. We had a good life in Israel, and moving across the ocean felt like taking several steps backward.

"He's got serious problems!" Rubin said of Leo, in Yiddish, on the phone to his aunt.

"Don't do anything!" Sara insisted. She knew what Rubin was talking about but didn't want him making any rash decisions he might come to regret.

Immediately after hanging up with him, Sara phoned her daughter, Rae, and told her to bring Rubin to their home.

I'm not sure what she said, or how she convinced him to stay, but in Rubin's next letter he wrote he was not returning to Israel after all and would wait for his green card. He also told me he had moved out of his brother's apartment and gone to live with Sara. And instead of the gloomy health news about Dora, this time the letter ended with joy: Rubin's cousins, Fred and Arline, had welcomed a baby boy into the family.

Moving in with Sara gave Rubin somewhat of a purpose. He didn't yet have his green card or a job, but he couldn't sit still either. He painted her apartment, fixed anything that needed to be fixed, and did everything he could to earn his keep. The day he climbed to the top of a tree to rescue a kitten, he not only secured a permanent place in Sara's heart but endeared himself to the entire family. Rubin was an Eber, he was one of them, and he was home.

Rubin's third letter was short and sad. He spoke about being hired by his cousin Max in a dress-manufacturing company that he owned, and about Dora's death. His brother's wife had fought long and hard but couldn't defeat the disease.

Over the next few months, Rubin began establishing himself in the new world. He worked tirelessly, learning the dress cutter's trade and hoping to build roots. Sara's children welcomed him into their lives and helped replace the family and siblings he had lost in the war.

With a job, a supportive family, and at long last, a green card, Rubin sent for Jacob and me to join him. I missed my husband more than words can say but had been dreading the trip to America. It would be a much longer boat ride than the one to Israel, and without Rubin to help with Jacob, I was terrified.

But I didn't need to be, and I never had to step on a ship either. When Max and his wife, Marcia, heard of my ordeal on the seas, they insisted on paying the additional cost that would allow Jacob and me to fly instead. I was stunned and greatly appreciative. *Who does that for someone they've never met, Just because you happen to share a bloodline with the person they married?* The Ebers were and are a rare breed. To this day, I am glad Rubin listened to his aunt and Cousin Rae, and decided to stick it out a while longer.

After seven months apart, Rubin and I were reunited. On September 22, 1955, I got off a plane and stepped onto American soil—the place where dreams really do come true, the *land* of the *free*. And I've never felt more at home.

CHAPTER 75

STARTING OVER IN A NEW PLACE—again—wasn't easy, but Rubin and I didn't have to do it alone. Not everyone who immigrated to the United States, including many of those I knew, were as lucky. To do it legally, you had to be sponsored by a family member already living here, but more often than not, there was very little interaction afterwards. The sponsoring family member would come to greet you at a pier or gate, offer their phone number, and have little or nothing to do with you after that day.

But the Ebers were a different kind of family. They knew, or had been taught, that family is more than just sharing common ancestry, but a warm and loving relationship emanating from the heart. Aunt Sara managed to instill into all five of her children the true definition of family, which has trickled down from generation to generation.

Some of Rubin's cousins came with him to meet Jacob and me at the airport, and then that night there was a huge celebration in our honor. Twenty to thirty members of the family came over to welcome us into their country and their lives. I was astonished by the welcome, and the warmth and acceptance, from that day on, has never stopped. Without realizing it, the Eber family gave me the thing that I craved most of all—the feeling of *permanence*. I had a home, a special place in the world, and people to share it with, and for those things I am eternally grateful.

Sara didn't think twice about inviting the three of us to live in her home—in a quiet manner that inferred that it was a done deal, and we had no choice in the matter—and during the three months that followed, she helped us become acquainted with our new surroundings. We acclimated to our new life and bonded with the family. Everyone helped us, all of Sara's children, and even those who were not bound by blood—the Sadins, Mickey and Sylvia (Sara's niece—but they were family anyway. It was Mickey who loaned us money when Rubin wanted to start his own business, and who was disappointed when the loan was paid back earlier than expected. For years afterwards, Mickey would often joke about never doing business with immigrants again—"You can't make money with them!") In any case, the Ebers and the Sadins welcomed us into their world with open arms and gave both Rubin and me a feeling of belonging that we had lost.

Not long after we moved into our first apartment in Brooklyn, Max and Marcia gave us a television set as a present. We thought it was too expensive, especially after they had seen to it that Jacob and I flew to America instead of on the high seas for fourteen days, but, Marcia insisted, "It's not for you, it's for Jacob. He'll learn English much quicker, and that will help him adapt to America."

She was right. Jacob fell in love with the TV, began watching American shows like *I Love Lucy* and *The Honeymooners*, and he did pick up the language faster than expected.

The three of us went through a lot of changes in those early years in America, but Rubin and I succeeded in building a life for ourselves and our son. We moved out of Sara's home but stayed in Brooklyn for several years before settling into an apartment in Queens at the insistence of Rubin's cousins Tom and Reba, who wanted us near them—the place that is still my home, some fifty-plus years later.

Rubin went through a lot of changes over the years. His first job, working for Max in the garment industry, proved to be only a stepping stone, and he eventually went into business for himself. With a loan from Mickey—the one he paid back too soon—he partnered with two

Betty and Rubin, 1979

men in the opening of a supermarket. But Rubin's first attempt at American entrepreneurship did not go as planned when one of the partners embezzled company funds, bankrupting the store.

Rubin was not deterred, though; soon afterward, he opened a second supermarket, which he successfully operated for several years. But luck wasn't on his side, and one year, during Passover, the store burned to the ground.

That time, he wound up out of work for almost nine months. There was no money coming in, and with bills that needed to be paid, things were tough. But he and I made it work. We had always been frugal, spending less than we earned and saving for a rainy day. We cut corners, saved wherever we could, but made sure there was food on the table, a roof over our heads, and that Jacob didn't feel the strain. We didn't want him to suffer the way we had; we wanted him to prosper and flourish, to experience only the joys and good things in life.

Eventually, Rubin found his way into another business, this time a dry-cleaning establishment, a successful partnership with a survivor acquaintance. The store had two Manhattan locations, just blocks apart. One location was the cleaning and processing plant; the other the location Rubin took over, was the customer service store, where drop-offs and pickups occurred.

In quick fashion, Rubin made the location his own, becoming friendly with the regulars and simplifying the process for many customers. He hired runners to transfer the clothes back and forth, and when they were busy or unavailable he did it himself. He never backed down from a challenge.

Rubin was a terrific man, a hard worker, and the love of my life. Without him I don't know where I would have ended up. As I sit back and think about all the things that he meant to me, to Jacob, and to the rest of the Eber family, I can't help but miss him even more.

He was a man who had gone through horrors similar to mine or those of any other Jew who crossed paths with the Nazi regime, yet his scars seemed to burn deeper. He had difficulty talking about what had happened to him and could never relate any details to anyone who hadn't lived through it, too.

I, on the other hand, can discuss those events with anyone interested but have never been able to fully let go of what happened to me—either physically or emotionally. Rubin's injuries caused him far more pain throughout his life. It was only during the final five years of his life that he had any physical relief from the pain of the slipped disc, relief that came from acupuncture therapy recommended by a dry-cleaning customer.

He gave me more than I believed I would ever have and whose mere presence in my life opened so many doors for me. He was the only man who, with one special look, could exude warmth and protectiveness—a look of total adoration. He was the only man who could make me woozy when he kissed me and, with a touch of his gentleness, could inflame many parts of my body at once. We have always been on the same wavelength. We had what today's generation calls "chemistry," a chemistry that never faded. We had a beautiful three-and-a half-decade love affair. Together, we built a home, raised a son, and watched him grow into a smart, educated man who reminds me more and more of a combination of his father and myself with each passing day.

Rubin was also a man who kept his feelings to himself and rarely showed unnecessary emotion. I remember the day his brother left for California. They had only been back in contact a short time after thirty years apart, and suddenly, they were going to be separated by thousands of miles—again. Rubin was devastated but took it in stride. He wished his brother well, and while they remained in constant contact, speaking on the phone every Sunday and vacationing together whenever possible, things were never the same. But, Rubin did not show his disappointment to the world.

In fact, in all the years we were together, the only time I remember him visibly displaying emotion in public was the day Jacob graduated from high school. Rubin hadn't been able to finish school when he was younger and in some ways lived vicariously through his son. When Jacob crossed the stage to accept his diploma, I looked at Rubin as he squeezed my hand, and there were tears in his eyes.

My life with Rubin was everything I dreamed it could be and more. When we first met in the remnants of what had been Poland, neither of us had any long-term plans. After what we had been through, we didn't dare to dream any dream and hoped only to survive another day. If we were lucky enough, then maybe someday in the future we'd get back to normalcy and perhaps even have a life worth living.

Rubin and I accomplished much more than that. Together, we built a fine family, impacted many lives, and lived a life worthy of envy. There were times of struggle, but we found our way through them because we had each other. We had so many plans—things we wanted to do, places we wanted to go. We had always prepared for tomorrow, scrimping and saving so that one day he could retire, and we would enjoy our life.

We had certainly earned it.

We had everything we needed.

Except *time*.

Rubin didn't have any left.

CHAPTER 76

JUST DAYS AFTER RINGING IN 1980, Rubin suffered a massive heart attack and died at the age of sixty-two. My best friend, my lover, my partner, was gone. I was a widow far too young.

Losing him hit me harder than I could ever have imagined. I had been through the worst of the worst and survived. I had lost everyone I ever cared about and built a wall around my heart and my feelings that I never planned on opening again. Rubin changed that. My love and adoration for that man gave me the strength to open myself up. . .and to get through his death.

I loved him dearly, and still do, and what he gave me enabled me to go on living without him. In the weeks and months that followed, I took on new and different responsibilities. I stepped into his shoes and continued his work at the dry-cleaning business. Working six days a week, I took the New York subway—since I never drove, the New York subway system was my limousine—from Queens to Manhattan. I was on my feet fifteen hours a day, up at 5:00 a.m. every morning and home at 8:00 p.m. It was a grueling schedule, yet the transition was as smooth as a pilot gliding an airplane to a safe landing.

Overnight, I seemed to have blossomed into a successful business woman—still the housewife, still the caretaker, but much more.

Again, I grabbed life by its horns, like an equestrian who keeps a tight rein on a horse. I held it all together to direct and control my destiny. I took on the responsibility of the business with a smile and never showed the depth of the sorrow I felt. My son, the Ebers, and my friends were aware of it, respected my wishes, and allowed me to keep it hidden. I let it out when I came home to an empty apartment, but I was not alone. Rubin was, and always will be, there.

At work, the customers called me "Miss Sunshine" because of my pleasant demeanor and never-fading smile. The customers, like so many others, acknowledged my special quality, an indescribable magnetism that make people gravitate towards me. I often wondered what they would think if they knew all the pain and loss hidden behind that smile. But that's who I am, who I have always been, and a big reason why I survived.

Eventually, we sold the business and I had to re-establish myself. I was still a valued member of the Eber family—these days serving as a family matriarch—and I developed an active lifestyle. I am approaching ninety-six and am as busy as ever. I live alone, visit and lunch with friends almost daily, and am hardly ever home. My group of friends has gotten smaller, but those who remain are very dear to me.

Following my business years, I joined many of my friends and vacationed in Florida in February. It was a yearly reunion where survivors and friends from Chicago, Los Angeles, St. Paul, and other parts of the United States gathered together to party, dance, lunch, play cards, and reminisce. After all the time that has passed, I am astonished that I still occupy an influential place among my friends and many of the survivors. Years after I started going, I learned that, several weeks prior to my arrival each year, the air was filled with anticipation. The buzz around town was, "Betty's coming." Every meeting, every gathering, every conversation included that tidbit of information.

After Rubin's death, I was included by family or friends in everything from an evening at the movies to a card game, from a concert or show to shopping or dinner. Never a fifth wheel, I remained a welcome cousin or friend. I have devoted people around me who are always a phone call away.

In 1982, "The Group," as we called ourselves—the twenty-plus families who had survived the Holocaust together and become lifelong friends due to the most extreme and unusual circumstances—bought

The Eber family—four generations

units at a bungalow colony in the Catskill Mountains. We named it "Silver Gate" and have been vacationing there ever since.

That colony has been my summer haven for the past thirty-five years. With bed covers I sewed from calico fabric, embroidered curtains, crocheted accessories, and silk flowers, I have transformed a tiny one-bedroom cottage into my personal doll house. Bungalow 21, surrounded by friends, has a picture of Betty Boop, that iconic cartoon character I have been linked to all my life, hanging at the entrance that welcomes all.

I have loved every one of the summers I've spent at Silver Gate. It gets me out of the heat of the city and gives me the chance to reunite with friends I don't see during the year whom I have known for a lifetime, men and women who survived hell and who have meant so much to each other over the years.

At its height, the Silver Gate community housed upwards of fifty families. Monday through Friday, we lived a fulfilling existence—we talked, laughed, reminisced, swam, played cards, but mostly enjoyed being together. Over the years, I have watched my grandchildren and now my great-grandchildren run and play on the grass, swim in the pool, dance in the casino (community center), and enjoy the camaraderie and warmth of the colony.

Every Saturday morning, the casino becomes a place of worship where families pray. Every Saturday night, the place of worship is transformed into a party room. With everyone dressed to the nines, it comes alive with music and dancing to a band while celebrating life.

It was our little corner of the world, and everyone worked hard to make it special. I worked endlessly behind the scenes, refusing to run for the board, to make sure everything runs smoothly. Friends and acquaintances came to me for opinions and advice on all sorts of issues from personal to bungalow colony business. Since 1942, "Let's ask Betka" has been a popular solution and continues now—seventy-plus years later.

It's been thirty-five years since I lost Rubin, and I still live in the same apartment we shared for two decades. Not a day has gone by when I haven't missed him or thought about him. And I still talk to Rubin every day, and I know he hears me and guides me as I venture on without him.

Everything I have today is because of him and his love for me. We have a wonderful son who has given us two grandchildren and great-grandchildren, and Rubin's family is still *my* family, too.

Oh Rubin! I wish you were still here. I wish you could see the man your son has become and feel the same gush of pride I do when people tell me what an exceptional person he is. I wish you could have gotten to meet your grandchildren. Robin, your namesake, was born less than a year after your death. She is smart, beautiful, and talented, and I see a lot of you in her. She's a determined young woman, and like both of us, she accomplishes anything she puts her mind to.

The day of her wedding was a glorious moment, and I would have loved to have shared it with you. As did I, she married the man of her dreams, the man who completes her and makes her whole. Together, they are building a life like we had—a life of commitment, love, and happiness. It was at her wedding, as I watched Robin and Tom Mechin exchange vows and rings, promise to love each other forever, that I finally felt a heavy weight lifted off my shoulders. When I saw the happiness in our granddaughter's eyes, it awakened something inside me that had been gone far too long.

I stood up, took the hand of our grandson, Joshua, and danced. It was the first time I had done so with anyone since you—the only dance partner I ever wanted—died. I could feel you with me, with us, and an overwhelming sense of peace. I thank you and Joshua for that.

You were with me the day he was born. Today he is a happy, delightful thirty-two-year-old with a variety of interests and talents, but when he was born with Down Syndrome, I worried. I didn't know what kind of life or limitations he would have, and it scared me.

That night I was awakened from a deep sleep, although this time I wasn't shaking, and I didn't have any nightmares. You, Rubin, awoke me. You were standing at the foot of our bed, looking down at me. In your usual calm voice, you reassured me as only you could. "Stop worrying," you said. "He'll be okay."

So I did, and he is. Joshua has grown into an incredible young man—sensitive and caring and undaunted. He has Jacob's personality and was born to entertain. He's been on Sesame Street, in movies, commercials, and off-Broadway. He loves being on a stage and making people happy, and he's proud to wear his Screen Actors Guild pin. He is a very determined young man. He was determined to have a bar mitzvah like all other young Jewish teens at thirteen. He studied diligently and succeeded in inspiring everyone. He is blessed with a wonderful imagination and unlimited dreams.

Joshua and I have always had a close and joyous relationship. When he was younger we bonded over I Love Lucy and making a "potato-nik" (large potato pancake) together. As he grew older, we advanced to UNO and Rummy-Q.

As the years have passed, things have changed, but we are still close and have a terrific relationship.

Like us, both our grandchildren have the strength to overcome obstacles, and face their own challenges.

Oh, Rubin! I wish you could be here to share in the legacy you left. You would be proud. Robin, now known to the world as Ruvina, her Hebrew name, is the mother of two children, our great-grandchildren. You would love them as I do. Spencer is a beautiful seven-year-old girl with blue eyes and blonde hair, and she lights up a room with her smile. She's fearless and fun-loving, and I have no doubt she would have stolen your heart. Her younger brother, Braden, just turned four. He's an affectionate little boy, shy and sensitive with a never-ending supply of energy and a devilish gleam in his eyes. As sure as I am that Spencer would have stolen your heart, Braden has stolen mine. All in all, our great-grandchildren are all I could have wished for.

LET'S ASK BETKA

I am ninety-five now, and I have lived a long and full life. It's been a long time since that Friday night dinner when Vanda first brought Stasiek home to meet the family. In the years since, everything has happened, I've traveled from Poland to Germany to Israel to America. I've gone by different names at different times. The world has known me as Regusha Wygodska, Albina Sofia Voitchuk, Betka Wygodska, and Regina Betty Eber, but it is the final moniker that gives me the most satisfaction—Nana. It is the term my grandchildren and great-grandchildren use to refer to me, affectionately.

As I look back on all the years, I have come to realize that life is made up of individual moments and feelings bottled up together. I try to remember the wonderful ones, the special ones, the ones that made me glow on the inside. My life is filled with great moments, not just because of Jacob, his children and my great-grandchildren, but due to all the friends that survived with me, and mostly family—Max and Marcia, Rae and Irwin Finn, Tom and Reba, Jack and Evelyn, Fred and Arline, Clair and Larry (Rubin's uncle), and Sylvia and Mickey Sadin. They gave me the unconditional love and *permanence* I craved. I know I'll never be free of horrible memories—captivity, beatings, and torture—but I know how to live with them better. The nightmares still wake me up, but they'll never get the better of me.

Sometimes when I can't sleep, I drift back to those early years, remembering my family. I try to get inside my head and remember what I was thinking. At the time, I was just a little girl who had her whole future ahead of her. I had a wonderful family, loving parents, and I could dream any dream I wanted.

In the years that followed, I probably shouldn't have survived, but I did. Something more powerful than I am was driving me, guiding me, leading me to where I am today. Along the way, I made several stops, and at each junction my strengths, capabilities, and determination were tested. I survived on luck, love, respect, and humor. As I reach the conclusion of my arduous journey of endurance, I now understand that family and love are the foundation and basis of my existence. Without you, all of you, nothing matters.

And even after everything, I'm still the same little girl. I want to crawl into my father's lap and laugh and play. I'm still an optimist, seeing the glass as half full and believing in the good in the world. I spent most of the twentieth century battling the atrocities of the Holocaust, but even that couldn't get the best of me. As I look forward to my ninety-sixth birthday, I can honestly say I have the most inexplicable feelings of happiness.

www.ingramcontent.com/pod-product-compliance
Lightning Source LLC
Chambersburg PA
CBHW031313160426
43196CB00007B/516